POST OFFICE JOBS

Explore and Find Jobs,
Prepare for the 473 Postal Exam,
and Locate ALL Job Opportunities

Dennis V. Damp

Fourth Edition, Completely Revised

BOOKHAVEN PRESS LLC
Mckees Rocks, PA

POST OFFICE JOBS

Explore and Find Jobs, Prepare for the 473 Postal Exam,
and Locate ALL Job Opportunities

By Dennis V. Damp

Copyright © 2005 by Dennis V. Damp

First Printing 1996	Fourth Printing 2003 (**Revised**)
Second Printing 1997	Fifth Printing 2003
Third Printing 2000 (**Revised**)	Sixth Printing 2005 (**Revised**)

Printed and bound in the United States of America
Published by
BOOKHAVEN PRESS LLC
249 Field Club Circle, Mckees Rocks, PA 15108

Disclaimer of All Warranties and Liabilities

The author and publisher make no warranties, either expressed or implied, with respect to the accuracy or completeness of the information in this book. Federal and Postal Service policies, regulations, laws, statistics, addresses and phone numbers continually change. The author and publisher shall not be liable for any incidental or consequential damages in connection with, or arising out of, the use of material in this book.

Library of Congress Catalog-in-Publication Data

Damp, Dennis V.
    Post Office jobs : explore and find jobs, prepare for the 473 Postal Exam, and locate all job opportunities /
Dennis V. Damp.-- 4th ed., completely rev.
        p. cm.
    Includes bibliographical references and index.
    ISBN-10: 0-943641-24-1 (isbn-10 : alk. paper)
    ISBN-13: 978-0-943641-24-9 (isbn-13 : alk. paper)
    1. Postal service--Vocational guidance--United States.
    2. Postal service--United States-- Employees.
    3. Postal service--United States-Examinations, questions, etc. I. Title.
HE6499.D18 2005
383'.4973'023--dc22   2005006751

For information on distribution or quantity discount rates, Telephone 412/494-6926 or write to: Sales Department, Bookhaven Press LLC, P.O. Box 1243, Moon Township, PA 15108. Distributed to the trade by Midpoint Trade Books, 27 West 20th Street, Suite 1102, New York, NY 10011, Tel: 212-727-0190. Individuals can order this title with credit card toll free (ORDERS ONLY) at 1-800-782-7424.

Table of Contents

Chapter Four
Customer Service and Sales District Offices 37

Chapter Five
Postal Exams 43

Chapter Six
The 473 & 473-C Postal Exam 103

Preface

Generating over 68 billion dollars in sales annually, the U. S. Postal Service employs 773,000 workers nationwide to process and deliver 10.5 million pounds of mail daily. The average pay and benefits for career bargaining unit employees now exceeds $57,000 per year and the jobs are highly competitive.

This book guides readers step-by-step through the Postal Service's recruitment system and provides the information needed to explore and find jobs, prepare for the 473 Postal Exam, and locate all job opportunities. The author writes from first hand experience, he spent 35½ years working for Uncle Sam. He provides an insider's perspective on what it takes to go from job hunter to hired, and everything in between to improve your chances of landing a high-paying government job.

The all new fourth edition provides an overview of what is available, including many jobs that don't require written tests and how to apply for them. Over half of all workers are mail carriers and clerks, however, postal workers are employed in hundreds of diverse occupations, from janitors and truck drivers to accountants, personnel specialists, electronics technicians, and engineers.

The Postal Service continues to improve its recruiting process, including useful on-line testing schedules and job announcements. *Post Office Jobs* explains these improvements and provides abundant information, study guides, resources and easy-to-follow checklists that will assist you with your job search. You will also learn about postal corporate jobs and viable job options that you can explore in the competitive federal civil service.

The Postal Service initiated a new test for major entry-level jobs in December of 2004, called the 473 Battery Exam or 473 Major Entry-Level Exam. This new exam tests applicants for general aptitude and characteristics. The 473 Major Entry-Level Exam screens applicants on job-related characteristics and it permits applicants to compete for job vacancies.

This new edition includes a comprehensive study guide for both the 473 and 473-C test versions. The only difference between the two exams is the target audience. The 473-C exam is advertised when the Postal Service is primarily recruiting city mail carriers. The 473 exam is used to recruit for all major entry-level jobs including city carrier, mail processing clerks, mail handlers, and sales, service, and distribution associates.

Post Office Jobs is the only Post Office career guide that includes a comprehensive 473 Battery Test study guide and job descriptions for the top 28 Post Office occupations. It also lists 2,000 Postal Service job classifications, offers guidance on how to explore alternative civil service occupations, and includes a chapter on how to apply for Postal Inspector positions.

Postal employees are interviewed prior to appointment by the selecting official and Chapter Seven provides detailed guidance on how to successfully handle this often nerve-racking face-to-face encounter. The interview chapter guides you step-by-step through the interview process and provides sample questions to help you prepare and reduce your stress level.

Many professional and administrative occupations do not require written examinations. Your background, work experience and education will be used to determine your eligibility for the job. You'll learn how to locate vacancies and apply for these positions nationwide. An updated list of Customer Service Districts is included in Chapter Four that you can contact concerning test results and to learn when exams will be scheduled in your area.

Visit http://postofficejobs.info for up-to-date guidance on Postal Service job options including direct links to key Postal Service recruiting sites. Also visit http://federaljobs.net to explore other civil service opportunities. This site includes extensive assistance for job seekers and covers many topics for people interested in exploring all federal careers.

If you are seeking a job with the Postal Service you should also be aware of the many scams that offer or guarantee postal employment for a fee. The Postal Service does not charge application fees and no one can guarantee you a federal job. All jobs are filled competitively.

If you're looking for good pay with excellent benefits, pursue the Postal Service job market. Use this book's resources, including the Job Hunter's Checklist in Appendix A, to begin your personal job search.

Chapter One
The U.S. Postal Service

The U.S. Postal Service's annual operating revenue exceeds $68 billion and they pay $2 billion in salaries and benefits every two weeks. There are more than 773,000 workers in 300 job categories for positions at 37,000 post offices, branches, stations, and community post offices throughout the United States. Approximately 40,000 postal workers are hired each year to backfill for retirements, transfers, deaths and employees who choose to leave the Postal Service.

Vacancies are advertised internally by the USPS and not by the Office of Personnel Management. Visit their web site at http://usps.com/employment for exam schedules and job vacancy lists. In 1971, the Postal Service became independent. Pay scales are determined by the Postal Pay Act.

Informative Sites:
www.usps.com/employment
www.postofficejobs.info

Pay starts at $25,871 per year for full time career employees at the PS-1-BB pay grade and increases to $53,551 at the PS-10-P pay grade. The average pay and benefits for career bargaining unit employees was $57,051 per year, excluding corporate-wide expenses, in 2003.[1] The largest pay system in the Postal Service is predominately for bargaining unit employees. There are also Executive and Administrative Schedules for non-union members that range from $20,875 up to an authorized maximum of $98,514.

Adding benefits, overtime, and premiums, the average bargaining unit annual compensation rate was $57,051.

[1]Comprehensive Statement on Postal Operations, 2003 — USPS

BENEFITS

Postal employees receive the same general benefits provided to federal employees for the most part. However, USPS employees pay considerably less for their health care bi-weekly premiums than the competitive Civil Service does.

Vacation & Sick Leave

All employees receive: 10 paid holidays, 13 days of vacation for the first three years, twenty days of vacation with three to fifteen years service and after fifteen years twenty-six days. Additionally, 13 sick days are accrued each year regardless of length of service. Military time counts toward benefits. If you have three years of military service, you begin with four weeks paid vacation and three years toward retirement.

Health Benefits & Life Insurance

Medical health plans and the *Federal Employees' Group Life Insurance* (FEGLI) programs are available to all employees. The medical plan is an employee-employer contribution system and includes HMO and Blue Cross and Blue Shield programs. There are hundreds of plans to choose from. The FEGLI program offers low cost term life insurance for the employee and basic coverage for the family. FEGLI offers up to five times the employee's salary in death benefits.

One of the primary benefits of Postal Service employment is the satisfaction you experience from working in a challenging and rewarding position. Positions are available with the level of responsibility and authority that you desire.

Retirement

The Postal Service retirement system was significantly changed for individuals hired after January 1, 1984. Social Security is withheld and a new employee contribution system is fashioned after a 401k defined contribution plan. You can elect to contribute into a *THRIFT savings 401k plan*. The government will match your contribution up to 5 percent. This is effectively a 5 percent pay increase. Your contributions are tax deferred and reduce your taxable income by the amount contributed. The retirement benefit is determined by the amount that has accumulated during the employee's career. This includes the interest earned and capital gains realized from the retirement fund.

There are many withdrawal options including lump sum and various fixed term annuities. The contribution plan payout is in addition to the social security benefits that you will be eligible for at retirement. Postal workers pay considerably less for their health benefits than competitive federal civil service employees due to their negotiated union contracts.

EMPLOYEE CLASSIFICATIONS

Initial appointments are either casual (temporary) or Part-Time Flexible (Career). Hourly rates for Part-Time Flexible employees vary depending upon the position's rate schedule. Some positions are filled full-time, such as the Maintenance (Custodial) classification.

- Full-Time and Part-Time Flexible (career) employees comprise the *Regular Work Force*. This category includes security guards. Part-Time Flexible employees are scheduled to work fewer than 40 hours per week and they must be available for flexible work hours as assigned. Part-Time Flexible employees are paid by the hour. Hourly rates vary from $12.29 for PS Grade 1 Step BB to $27.26 for PS Grade 11 step P. See page 15 for a complete pay scale listing.

- A *Supplemental Work Force* is needed by the Postal Service for peak mail periods and offers casual (temporary) employees two 89-day employment terms in a calendar year. During Christmas an additional 21 days of employment can be offered to Supplemental Work Force employees.

College students may be considered for casual (temporary) employment with the Postal Service during the summer months. The rate of pay now exceeds $11.50 per hour. Tests are not required and appointments cannot lead to a career position. Apply early for summer work. Contact Post Offices in your area by no later than February for summer employment applications. Casual temporary positions are also advertised on the Postal Service's excellent employment and job listing web site at http://usps.com/employment.

QUALIFICATION REQUIREMENTS

Various standards from age restrictions to physical requirements must be met before you can take one of the Postal Service exams.

Age Limit

You must be eighteen to apply. Certain conditions allow applicants as young as sixteen to apply. Carrier positions, requiring driving, are limited to age 18 or older. High school graduates or individuals that terminated high school education for sufficient reason are permitted to apply at age 16.

Entrance Exams

Clerk, carrier and other specific postal job applicants must pass an entrance exam. Specialties such as mechanic, electronic technician, machinist, and trades must also pass a written test. The overall rating is based on the test results and your qualifying work experience and education. Professionals and certain administrative positions don't require an entrance exam or written test. They are rated and hired strictly on their prior work experience and education. The clerk and carrier exam was updated in December of 2004 to the new 473 and 473 C Battery Exam. The only difference between the two is that the 473 C is used for city mail carriers.

The **473 and 473 C Battery examination** covers the following major entry level positions including:

✔ **City Carrier**
✔ **Mail Processing Clerk**
✔**Sales, Service, and Distribution Associates**
✔ **Mail handler**

The *473 Battery Examination* covers the majority of entry level hiring although some offices also maintain custodial registers, which by law, are reserved for veteran preference eligibles. The USPS also maintains *motor vehicle* and *tractor trailer registers* and some highly skilled maintenance positions such as *Building Equipment Mechanic, Engineman, Electronics Technician, and General Mechanic*. All of the skilled maintenance positions require examination 931. A separate announcement, examination number 932, is required for Electronics Technician positions.

Six sample exams are presented in Chapter Five and a sample *473 Battery Test* is included in Chapter Six to help you prepare for this test. The 473 examination and completion of forms will require approximately two hours and fifteen minutes. Jobs with the U.S. Postal Service are highly competitive due to the excellent salary and benefits offered. It's essential that you pass the test with the highest score possible to improve your chances. Applicants scoring between 90% -100% have a better chance of being hired.

Citizenship

Applicants do not have to be U.S. citizens. If you have permanent alien resident status in the United States of America or owe allegiance to the United States of America you can apply for Postal Service Jobs.

Physical Requirements

Physical requirements are determined by the job. Carriers must be able to lift a 70-pound mail sack and all applicants must be able to efficiently perform assigned duties. Eyesight and hearing tests are required. Applicants must have at least 20/40 vision in the good eye and no worse than 20/100 in the other eye. Eyeglasses are permitted.

State Drivers License

Applicants must have a valid state driver's license for positions that require motor vehicle operation. A safe driving record is required and a Postal Service road test is administered for the type of vehicle that you will operate.

DRUG TESTING (SUBSTANCE ABUSE)

The Postal Service maintains a comprehensive program to insure a drug-free workplace. A qualification for postal employment is to be drug free, and this qualification is determined through the use of a urinalysis drug screen. When you are determined to be in the area of consideration for employment, you will be scheduled for a drug screening test.

APPLICATION PROCEDURES

Positions Requiring Written Examinations

The USPS maintains a directory or register of openings by location. The Postal Service has a decentralized hiring process for personnel and examination related matters. The examinations are administered by examination center personnel from local Customer District Human Resources offices located in most large cities. A comprehensive listing of Customer Service District offices is provided in Chapter Four.

To apply for postal positions visit the Postal Service's online employment and job listing site at **http://usps.com/employment/** and their test scheduling site at **http://uspsapps.hr-services.org/**. You can also call 1/866-999-8777 and follow the prompts. You must have the job announcement number to use the phone system. If you don't have an announcement number, which is readily available for current openings on the Internet, contact your local Post Office, Management Sectional Center (MSC), General Mail Facilities or a Customer Service District Office in your area. You can also obtain computer access to the USPS web site at many local libraries. Job opportunities are also advertised at local post offices, in national and local newspapers, journals and periodicals.

A passing score of 70 percent or better on an exam will place the applicant's name on an eligible *register* for a period of two years. Registers are lists of job applicants who have passed an exam or evaluation process. Your score determines your placement on the register. Applicants can write to the Postal Examination office for a one-year extension. Requests for extension must be received between the eighteenth-and twenty-fourth month of eligibility. Most people hired have a score of between 90% and 100%. There is a separate register for each job classification. To improve your chances, test for as many different positions that you can qualify for.

Positions That Don't Require a Written Exam

Vacancies in these positions — generally professional and administrative — are announced (advertised) first within the Postal Service. Postal employees who have the knowledge, education, credentials, and skills may apply for these openings. If there aren't any qualified internal applicants (called bidders in the federal sector), then the postal service will advertise the vacancies to the general public and accept resumes and applications for rating. All applicants must pass an entrance examination and/or an evaluation process to be placed on a register in numerical score order. Corporate positions that don't require entrance exams are covered in Appendix B.

It is generally recommended that job applicants seeking entry level professional and administrative positions take the 470 Battery Exam to get their foot in the door. Once hired, as vacancies open in their specialty such as accounting, budget, and engineering, they will have first crack at the jobs through internal Postal Service job announcements. You can view the diverse lists of job advertisements online at http://usps.com/employment. There are lists of jobs reserved for current federal employees only. Once you get your foot in the door you can bid on these restricted announcements and the experience that you will gain from the entry level position will help you to better understand the postal system.

Realistically, many professional jobs won't be filled internally. Few postal clerks and non professional employees will have law degrees, engineering credentials or doctorates, for example. Review the list of more than 2,000 job classifications in Chapter Ten to see the scope of available jobs. This list also includes the total number employed and the pay for that occupation.

These job openings will generally be advertised in local papers and on the USPS web site. You should also contact local Customer Service & Sales District (CSSD) personnel offices listed in Chapter Four to identify upcoming job vacancies for your speciality. You can also call your local CSSD office to check on the status of your application or to follow up on interviews.

You will be rated on a point system (maximum of 100 points) even without a written test. Therefore, your resume and *Application For Employment* (PS Form 2591) must be thoroughly completed and include all key information such as degrees, training, credentials, and detailed work experience. Only the top three candidates will generally be referred to the selecting official for consideration.

VETERANS PREFERENCE

Veterans receive five or ten point preference. Those with a 10% or greater compensable service-connected disability are placed at the top of the register in the order of their scores. All other eligibles are listed below the disabled veterans group in rank order. The Veterans Preference Act applies to all Postal Service positions. Refer to Chapter Eight for detailed information on veterans preference.

Custodial exams for the position of cleaner, custodian, and custodial laborer are exclusively for veterans and present employees. This exam is open only to veterans preference candidates.

PAY SCALES

There are several pay schedules in the Postal Service. The Postal Service (PS) pay scale for bargaining unit employees and the Executive and Administrative Schedule (EAS) pay scale for non-bargaining unit employees are presented in this chapter. Special pay scales are also used for rural letter carriers. The Postal Service also pays extra compensation, overtime, and night shift differential to workers. A Cost of Living Adjustment (COLA) is added to the base salary of employees at the rate of one cent per hour for each increase of a .4 point increase in the Consumer Price Index. Additional pay scales are posted on **http://postofficejobs.info** and they are updated as changes occur. Visit this site for updated information. Explore other federal job options at **http://federaljobs.net**/.

POSTAL SERVICE (PS) Full Time Annual Rates (11/27/2004)

STEPS	1	2	3	4	5	6	7	8	9	10	11
BB	25,871	26,983	28,089								
AA	26,833	27,935	29,032								
A	27,795	28,887	29,975	31,663	33,301	35,044	35,851				
B	28,757	29,839	30,918	32,550	34,141	35,836	36.667				
C	29,719	30,791	31,861	33,437	34,981	36,628	37,483				
D	30,681	31,743	32,804	34,324	35,821	37,420	38,299	41,825	42,777	43,780	44,839
E	31,643	32,695	33,747	35,211	36,661	38,212	39,115	42,436	43,442	44,466	45,565
F	32,605	33,647	34,690	36,098	37,501	39,004	39,931	43,047	44,067	45,152	46,291
G	33,567	34,599	35,633	36,985	38,341	39,796	40,747	43,658	44,712	45,838	47,017
H	34,529	35,551	36,576	37,872	39,181	40,588	41,563	44,269	45,357	46,524	47,743
I	35,491	36,503	37,519	38,759	40,021	41,380	42,379	44,880	46,002	47,210	48,469
J	36,453	37,455	38,462	39,646	40,861	42,172	43,195	45,491	46,647	47,896	49,195
K	37,415	38,407	39,405	40,533	41,701	42,964	44,011	46,101	47,292	48,582	49,921
L	38,377	39,359	40,348	41,420	42,541	43,756	44,827	46,713	47,937	49,269	50,647
M	39,339	40,311	41,291	42,309	43,381	44,548	45,643	47,324	48,582	49,954	51,373
N	40,301	41,263	42,234	43,194	44,221	45,340	46,459	47,935	49,227	50,640	52,099
O	41,546	42,330	43,177	44,081	45,061	46,132	47,275	48,546	49,872	51,326	52,825
P								49,157	50,517	52,012	53,551
RC	42,508	43,282	44,120	44,968	45,901	46,924	48,091	49,768	51,162	52,698	54,277

Step Increases BB-P are awarded on time in service and range from 24 weeks to 96 weeks between increases.

EXECUTIVE & ADMINISTRATIVE STEP SCHEDULE (EAS) 12/272003

EAS GRADE	MIDPOINT	EAS GRADE	MIDPOINT
1	$23,693.00	15	$45,277.00
2	24,470.00	16	48,882.00
3	25,275.00	17	51,049.00
4	26,295.00	18	53,292.00
5	27,171.00	19	55,817.00
6	28,150.00	20	58,845.00
7	29,304.00	21	61,704.00
8	30,478.00	22	66,088.00
9	31,699.00	23	69,690.00
10	32,837.00	24	73,139.00
11	37,193.00	25	76,777.00
12	38,978.00	26	80,606.00
13	40,796.00		
14	42,927.00		

POSTAL OCCUPATIONS WITH OVER 1,000 EMPLOYEES

OCCUPATION	NUMBER EMPLOYED
Accounting Clerk	1,193
Auto Mechanic	2,762
Bldg. Equipment Mechanic	1,928
Bldg. Maintenance Custodian	1,004
Bulk Mail Clerk	1,350
Bulk Mail Technician	1,864
Carrier City	223,562
Carrier Technician	28,240
Clerk Finance	1,137
Custodian	1,844
Customer Service Manager/Supr.	17,138
Data Collection Technician	1,183
Data Conversion Operator	8,078
District Clerk	36,014
Distribution Clerk	95,706
Distribution Operations Mgr./Supr.	15,520
Electronics Technician	6,467
Flat Sorting Mach. Operator	19,940
General Clerk	3,350
General Expediter	3,747
Human Resource Specialists	2,361
Laborer Custodial	13,134
Mail Handler/Tech/Operator	52,165
Maintenance Control Clerk/Tech	1193
Maintenance Managers/Supervisors	2,447
Maintenance Mechanic/MPE	8,221
Markup Clerk	6,124
Motor Vehicle Operator	3,475
Parcel Post Dist-Machine	9,572
PM/Relief/Replacement	12,951
Postal Police Officer	1,313
Postmaster	26,803
Postal Inspector	1,674
Rural Delivery Carriers	45,049
Sack Sorting Mach. Operator	1,616
Secretary	1,115
Special Delivery Messenger	1,555
Tractor Trailer Operator	4,633
Vehicle maintenance	4,689
Window service Clerk/Tech	8,435

Chapter Two
The Hiring Process

The Postal Service's selection, evaluation and recognition system was recently overhauled. This progressive initiative has streamlined and standardized the application and exam scheduling process for applicants. In 2001, more than 843,147 applicants applied for postal exams or for casual/temporary employment through this new system.[1] It is now easy to identify and apply for exams online or by phone.

The U.S. Postal Service is an Equal Opportunity Employer. Hiring and advancement in the Postal Service is based on qualifications and performance regardless of race, color, creed, religion, sex, age, national origin, or disability. Applicants do not have to be U.S. citizens. If you have permanent alien resident status in the United States of America or owe allegiance to the United States of America you can apply for Postal Service jobs. The majority of positions require passing a postal exam. Professionals such as doctors, engineers, and others are employed through an application and interview process.

Postal installation managers are generally appointing officials and are delegated the authority to fill vacancies by transfer, reassignment, reinstatement of a former federal or postal employee, promotion, or from an entrance register of eligibles. Regardless of the recruitment source, the applicant must meet the qualifications of the position, including passing the appropriate examination. Examinations can be either written or a rated application process such as that used for professional positions.

EMPLOYEE CLASSIFICATIONS

There are two employee classifications; Regular Work Force (PS) and Supplemental Work Force. The regular work force comprises two groups; full-time and part-time flexible. All new hires except technician positions and professionals

---

[1] Compensation with Statutory Policies, 39 U.S.C. 101 (c)

start as part-time flexibles. Part-time flexibles are not guaranteed 40 hours per week but generally work five to six days per week and will be required to work up to 50 hours per week during peak periods.

The Postal Service's hiring process comprises four components, the suitability and selection component is separated into three sub groups as specified below:[2]

- Recruitment
- Examinations
- Registers
- Suitability Review
  - The applicant's work history
  - Criminal conviction history[3]
  - Personal interviews (See Chapter Seven)
  - Medical assessment

RECRUITMENT

The demands of many postal jobs in today's work environment have changed the Postal Service's recruitment efforts. They updated their recruitment programs to hire qualified candidates through the use of fair and efficient employee assessment systems. Their goal for recruitment is to attract an adequate number of qualified applicants to consider for postal employment. Local management evaluates its hiring needs. Evaluation consists of forecasting future hiring needs, assessing existing applicant pools, considering other hiring options such as special emphasis programs, and reviewing any upcoming Postal Service organizational changes.

EXAMINATIONS

The majority of occupations require entrance examinations. They help identify applicants that meet pre-established qualification requirements for filling vacant positions. Examinations measure or evaluate knowledge, skills, and abilities to predict probable future work performance. Passing examination scores are between 70 and 100. Entrance examinations are offered at locations where hiring is anticipated. Test dates and times are advertised in local papers and at the mail facilities that are actively recruiting. See Chapter Four for a list of Customer Service District Offices that you can call or write for test dates.

REGISTERS

Registers are lists containing applicant names and other information, including an examination rating and/or results of an evaluation process. The names of applicants who pass an entrance examination and/or evaluation process are

---

[2] Reference the U.S. Postal Service's Self-Instruction Module

[3] Because of the critical nature of suitability screening, evaluation activities continue after you are hired.

The Hiring Process   19

placed on the register in numerical score order. That is why it is important for applicants to score as high as possible on their entrance exams. Passing grades are between70 and 100; however, most are hired with scores between 90 and 100.

Eligible applicants are ranked on a register according to final ratings (including veterans preference points - see Chapter Eight) and divided into two groups. The first group is made up of veterans who have a compensable service-connected disability. The second group is made up of everyone else.

An alternative recruitment source, called the general application file, can be used to fill temporary positions when it isn't feasible to announce an examination. A general application file is comparable to a one-time use or temporary register. Because no examination is given and to comply with the provisions of the veteran preference, applicants must be considered for employment by priority groups. Persons entitled to 10-point veteran preference who have a compensable service-connected disability are placed ahead of all other persons entitled to veteran preference and then placed ahead of all other applicants on the list.

SUITABILITY

Applicants are screened and evaluated to determine their overall suitability for postal employment prior to selection. This evaluation includes a review of:

✔ The applicant's work history
✔ Criminal conviction history
✔ Personal interviews (See Chapter Seven)
✔ Medical assessment

Medical assessment is an example of suitability screening that occurs after the job offer. The Rehabilitation Act of 1973 prohibits the Postal Service from inquiring into an applicant's medical suitability until a bona fide job offer is made. Medical assessment is done after selecting an applicant who has met all other suitability requirements.

After an applicant is hired, a career employee's job performance is evaluated during the probationary period. Fingerprints are submitted for a special agency check to be performed by the Office of Personnel Management (OPM) to ensure that there is no derogatory information about the individual that has not been discovered in the screening process. Thorough screening is done to ensure that individuals who do not meet Postal Service requirements are eliminated from the hiring process.

SELECTION

Selection is the process of identifying the best-qualified applicant for employment. Employing officials make selection decisions based on an evaluation of all information obtained during suitability screening. It is important to understand that a decision to select does not guarantee that the applicant will be appointed to the Postal Service. The applicant's medical assessment, which is completed after selection, or the identification of derogatory information about the applicant, may disqualify the individual before the appointment is effected.

APPOINTMENT

Appointment is the process of placing a selected applicant, who is totally qualified, on the Postal Service rolls. The appointment is made after suitability is confirmed.

GETTING IN THE FRONT DOOR

Getting in is half the battle. If you are qualified as a computer systems analyst and there are currently no openings, take the appropriate entrance exam and apply for entry level positions such as Postal Clerks and Mail Carriers. The Postal Service offers in-service examinations for various specialities and generally advertises jobs in-house first to offer qualified workers opportunities for advancement. You will have a good chance to bid on other jobs if you have the qualifications and a good track record.

There are two things to aim at in life: first, to get what you want; and after that to enjoy it. Only the wisest of people achieve the second.
— **Logan Smith**

INTERVIEWS

The Postal Service conducts interviews as part of the suitability recruitment process. You need to be prepared for these interviews. There are generally a good number of high scoring applicants and the selecting official will use the interview process to determine the best candidates for the jobs. Refer to Chapter Seven for guidance on how to prepare for interviews.

Chapter Three
What Jobs Are Available

This chapter provides detailed occupational descriptions for the largest Postal Service jobs. A list of occupations with more than 1,000 employees is available on page 16. Chapter Nine provides comprehensive job descriptions for 28 diverse occupations, Chapter Ten presents a comprehensive list of Post Office jobs including pay and Chapter Eleven features Postal Inspector jobs. You should also explore related occupations with the competitive federal Civil Service in Chapter Twelve. Use the *Job Hunters Checklist* in Appendix A to assist you with your job search.

The Postal Service initiated new streamlined application and testing procedures recently. Jobs are now posted on-line at http://usps.com/employment or visit http://uspsapps.hr-services.org/ to locate exams that are scheduled in your area. You can also call **1-866-999-8777** to access their *Interactive Voice Response* (IVR) system to locate job vacancies and to apply for exams by phone. If you call you will need the job announcement number which can be obtained from their web site or by calling your local Post Office or Customer Service District Sales office. Customer Service District Sales offices are listed in Chapter Four by area. Professional or administrative positions that may not require written exams are also posted on the listed web sites. The two primary application forms are the PS Form 2591 Application for Employment, a four page document and the PS Form 2181-A Pre-Employment Screening. Forms are printed in Appendix C. Use these forms to draft your application prior to receipt of the job announcement.

Postal recruitment notices are often advertised in national and local newspapers, publications, journals and periodicals. You can also visit the web site http://postofficejobs.info/ for direct links to the Postal web sites. You should also explore other related federal jobs by visiting http://federaljobs.net/. You will find links on this site to over 145 federal recruiting web sites. If there are no vacancies listed on the sites mentioned above, contact individual mail facilities in your area

Our business in life is not to get ahead of others, but to get ahead of ourselves — to break our own records, to outstrip our yesterdays by our today.

Susan B. Johnson

to find out when they intend to recruit. Otherwise you will have to visit these sites weekly to check for new job announcements.

IMPROVING YOUR CHANCES

The more contacts you make the greater your chances. **Don't get lost in the process.** Too many job seekers pin all their hopes on one effort. They take one exam then forget about the process until they receive a reply. Post Office jobs are highly competitive. The more positions that you apply for and examinations that you take the better your chances. There are also jobs that don't require entrance exams. Visit the USPS web site to explore all occupations that you may qualify for. A list of exams is located in Chapter Five. Also explore related occupations in the competitive federal civil service in Chapter Twelve.

Good things come to those who
wait, as long as they work like hell
while they wait.

The interviewing techniques presented in Chapter Seven will help you prepare for the suitability screening process discussed in Chapter Two. Prepare for the interview. The Postal Service requires that each individual be interviewed prior to making an offer of appointment. They use Form 2591, Application for Employment, as a guide during the interview process to verify education, job history, specialized skills, and to clarify reasons for leaving previous jobs. Take time to thoroughly complete the job application. Type the application if possible or print legibly. You can copy and use the sample forms provided in Appendix B to prepare your application.

You aren't locked into the first job or, for that matter, location that you are originally selected for. Once hired, you'll have opportunities to bid for jobs in-house. Post Offices, General Mail Facilities, and District Offices are located throughout the country and you can bid to many locations for future promotions or to enter a related or new career field. There are over 39,000 postal facilities nationwide.

POSTAL CLERKS AND MAIL CARRIERS
(The Largest USPS Occupations)

Nature of the Work

Each week, the U.S. Postal Service delivers billions of pieces of mail, including letters, bills, advertisements, and packages.[1] To do this in an efficient and timely manner, the Postal Service employs about 773,000[2] individuals. Most Postal

---

[1] This section excerpted from the Occupational Outlook Handbook 2004-2005 edition, U.S. Department of Labor

[2] Federal Civilian Workforce Statistics - March 2004

Service workers are clerks, mail carriers, or mail sorters, processors, and processing machine operators. Postal clerks wait on customers at post offices, whereas mail sorters, processors, and processing machine operators sort incoming and outgoing mail at post offices and mail processing centers. Mail carriers deliver mail to urban and rural residences and businesses throughout the United States.

Postal service clerks, also known as window clerks, sell stamps, money orders, postal stationary, and mailing envelopes and boxes. They also weigh packages to determine postage and check that packages are in satisfactory condition for mailing. These clerks register, certify, and insure mail and answer questions about postage rates, post office boxes, mailing restrictions, and other postal matters. Window clerks also help customers file claims for damaged packages.

Postal service mail sorters, processors, and processing machine operators prepare incoming and outgoing mail for distribution. These workers are commonly referred to as mail handlers, distribution clerks, mail processors, or mail processing clerks. They load and unload postal trucks and move mail around a mail processing center with forklifts, small electric tractors, or hand-pushed carts. They also load and operate mail processing, sorting, and canceling machinery.

Postal service mail carriers deliver mail, once it has been processed and sorted. Although carriers are classified by their type of route—either city or rural—duties of city and rural carriers are similar. Most travel established routes, delivering and collecting mail. Mail carriers start work at the post office early in the morning, when they arrange the mail in delivery sequence. Automated equipment has reduced the time that carriers need to sort the mail, allowing them to spend more time delivering it.

Mail carriers cover their routes on foot, by vehicle, or a combination of both. On foot, they carry a heavy load of mail in a satchel or push it on a cart. In most urban and rural areas, they use a car or small truck. Although the Postal Service provides vehicles to city carriers, most rural carriers must use their own automobiles. Deliveries are made house-to-house, to roadside mailboxes, and to large buildings such as offices or apartments, which generally have all of their tenants' mailboxes in one location.

Besides delivering and collecting mail, carriers collect money for postage-due and COD (cash-on-delivery) fees and obtain signed receipts for registered, certified, and insured mail. If a customer is not home, the carrier leaves a notice that tells where special mail is being held. After completing their routes, carriers return to the post office with mail gathered from street collection boxes, homes, and businesses and turn in the mail, receipts, and money collected during the day.

Some city carriers may have specialized duties such as delivering only parcels or picking up mail from mail collection boxes. In contrast to city carriers, rural carriers provide a wider range of postal services, in addition to delivering and picking up mail. For example, rural carriers may sell stamps and money orders and register, certify, and insure parcels and letters. All carriers, however, must be able to answer customers' questions about postal regulations and services and provide change-of-address cards and other postal forms when requested.

Working Conditions

Window clerks usually work in the public portion of clean, well-ventilated, and well-lit buildings. They have a variety of duties and frequent contact with the public, but they rarely work at night. However, they may have to deal with upset customers, stand for long periods, and be held accountable for an assigned stock of stamps and funds. Depending on the size of the post office in which they work, they also may be required to sort mail.

Despite the use of automated equipment, the work of mail sorters, processors, and processing machine operators can be physically demanding. Workers may have to move heavy sacks of mail around a mail processing center. These workers usually are on their feet, reaching for sacks and trays of mail or placing packages and bundles into sacks and trays. Processing mail can be tiring and boring. Many sorters, processors, and machine operators work at night or on weekends, because most large post offices process mail around the clock, and the largest volume of mail is sorted during the evening and night shifts. Workers can experience stress as they process ever-larger quantities of mail under tight production deadlines and quotas.

Most carriers begin work early in the morning—those with routes in a business district can start as early as 4:00 a.m. Overtime hours are frequently required for urban carriers. A carrier's schedule has its advantages, however. Carriers who begin work early in the morning are through by early afternoon and spend most of the day on their own, relatively free from direct supervision. Carriers spend most of their time outdoors, delivering mail in all kinds of weather. Even those who drive often must walk periodically when making deliveries and must lift heavy sacks of parcel post items when loading their vehicles. In addition, carriers must be cautious of potential hazards on their routes. Wet and icy roads and sidewalks can be treacherous, and each year dogs attack numerous carriers.

Employment

The U.S. Postal Service employed 77,000 clerks, 334,000 mail carriers, and 253,000 mail sorters, processors, and processing machine operators in 2002. Most of them worked full time. Most postal clerks provided window service at post office branches. Many mail sorters, processors, and processing machine operators sorted mail at major metropolitan post offices; others worked at mail processing centers. The majority of mail carriers worked in cities and suburbs, while the rest worked in rural areas.

Postal Service workers are classified as either casual, part-time flexible, part-time regular, or full time. Casuals are hired for 90 days at a time to help process and deliver mail during peak mailing or vacation periods. Part-time flexible workers do not have a regular work schedule or weekly guarantee of hours but are called as the need arises. Part-time regulars have a set work schedule of fewer than 40 hours per week, often replacing regular full-time workers on their scheduled day off. Full-time postal employees work a 40-hour week over a five-day period.

Training, Other Qualifications, and Advancement

Postal Service workers must be at least 18 years old. They must be U.S. citizens or have been granted permanent resident-alien status in the United States, and males must have registered with the Selective Service upon reaching age 18. Applicants should have a basic competency of English. Qualification is based on a written examination that measures speed and accuracy at checking names and numbers and the ability to memorize mail distribution procedures. Applicants must pass a physical examination and drug test, and may be asked to show that they can lift and handle mail sacks weighing 70 pounds. Applicants for mail carrier positions must have a driver's license and a good driving record, and must receive a passing grade on a road test.

Job seekers should contact the post office or mail processing center where they wish to work to determine when an exam will be given. Applicants' names are listed in order of their examination scores. Five points are added to the score of an honorably discharged veteran and 10 points are added to the score of a veteran who was wounded in combat or is disabled. When a vacancy occurs, the appointing officer chooses one of the top three applicants; the rest of the names remain on the list to be considered for future openings until their eligibility expires — usually two years after the examination date.

Relatively few people become postal clerks or mail carriers on their first job, because of keen competition and the customary waiting period of one to two years or more after passing the examination. It is not surprising, therefore, that most entrants transfer from other occupations.

New Postal Service workers are trained on the job by experienced workers. Many post offices offer classroom instruction on safety and defensive driving. Workers receive additional instruction when new equipment or procedures are introduced. In these cases, workers usually are trained by another postal employee or a training specialist.

Postal clerks and mail carriers should be courteous and tactful when dealing with the public, especially when answering questions or receiving complaints. A good memory and the ability to read rapidly and accurately are important. Good interpersonal skills also are vital, because mail distribution clerks work closely with other postal workers, frequently under the tension and strain of meeting dispatch or transportation deadlines and quotas.

Postal Service workers often begin on a part-time, flexible basis and become regular or full time in order of seniority, as vacancies occur. Full-time workers may bid for preferred assignments, such as the day shift or a high-level non supervisory position. Carriers can look forward to obtaining preferred routes as their seniority increases. Postal Service workers can advance to supervisory positions on a competitive basis.

Job Outlook

Employment of Postal Service workers is expected to decline through 2012. Still, many jobs will become available because of the need to replace those who retire or leave the occupation. Those seeking jobs as Postal Service workers can expect to encounter keen competition. The number of applicants should continue to exceed the number of job openings due to low entry requirements and attractive wages and benefits.

A small decline in employment is expected among window clerks over the 2002-12 projection period. Efforts by the Postal Service to provide better service may somewhat increase the demand for window clerks, but the demand for such clerks will be offset by the use of electronic communications technologies and private delivery companies. Employment of mail sorters, processors, and processing machine operators is expected to decline because of the increasing use of automated materials handling equipment and optical character readers, barcode sorters, and other automated sorting equipment.

Several factors are expected to influence demand for mail carriers. The competition from alternative delivery systems and new forms of electronic communication could decrease the total volume of mail handled. Most of the decrease is expected to consist of first-class mail. The Postal Service expects an increase in package deliveries due to the rising number of purchases made through the Internet. Although total mail volume may decrease, the number of addresses to which mail must be delivered will continue to grow. However, increased use of the "delivery point sequencing" system, which allows machines to sort mail directly by the order of delivery, should reduce the amount of time that carriers spend sorting their mail, allowing them more time to handle longer routes. In addition, the Postal Service is moving toward more centralized mail delivery, such as the use of cluster boxes, to cut down on the number of door-to-door deliveries. These trends are expected to increase carrier productivity, resulting in a small decline in employment among mail carriers over the projection period. The increasing number of delivery points may result in greater demand for rural mail carriers than for city mail carriers, as much of the increase in delivery points will be seen in less urbanized areas.

Earnings

Median annual earnings of postal mail carriers was $39,530 in 2002. The middle 50 percent earned between $36,020 and $43,040. The lowest 10 percent had earnings of less than $31,180, while the top 10 percent earned more than $47,500. Rural mail carriers are reimbursed for mileage put on their own vehicles while delivering mail.

Median annual earnings of Postal Service clerks were $39,700 in 2002. The middle 50 percent earned between $37,160 and $42,230. The lowest 10 percent had earnings of less than $35,640, while the top 10 percent earned more than $43,750.

Median annual earnings of mail sorters, processors, and processing machine operators were $38,150 in 2002. The middle 50 percent earned between $30,140 and $41,450. The lowest 10 percent had earnings of less than $21,680, while the top 10 percent earned more than $43,430.

Postal Service workers enjoy a variety of employer-provided benefits similar to those enjoyed by federal government workers. The American Postal Workers Union, the National Association of Letter Carriers, the National Postal Mail Handlers Union, and the National Rural Letter Carriers Association together represent most of these workers.

Related Occupations

Other occupations with duties similar to those of postal clerks include cashiers; counter and rental clerks; file clerks; and shipping, receiving, and traffic clerks. Others with duties related to those of mail carriers include couriers and messengers and truck drivers and driver/sales workers. Occupations whose duties are related to those of mail sorters, processors, and processing-machine operators include inspectors, testers, sorters, samplers, and weighers, and material moving occupations. Review related federal civil service occupations and hiring options in Chapter Twelve.

Sources of Additional Information

Local post offices and state employment service offices can supply details about entrance examinations and specific employment opportunities for postal clerks and mail carriers. Visit http://usps.com/employment for complete information on all occupations including jobs that don't require entrance examination. Also visit http://federaljobs.net for direct links to over 150 federal agency personnel recruiting offices and for guidance on how to locate related jobs in the competitive federal civil service. If you are looking for secretarial, general or entry level healthcare work visit http://healthcarejobs.org for other viable hiring options.

CUSTODIAN AND CUSTODIAL LABORER

Note: These positions are restricted to veteran preference eligibles.

The Job:

Custodian duties include manual cleaning, housekeeping, and buildings and grounds maintenance. Custodial laborers perform manual labor in connection with the maintenance and cleaning of the buildings and grounds. All positions may include irregular hours.

General Qualifications:

All applicants will be required to take a written examination. The examination and completion of forms will require approximately one hour and 30 minutes.

Custodial positions require prolonged standing, walking, climbing, bending, reaching and stooping. Employees must lift and carry heavy objects on level surfaces, on ladders and/or stairways. Custodial positions may require the use of hand tools and power cleaning equipment.

A qualification for postal employment is to be drug-free. This is determined through the use of a urinalysis drug screen. Applicants who qualify on the examination and are in the area of consideration for employment will be scheduled for the drug test.

Applicants must have vision of 20/40 (Snellen) in one eye and the ability to read without strain, printed material the size of typewritten characters, glasses permitted.

How to Apply:

Visit http://usps.com/employment or call 1/866-999-8777 for job vacancy announcements and application procedures. If you call you must first have the announcement number to apply by phone. You can now apply on-line for many entrance exams.

Applicants will be notified of the date, time, and place of the examination and will be sent material to prepare for the examination.

Selection Process:

A minimum score of 70 points (exclusive of Veteran Preference) on the examination places the applicant's name on a list of eligibles for two years. Names are placed on the hiring list according to the score on the examination.

DATA CONVERSION OPERATOR

The Job

Data Conversion Operators extract information from source documents, transfer that information to computer input forms, and enter data using a keyboard.

General Qualifications

All applicants will be required to take a written examination. The examination and completion of forms will require approximately two hours.

Applicants must have six (6) months or equivalent of clerical or office machine operating experience, preferably on a data conversion machine. Typing is required.

A qualification for postal employment is to be drug-free. This is determined through the use of a urinalysis drug screen. Applicants who qualify on the examination and are in the area of consideration for employment will be scheduled for the drug-test.

Applicants must have vision of 20/40 (Snellen) in one eye and the ability to read without strain, printed material the size of typewritten characters, corrective lenses permitted. The ability to distinguish basic colors and shades is desirable.

Applicants must be able to hear the conversational voice, hearing aids permitted.

How to Apply

Visit http://usps.com/employment or call 1/866-999-8777 for job vacancy announcements and application procedures. If you call you must first have the announcement number to apply by phone. You can now apply on-line for many entrance exams.

Applicants will be notified of the date, time, and place of the examination and will be sent material to prepare for the examination.

Selection Process

Applicants must first attain a minimum score of 70 points (exclusive of Veteran Preference) on the written examination. The applicants' names are then placed, by score, on a hiring list of eligibles for a period of two years. Applicants who qualify on the examination and are in the area of consideration for employment will be scheduled for a job simulated typing performance test.

MAINTENANCE POSITIONS

The Job

Maintenance positions require highly skilled and experienced individuals. All applicants must meet the Knowledge, Skills, and Abilities listed on the job description.

General Qualifications

All applicants will be required to pass a three hours written examination, complete a Candidate Supplemental Application booklet and successfully complete an interview.

A qualification for postal employment is to be drug-free. This is determined through the use of a urinalysis drug screen. Applicants who qualify on the examination and are in the area of consideration for employment will be scheduled for the drug test.

Maintenance positions require prolonged standing, walking, climbing, bending, reaching and stooping. Employees must lift and carry heavy objects on level surfaces, on ladders and/or stairways.

For positions requiring driving, applicants must have a valid state driver's license and a safe driving record. They must be able to obtain a Government Motor Vehicle Operator's Identification Card. Applicants may be required to qualify on industrial powered lifting equipment.

Applicants must have vision of 20/40 (Snellen) in one eye and the ability to read without strain, printed material the size of typewritten characters, glasses permitted. The ability to distinguish basic colors and shades is required.

How to Apply

Visit http://usps.com/employment or call 1/866-999-8777 for job vacancy announcements and application procedures. If you call you must first have the announcement number to apply by phone. You can now apply on-line for many entrance exams.

Applicants will be notified of the date, time, and place of the examination and will be sent material to prepare for the examination..

Selection Process

Applicants must first attain a minimum score of 70 points (exclusive of Veteran Preference) on the written examination. They must then complete a Candidate Supplemental Application booklet and successfully complete an interview. The applicants' names are then placed, by score, on a hiring list of eligibles for a period of two years.

VEHICLE OPERATOR/ TRACTOR-TRAILER OPERATOR

The Job:

Motor Vehicle Operators operate mail trucks to pick up and transport mail in bulk. Tractor-Trailer Operators operate heavy duty tractor-trailers either in over-the-road service, city shuttle service or trailer operations. May include irregular hours.

General Qualifications:

Applicants for Motor Vehicle Operator and Tractor-Trailer Operator positions must have at least two years of driving-experience, with at least one year of full-time experience (or equivalent) driving at least a seven-ton capacity truck or 24-passenger bus.

For Tractor-Trailer Operators, at least six months of the truck driving experience must be with tractor-trailers. Only driving experience in the United States, its possessions, territories, or in any United States military installation worldwide will be considered.

At the time of appointment, applicants must have a valid commercial driver's license, with air brakes certification, for the type(s) of vehicle(s) used on the job from the state in which they live. After being hired, applicants must be able to obtain the appropriate certification to operate specific postal vehicles.

Applicants will be required to pass a two hour and 30 minutes written examination and must also complete forms detailing their employment history, driving record, and other qualifying factors, to demonstrate possession of the following abilities: 1) Ability to drive trucks safely. 2) Ability to drive under local conditions. 3) Ability to follow instructions and prepare trip and other reports.

A qualification for postal employment is to be drug-free. This is determined through the use of a urinalysis drug-screen. Applicants who qualify on the examination, and are in the area of consideration for employment, will be scheduled for the drug test.

Applicants must have a vision of at least 30/30 (Snellen) in one eye and 20/50 (Snellen) in the other eye and the ability to read, without strain, printed material the size of typewritten characters, corrective lenses permitted. Operators must also be able to hear the conversational voice, hearing aids permitted.

How to Apply:

Visit http://usps.com/employment or call 1/866-999-8777 for job vacancy announcements and application procedures. If you call you must first have the announcement number to apply by phone. You can now apply on-line for many entrance exams.

Applicants will be notified of the date, time, and place of the examination and will be sent material to prepare for the examination.

Selection:

Applicants receive scores based on their examination results and a rating of their qualifications process: listed on the U.S. Postal Service Application for Employment Form, Driving Record, and Supplemental Experience Statement. The application must contain pertinent information detailed enough to establish that the applicant meets all the requirements listed in this announcement. Applicants must provide full details about the types and weight of vehicles they have driven and the companies for which they worked as well as the length of their experience. A score of 70% (exclusive of Veteran Preference) places the applicant's name on a list of eligibles for two years. Names are placed on the hiring list in the order of their scores.

PROCESSING, DISTRIBUTION & DELIVERY POSITIONS

All eligibilities previously established will be canceled upon receipt of the new examination results. Therefore, all applicants must reapply and compete in the new examination to reestablish eligibility.

General Qualifications:

A qualification for postal employment is to be drug-free. This is determined through the use of a urinalysis drug screen. Applicants who qualify on the examination and are in the area of consideration for employment will be scheduled for the drug test. All applicants will be required to take a written examination. The examination and completion of forms will require approximately two hours and fifteen minutes.

At the time of the examination, the applicant may select any or all of the seven different jobs listed below.

Job Choices:

CITY CARRIER   **MAIL HANDLER**
CLERK   **MAIL PROCESSOR**
DIST. CLERK, MACHINE   **MARK UP CLERK**
FLAT SORTING MACH. OPER.

How to Apply:

Visit http://usps.com/employment or call 1/866-999-8777 for job vacancy announcements and application procedures. If you call you must first have the announcement number to apply by phone. You can now apply on-line for many entrance exams.

Applicants will be notified of the date, time, and place of the examination and will be sent material to prepare for the examination.

CITY CARRIER AND CLERK

The Jobs:

Clerks work indoors sorting and distributing mail. They may be required to work with the public selling stamps and weighing parcels, and are responsible for all money and stamps. May include irregular hours.

City Carriers collect and deliver mail in all kinds of weather, and walk and/or drive on their route.

Carrier and clerk positions require prolonged standing, walking, reaching and the ability to lift 70 pounds. Carriers are also required to carry a mail bag weighing as much as 35 pounds.

For positions requiring driving, applicants must have a valid state driver's license and a safe driving record. They must be able to obtain a Government Motor Vehicle Operator's Identification Card.

Applicants must have a vision of 20/40 (Snellen) in one eye and the ability to read without strain, printed material the size of typewritten characters, glasses permitted. Clerks working with the public must be able to hear the conversational voice.

DISTRIBUTION CLERK, MACHINE AND FLAT SORTING MACHINE OPERATORS

The Jobs:

Distribution Clerk, Machine and Flat Sorter Machine Operators are required to operate machinery which sorts and distributes letters or flats (magazines, over-sized envelopes etc.). Individuals must read address ZIP Codes and enter codes, using special purpose keyboards. Operators must also load and unload the machines and the job may include irregular hours.

Distribution Clerk, Machine applicants must pass a vision test and possess the manual dexterity required to operate a two-handed keyboard. Vision requirements are: 20/40 (Snellen) in one eye and at least 20/100 (Snellen) in the other, and the ability to read without strain printed material the size of typewritten characters, corrective lenses permitted.

Flat Sorting Machine Operator applicants must pass a vision test and possess the manual dexterity required to operate a one-handed keyboard. Vision requirements are: 20/30 (Snellen) in one eye and 20/50 (Snellen) in the other, corrective lenses permitted. The ability to distinguish basic colors and shades is desirable.

MAIL HANDLER

The Job:

Mail Handlers work in an industrial environment. Duties include the loading, unloading and moving of sacks of mail and packages weighing up to 70 pounds. May include irregular hours.

Prior to appointment, applicants will be required to pass a test of physical abilities. Applicants must demonstrate they can lift and carry up to 70 pounds.

Applicants must have a vision of 20/40 (Snellen) in one eye and the ability to read without strain, printed material the size of typewritten characters, corrective lenses permitted. The ability to distinguish basic colors and shades is desirable.

MAIL PROCESSOR

The Job:

Mail Processors are required to stand for prolonged periods of time loading and unloading mail from a variety of automated mail processing equipment. May include irregular hours.

Applicants must have a vision of 20/40 (Snellen) in one eye and the ability to read without strain, printed material the size of typewritten characters, corrective lenses permitted. The ability to distinguish basic colors and shades is desirable.

AUTOMATED MARK UP CLERK

The Job:

Automated Mark Up Clerks enter change of address data into a computer data base, process mail and perform other clerical functions. May include irregular hours.

Applicants must have six (6) months or equivalent of clerical or office machine operating experience. Typing is required.

Applicants must have a vision of 20/40 (Snellen) in one eye and the ability to read without strain, printed material the size of typewritten characters, corrective lenses permitted. The ability to distinguish basic colors and shades is desirable.

Selection Process:

A minimum score of 70 points (exclusive of Veteran Preference) on the examination places the applicant's name on a list of eligibles for two years. Names are placed on the hiring list according to the score on the examination. An applicant who qualifies on the examination and is in the area of consideration for employment for a certain job will be scheduled for job simulated performance exercises or an additional test. Distribution Clerk, Machine and Flat Sorter Machine Operators will be scheduled for Dexterity Exercises, Mail Handlers for a Strength and Stamina Test and Automated Mark Up Clerks for a Typing Test.

Veteran Preference:

Veteran preference is granted for employment in the Postal Service. Those with a 10-percent or greater compensable service-connected disability are placed at the top of the hiring list in the order of their scores. Other eligibles are listed below this group in rank order.

Age Requirement:

The general minimum age requirement for positions in the Postal Service is 18 at the time of appointment or a high school graduate.

Citizenship:

All applicants must be citizens of or owe allegiance to the United States of America, or have been granted permanent resident alien status in the United States. Verification is required.

Selective Service:

To be eligible for appointment to a position in the Postal Service, males born after December 31, 1959 must (subject to certain exceptions) be registered with the Selective Service System in accordance with Section 3 of the Military Selective Service Act. Males between 18 and 26 years of age (have not reached their 26th birthday) can register with the Selective Service System at any U.S. Post Office or consular officer if outside the United States. Your registration status can be verified with the Selective Service System by calling (708) 688-6888 for information.

OCCUPATIONS LIST
(Partial Listing)

Craft & Wage per hour positions:

Administrative Clerk	General Mechanic
Auto Mechanic	Letter Box Mechanic
Blacksmith-Welder	Letter Carrier
Building Equipment Mechanic	LSM Operator
Carpenter	Machinist
Carrier	Mail Handler
Cleaner, Custodian	Maintenance Mechanic
Clerk Stenographer	Mark Up Clerk
Data Conversion Operator	Mason
Distribution Clerk	Mechanic Helper
Electronic Technician	Motor Vehicle Operator
Elevator Mechanic	Painter
Engineman	Plumber
Fireman	Scale Mechanic
Garageman-Driver	Security Guard

Professional

Accounting Technician	Electronic Engineer
Architect/Engineer	Transportation Specialist
Budget Assistant	Industrial Engineer
Computer Programmer	Technical Writer
Computer System Analyst	Stationery Engineer

Management

Administrative Manager	Postmaster-Branch
Foreman of Mail	Safety Officer
General Foreman	Schemes Routing Officer
Labor Relations Representative	Supervisor-Accounting
Manager Bulk-Mail	Supervisor-Customer Service
Manager-Distribution	System Liaison Specialist
Manager-Station/Branch	Tour Superintendent

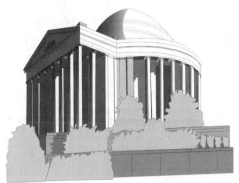

Chapter Four
Customer Service & Sales District Offices

In addition to the national headquarters, there are area and sales district offices supervising approximately 39,000 post offices, branches, stations, and community post offices throughout the United States. The Postal Service has approximately 773,000 employees and handles about 200 billion pieces of mail annually generating more than $68 billion in operating revenues.

If you need to determine when exams will be offered in your area or to check on test results call your local CSSD.

Government jobs offer abundant opportunities in all 50 states and U.S. Territories. With more than 39,000 postal facilities individuals have an excellent opportunity to apply for positions in thousands of small towns and in all major metropolitan areas.

CUSTOMER SERVICE AND SALES DISTRICTS

To determine what job vacancies are available and when exams are scheduled, visit the web sites or call the number listed in Chapter Three. You can also contact the Customer Service and Sales District (CSSD) office nearest you to inquire when specific exams will be scheduled in your area. The Postal Service has established nine Customer Service District areas: Eastern, Great Lakes, Capital Metro Operations, New York Metro, Northeast, Pacific, Southeast, Southwest, and Western. The following list, updated December 9, 2004, provides the District

Manager's name, address, phone and fax numbers. Call this number and have them direct you to their Human Resource Department. Human Resources is responsible for administering exams and hiring. You can also query local CSSD offices to find out what occupations are needed in your area and when they anticipate recruiting if no current vacancies exist or exams aren't scheduled.

Disabled veterans can apply at any time regardless of whether or not exams are scheduled or vacancies exist. This list does not include every Postal Service testing center. Examinations can be given at General Mail Facilities (GMF), Sectional Center Facilities (SCF), Management Sectional Centers (MSC), or Bulk Mail Centers in your area. Call the CSSD nearest you to identify all available testing centers for your location.

CUSTOMER SERVICE DISTRICTS

EASTERN AREA

Lori Wigley
District manager
Appalachian District
P.O. Box 59992
Charleston, WV 25350-9992
(304) 561-1200
(304) 561-1209 (FAX)

Roger Nienaber
District Manager
Cincinnati District
1591 Dalton Street
Cincinnati, OH 45234-9990
(513) 684-5360
(513) 684-5197 (FAX)

Kathleen Ainsworth
District Manager
Northern Ohio District
2200 Orange Avenue, Room 210
Cleveland, OH 44104-9993
(216) 443-4573
(216) 443-4577 (FAX)

Richard Cellino
District Manager
Columbus District
850 Twin Rivers Drive
Columbus, OH 43216-9993
(614) 469-4300
(14) 469-7605 (FAX)

Tammy Autenrieth
District Manager
Erie District
2700 Legion Road
Erie, PA 16515-9997
(814) 836-7201
(814) 836-7215 (FAX)

Nicholas Rinaldi
Greater SC District
PO Box 929998
Columbia, SC 29292-9998
(803) 926-6469
(803) 926-6470 (FAX)

David C. Fields Sr.
District Manager
Greensboro District
418 Gallimore Dairy Road
P.O. Box 27499
Greensboro, NC 27498-9900
(336) 668-1201
(336) 668-1366 (FAX)

Edward B. Burke
District Manager
Central Pennsylvania District
1425 Crooked Hill Road
Harrisburg, PA 17107-0001
(717) 257-2104
(717) 257-2302 (FAX)

Dennis M. Baca
District Manager
Kentuckiana District
PO Box 31000
Louisville, KY 40231-1000
(502) 454-1814
(502) 454-1990 (FAX)

Greg Gaamble
District Manager
Mid-Carolinas District
2901 Interstate 85 Service Rd
Charlotte, NC 28228-9980
(704) 424-4400 or 4570
(704) 424-4489 (FAX)

Jordan M. Small
District Manager
Philadelphia Metro District
2970 Market St., Room 306A
Philadelphia, PA 19104-9997
(215) 895-8607
(215) 895-8611 (FAX)

Keith J. Beppler
District Manager
Pittsburgh District
1001 California Avenue, Rm 2001
Pittsburgh, PA 15290-9996
(412) 359-7771
(412) 321-3373 (FAX)

Joanna Korker
District Manager
South Jersey District
PO Box 9001
Bellmawr, NJ 08099-9998
(856) 933-4400
(856) 933-4440 (FAX)

GREAT LAKES AREA

James M. Holmes
District Manager
Central Illinois District
6801 West 73rd Street
Bedford Park, IL 60499-9998
(708) 563-7800
(708) 563-2013 (FAX)

Akinyinka Akinyelle
District Manager
Chicago District
433 West Harrison
Chicago, IL 60607-9998
(312) 983-8030
(312) 983-8010 (FAX)

Gloria Tyson
District Manager
Detroit District
1401 West Fort Street
Detroit, MI 48233-9992
(313) 226-8605
(313) 226-8005 (FAX)

Danita Aquiningoc
District Manager
Gateway District
1720 Market Street, Rm 3027
St. Louis, MO 63155-9900
(314) 436-4114
(314) 436-4565 (FAX)

Peter R. Allen
District Manager
Greater Indiana District
3939 Vincennes Road
PO Box 9850
Indianapolis, IN 46298-9850
(317) 870-8201
(317) 870-8688 (FAX)

Charles E. Howe
District Manager
Greater Michigan District
PO Box 999997
Grand Rapids, MI 49599-9997
(616) 336-5300
(616) 336-5399 (FAX)

Lynn Smith
District Manager
North Illinois District
500 East Fullerton Ave.
Carol Stream, IL 60199-9998
(630) 260-5225
(630) 260-5130 (FAX)

Dave L Barthel
District Manager
Royal Oak District
P.O. Box 9000
Birmingham, MI 48009-9000
(248) 546-1370
(248) 546-0700 (FAX)

William J. Mitchell
District Manager
Lakeland District
PO Box 5000
Milwaukee, WI 53201-5000
(414) 287-2238
(414) 287-2296 (FAX)

*CAPITAL METRO
OPERATIONS*

Bill C. Miner
District Manager
Baltimore District
900 East Fayette Street, Rm 309
Baltimore, MD 21233-9990
(410) 347-4314
(410) 347-4289 (FAX)

Tim Haney
District Manager
Capital District
900 Brentwood Road, N.E.
Washington, DC 20066-7000
(202) 636-2210
(202) 636-5301 (FAX)

Michael S. Furey.
District Manager
Northern Virginia District
8409 Lee Highway
Merrifield, VA 22081-9996
(703) 698-6464
(703) 698-6500 (FAX)

Jeff Becker
District manager
Richmond District
1801 Brook Road
Richmond, VA 23232-9990
(804) 775-6365 or 6364
(804) 775-6058 (FAX)

NEW YORK METRO AREA
Robert Perez de Leon
Area/District Manager
Caribbean District
585 FD Roosevelt Ave., Ste 201
San Juan, PR 00936-9998
(787) 662-1800
(787) 622-1803 (FAX)

Vito J. Cetta
District Manager
Central New Jersey District
21 Kilmer Road
Edison, NJ 08899-9998
(732) 819-3264
(732) 819-3837 (FAX)

Thomas Rosati
District Manager
Long Island District
PO Box 7800
Islandia, NY 11760-9998
(631) 582-7410
(631) 582-7413 (FAX)

Vinnie E. Malloy
District Manager
New York District
421 5th Avenue, Room 3018
New York, NY 10199-9998
(212) 330-3600
(212) 330-3934 (FAX)

Eugene H. Rear
District Manager
Northern New Jersey District
494 Broad Street, Rm 307
Newark, NJ 07102-9300
(973) 468-7111
(973) 468-7215 (FAX)

Lily Jung
District Manager
Triboro District
142-02 20th Avenue
Flushing, NY 11351-9998
(718) 321-5144
(718) 321-5999 (FAX)

Peter J. Mancinelli
District Manager
Westchester District
PO Box 9800
White Plains, NY 10610-9800
(914) 697-7104
(914) 697-7128 (FAX)

NORTHEAST AREA

Timothy C. Healy
District Manager
Albany District
30 Old Karner Road
Albany, NY 12288-9992
(518) 452-2201
(518) 452-2309 (FAX)

William Downers
District Manager
Boston District
25 Dorchester Avenue
Boston, MA 02205-0098
(617) 654-5007
(617) 654-5816 (FAX)

William P. Galligan
District Manager
Connecticut District
141 Weston Street
Hartford, CT 06101-9996
(860) 524-6137
(860) 524-6199 (FAX)

Elizabeth A. Johnson
District Manager
Main District
P.O. Box 7800
Portland, ME 04104-7800
(207) 828-8529
(207) 828-8447 (FAX)

Joanna B. Korker
District Manager
Middlesex-Central District
74 Main Street
North Reading, MA 01889-9800
(978) 664-7603
(978) 664-5998 (FAX)

James H. Adams
District Manager
New Hampshire District
955 Goffs Falls Road
Manchester, NH 03103-9990
(603) 644-3800
(603) 644-3896 (FAX)

Thomas G. Day
District Manager
Southeast New England District
24 Corliss Street
Providence, RI 02904-9998
(401) 276-6950
(401) 276-6967 (FAX)

Charles K. Lynch
District Manager
Springfield District
1883 Main Street
Springfield, MA 01101-9700
(413) 731-0528
(413) 731-0280 (FAX)

Nicholas Fabozzi
District Manager
Western NY District
1200 William Street
Buffalo, NY 14240-9990
(716) 846-2532
(716) 846-2407 (FAX

PACIFIC AREA

Charles M. Davis
District Manager
Arizona District
4949 East Van Buren Street
Phoenix, AZ 85026-9900
(602) 225-5401
(602) 225-3286 (FAX)

Edward L. Broglio
District Manager
Honolulu District
3600 Aolele Street
Honolulu, HI 96820-3600
(808) 423-3700
(808) 423-3708 (FAX)

Johnray Egelhoff
District Manager
Las Vegas District
1001 East Sunset Road
Las Vegas, NV 89199-1000
(702) 361-9280
(702) 361-9349 (FAX)

David Shapiro
District Manager
Long Beach District
2300 Redondo Avenue
Long Beach, CA 90809-9798
(562) 494-2200
(562) 494-2437 (FAX)

Bill Almaraz
District Manager
Los Angeles District
7001 South Central Avenue
Los Angeles, CA 90052-9998
(323) 586-1200
(323) 586-1248 (FAX)

Kirby Faciane
District Manager
Oakland District
1675 7th Street
Oakland, CA 94615-9987
(510) 874-8222
(510) 874-8301 (FAX)

Hugo Francia
District Manager
Sacramento District
3775 Industrial Boulevard
West Sacramento, CA
95799-0010
(916) 373-8001
(916) 373-8704 (FAX)

John Platt
District Manager
San Diego District
11251 Rancho Carmel Dr.
San Diego, CA 92199-9990
(858) 674-0301
(858) 674-0405 (FAX)

P. Scott Tucker
District Manager
San Francisco District
PO Box 885050
San Francisco, CA 94188-5050
(415) 550-5591
(415) 550-5327 (FAX)

Winton Burnett
District Manager
San Jose District
1750 Lundy Avenue
San Jose, CA 95101-7000
(408) 437-6750
(408) 437-6776 (FAX)

Ed Ruiz
District Manager
Santa Ana District
3101 West Sunflower
Santa Ana, CA 92799-9993
(714) 662-6300
(714) 557-5837 (FAX)

Richard Ordonez
District Manager
Van Nuys District
28201 Franklin Parkway
Santa Clarita, CA 91383-9990
(661) 775-6500
(661) 775-7184 (FAX)

SOUTHEAST AREA

Gloria E. Tyson
District Manager
Alabama District
351 24th Street, North
Birmingham, AL 35203-9997
(205) 521-0201
(205) 521-0058 (FAX)

Robert Hodges Jr.
District Manager
Atlanta District
PO Box 599300
North Metro, GA 30026-9300
(770) 717-3736
(770) 717-3735 (FAX)

Peter J. Captain
District Manager
Central Florida District
PO Box 999800
Mid Florida, FL 32799-9800
(407) 333-4809
(407) 333-4899 (FAX)

James A. Daily
District Manager
Mississippi District
PO Box 99990
Jackson, MS 39205-9990
(601) 351-7350
(601) 351-7504 (FAX)

Harold L. Swinton
District Manager
North Florida District
PO Box 40005
Jacksonville, FL 32203-0005
(904) 858-6605
(904) 858-6610 (FAX)

Jo Ann Feindt
District Manager
South Florida District
PO Box 829990
Pembroke Pines, FL 33082-9990
(954) 436-4466
(954) 450-3015 (FAX)

Lizabeth J. Dobbins
District Manager
South Georgia District
451 College Street
Macon, GA 31213-9900
(478) 752-8530
(478) 752-8664 (FAX)

Michael P. Jordan
District Manager
Suncoast District
2203 N. Lois Avenue, Ste. 1001
Tampa, FL 33607-7101
(813) 354-6099
(813) 877-8656 (FAX)

Dennis R. Unger
District Manager
Tennessee District
811 Royal Parkway
Nashville, TN 37229-9998
(615) 885-9252
(615) 885-9317 (FAX)

SOUTHWEST AREA

E. W. Waldemayer Jr.
District Manager
Arkansas District
420 Natural Resources Drive
Little Rock, AR 72205-9800
(501) 228-4100
(501) 228-4105

J. Eric Martinez
District Manager
Albuquerque District
500 Marquette Ave., NW Ste. 900
Albuquerque, NM 87102-9999
(505) 346-8501 or 3950
(505) 346-8503 (FAX)

Carlton January
District Manager
Dallas District
951 West Bethel Road
Coppell, TX 75099-9998
(972) 393-6787
(972) 393-6198 (FAX)

Michael Flores
District Manager
Fort Worth District
4600 Mark IV Parkway
Fort Worth, TX 76161-9100
(817) 317-3301
(817) 317-3320 (FAX)

Terry Wilson
District Manager
Houston District
PO Box 250001
Houston, TX 77202-0001
(713) 226-3717
(713) 226-3755 (FAX)

Anthony J. Ruda
District Manager
Louisiana District
701 Loyola Avenue
New Orleans, LA 70113-9800
(504) 589-1950
(504) 589-1432 (FAX)

William C. Rucker
District Manager
Oklahoma City District
3030 NW Expressway St.
Oklahoma City, OK 73198-9800
(405) 553-6211
(405) 553-6106 (FAX)

Larry K. James
District Manager
Rio Grande District
One Post Office Drive
San Antonio, TX 78284-9997
(210) 368-5548
(210) 368-5511 (FAX)

WESTERN AREA

Bill R. Fetterhoff
District Manager
Alaska District
3720 Barrow Street
Anchorage, AK 99599-0001
(907) 261-5418
(907) 273-54866(FAX)

Robert G. Klein
District Manager
Big Sky District
841 South 26th Street
Billings, MT 59101-8800
(406) 657-5701
(406) 657-5788 (FAX)

Michael T. Matuzek
District Manager
Central Plains District
PO Box 249500
Omaha, NE 68124-9500
(402) 255-3900
(402) 255-3897 (FAX)

George Boettger
District Manager
Colorado/Wyoming District
7500 East 53rd Place, Rm 2204
Denver CO 80266-9998
(303) 853-6160
(303) 853-6099 (FAX)

Richard S. Shaver
District Manager
Dakotas District
PO Box 7500
Sioux Falls, SD 57117-7500
(515) 333-2604
(515) 333-2777 (FAX)

Joleen Baxa
District Manager
Hawkeye District
PO Box 189800
Des Moines, IA 50318-9800
(515) 251-2100
(515) 251-2050 (FAX)

Ormer Rogers, Jr.
District Manager
Mid-America District
315 West Pershing Road
Kansas City, MO 64108-9000
(816) 374-9104
(816) 374-0487 (FAX)

Michele J. Daley
District Manager
Northland District
100 South 1st Street
Minneapolis, MN 55401-9990
(612) 349-3505
(612) 349-6377 (FAX)

William G. Jackson
District Manager
Portland District
P.O. Box 3079
715 NW Hoyt Street
Portland, OR 97208-3079
(503) 294-2500
(503) 294-2020 (FAX)

Stephen L. Johnson
District Manager
Salt Lake City District
1760 West 2100 South
Salt Lake City, UT 84199-8800
(801) 974-2947
(801) 974-2975 (FAX)

Dale R. Zinser
District Manager
Seattle District
415 First Avenue North
Seattle, WA 98109-9997
(206) 442-6270
(206) 442-6006 (FAX)

Clair A. Brazington
District Manager
Spokane District
707 W. Maine Avenue, Suite 600
Spokane, WA 99299-1000
(509) 626-6703
(509) 626-6920 (FAX)

Chapter Five
Postal Exams

Clerk, carrier, and other job applicants such as mechanic, electronic technician, motor vehicle operators, machinist, clerical, and trades must pass a written test. The overall rating is based on the test results and your qualifying work experience and education. Certain occupations, including many professionals, don't require a written exam. These groups are evaluated under the Postal Service's *Rated-Application Examinations* process. They are rated and hired strictly on their prior work experience, education, and how well they do on the interview.

Locate Exams On-line
http://usps.com/employment
http://uspsapps.hr-services.org
http://postofficejobs.info

You need to locate the exam testing schedule for your area on-line or if you know the announcement number you can call the Postal Service's job hotline at **1/866-999-8777.** Go to http://usps.com/employment and select the "job" link located at the bottom of the page. This will take you to the employment section of their web site. You can also go direct to the Postal Service's exam schedules located at http://uspsapps.hr-services.org/.

If you don't have an announcement number click the continue button to bring up the exam schedule page. Select your state from the drop down menu and select go. All exams that are currently available for your state will be listed on this site. If an exam is open in your area you can click on the exam and apply on-line to take the test. The Postal Service will send you an exam package several weeks before the scheduled exam date.

All exams, including the 473 and 473-C exams are advertised infrequently in most areas. Once the exam is given all recruiting for that area is pulled from the active list of applicants who passed the last exam. When the list is insufficient to sustain recruiting efforts a new examination is announced for that area to replenish the list of applicants.

> The 473 exams are often only advertised for one week, typically starting on a Monday. You either have to visit the sites listed in this section each week or call your local Customer Service District Office listed in Chapter Four to find out when the next exams will be scheduled for your area.

473 MAJOR-ENTRY LEVEL EXAM

The **New 473 and 473-C Exam** covers the following positions:

- ✔ **City Carrier**
- ✔ **Mail Processing Clerk**
- ✔ **Mail handler**
- ✔ **Sales, Services, and Distribution Associate**

The **473 Major Entry Level Jobs Exam** may also be referred to as the 473 Battery Exam. The main difference between the 473 and 473-C exam is the target audience. The 473-C exam is announced primarily when the Postal Service is recruiting large numbers of City Letter Carriers and the 473 is exam is used to cover all of the job categories listed above. The two exams are essentially the same.

Battery Examinations cover the majority of entry level hiring although some offices also maintain custodial registers which, by law, are reserved for veteran preference eligibles. The postal service is still using the *460 Battery Examination* for Rural Mail Carrier positions. The USPS also maintains *motor vehicle* and *tractor trailer registers* and some highly skilled maintenance positions such as *Building Equipment Mechanic, Engineman, Electronics Technician, and General Mechanic.* All of the skilled maintenance positions require examination 931. A separate announcement, examination number 932, is required for Electronics Technician positions.

Sample exams and test questions are provided in this chapter for most job categories except for the *473 Battery Test*. The *473 Battery Test* and completion of forms is covered in Chapter Six with additional practice exams and study tips.

SKILLS TESTS

Ability and skills tests (*performance tests*) are designed to predict future success, both in job training and job performance. The Postal Service uses these tests to obtain an indication of your potential to learn and perform particular job responsibilities. Skills tests measure specifically what you know about and can perform in a particular job—they test your mastery of tasks. The Postal Service administers skills tests when they are interested in filling a position with an applicant who knows the basics of the job and can perform job tasks as soon as he or she starts. Some performance tests are: the road test for operators of postal vehicles, the typing test, and the test of strength and stamina for mail handlers.

ROAD TEST EXAMINATION

The initial road test is a systematic way to measure an individual's ability and skill to drive safely and properly under normal operating conditions. This test is an important part of the overall selection process for positions that require motor vehicle operation, and it is also a practical test to determine whether or not an individual is a skilled and a safe driver. The test includes items that have been reported as actual causes of accidents and gives special emphasis to the driving deficiencies identified as major causes of postal motor vehicle accidents.

There is a comprehensive table of disqualifications that apply to the Road Test Examination such as:

1.   Applicant doesn't have at least two years of documented driving experience.
2.   Applicant has had driving permit suspended once (or more) in the last three years, OR twice (or more) in the last five years.
3.   Applicant has had driving permit revoked once (or more) in last five years.

Specific offenses such as reckless driving, hit-and-run offense, or use of drugs also are disqualifying factors. For the purpose of determining disqualifying violations, consider only offenses followed by a conviction.

STUDY HABITS

It's often helpful to study with a partner, someone to read the question and check your responses. It can be a fellow worker, a spouse, or just a good friend.

Try various study routines until you hit a combination that works. Try studying in 20 to 30 minute sessions with 5 minute breaks in between, or stretch it out to hour intervals. A good study routine will improve your test scores.

TEST TAKING STRATEGIES

The following strategies will help you improve your grades. Use these strategies on the practice tests in this book and when you take your actual Postal Service exam. If you practice these techniques now, when you take the postal exam they will become second nature.

- ✎   Eliminate the answers in multiple choice questions that make no sense at all. You can often eliminate half of the answers through this method. If you have to guess an answer, you improve your chances through the process of elimination.
- ✎   Be skeptical when an answer includes words like, always, never, all, none, generally, or only. These words can be a trap. Only select an

answer with these words in it if you are absolutely sure it is the right answer.

✎   If two answers have opposite meanings, take your time and look closer. Many times one of the two is correct.

✎   Place a mark next to answers that you are unsure about. After completing the remainder of the exam, go back and review these questions and make a final selection. Often, other questions that you've answered will jog your memory.

✎   One word can dramatically change the meaning of a sentence. Read each question word-for-word before answering.

✎   Don't let the test get the best of you. Build your confidence by answering the questions you know first. If the first question you read stumps you, skip it and go on to the next one. When you've completed most of the exam you can go back - if time permits - to the questions that you couldn't answer.

✎   Get plenty of rest the night before the exam.

SAMPLE EXAMS

Sample practice exams are sent to applicants by the Postal Service when you apply for a test. The Postal Service will only send sample exams and application forms if they are hiring/testing for that specialty. Refer to Chapter Four's Customer Services and Sales District Office lists that you can call to obtain job vacancy announcements, test schedules, and applications.

Sample exams are presented in this chapter for the following occupational groups:

EXAM 91 - Motor Vehicle Operator Exam
(Garageman, Motor Vehicle & Tractor Trailer Operators)

EXAM 710 - Clerical Abilities Exam
(Data Conversion Operator, Clerk-Typist, Clerk Stenographer)

EXAM 714 - Data Conversion Operator

EXAM 931 - Maintenance Specialists/Technicians, Engineman, Blacksmith-welder, Custodian, Building Equipment Mechanics, Carpenter, Elevator Mechanic, Fireman, General Mechanic, Machinist, Electrician, Mason, Painter, Oiler, Plumber, Stationary Engineer.

EXAM 932 - Electronic Technician Positions

EXAM 933 - Measures 16 Knowledge, Skills, and Abilities (KSAs) used by a variety of maintenance positions including Maintenance Mechanic and Overhaul Specialist.

SAMPLE EXAM 91

Motor Vehicle Operator Exam
(Garageman, Motor Vehicle & Tractor Trailer Operators)

The sample exam that follows illustrates the types of questions that will be used in Test M/M 91. The samples will also show how the questions in the test are to be answered. Job descriptions for these occupations are included in Chapter Nine.

T0352 000000   SQ 91

SAMPLE QUESTIONS FOR TEST 91

The sample questions in this booklet show the kinds of questions that you will find in the written test. By reading and doing these questions, you will find out how to answer the questions in the test and about how hard the questions will be.

Read the questions carefully. Be sure you know what the questions are about and then answer the questions in the way you are told to do. If you are told the answer to a question, be sure you understand why the answer is right.

Here are the sample questions for you to answer.

Question 1 is about picture 1, below. Look at the picture.

PICTURE 1

1.   How many vehicles are shown in the picture,

(Write your answer for question 1 here.)

GO ON TO THE NEXT PAGE.

Questions 2 and 3 are about picture 2, below. Look at the picture.

PICTURE 2

2.   Who is sitting on the motorcycle ?

\-

(Write your answer for question 2 here.)

3.   What is the policeman probably doing ?

\-

(Write your answer for question 3 here.)

Questions 4 and 5 are about picture 3, below. Look at the picture.

PICTURE 3

4.   What is happening in this picture ?

\-

(Write your answer for question 4 here.)

5.   Show the positions of the truck and the passenger car by drawing boxes like those shown below. (Your boxes will not be the same position as these.)

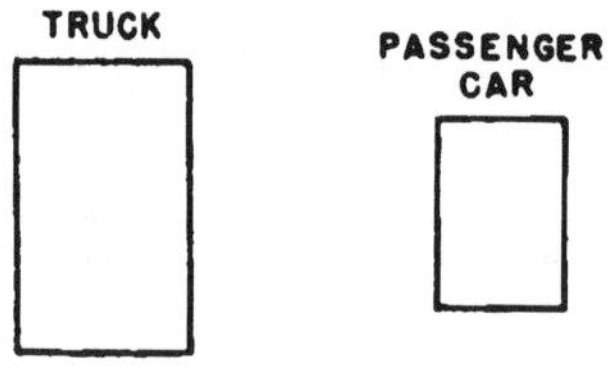

TRUCK   PASSENGER
                  CAR

Draw your boxes in the space below.

Questions 6 and 7 are about pictures of oilcans. Each picture has a letter. You are to tell what each picture shows by writing a short description of the picture on the answer line that goes with the question.

Now look at picture X.

6. What does picture X show ?

(Write your answer for question 6 here.)

Picture X shows two oilcans. So, you should have written something like "two oilcans" on the line under question 6.

Now look at picture Y.

7. What does picture Y show?

(Write your answer for question 7 here.)

Question 8 is filling in a chart. You are given the following information to put in the chart. Truck, license number 48-7128, had its oil changed last at speedometer reading 96,005.

Truck, license number 858-232, was greased last at speedometer reading 89,564.

Look at the chart below. The information for the first truck has already been filled in. For question 8, fill in the information for the other truck. You are to show, in the proper columns, the license number of the truck, the kind of service, and the speedometer reading when serviced.

Truck License Number	Kind of Service	Speedometer Reading When Serviced
48-7128	Oil Change	96,005

(For question 8, write the information for the second truck in the proper columns above.)

GO ON TO THE NEXT PAGE.

Questions 9 and 10 are about words that might appear on traffic signs.

In questions like 9, there is one numbered line and then, just below that line, four other lines which are lettered A, B, C, and D. Read the first line. Then read the other four linea. Decide which line—A, B, C, or D—means most nearly the same as the first line in the question. Write the letter of the line that means the same as the numbered line in the answer space.

Here is another example.
9. Speed Limit—20 Miles
A) Do Not Exceed 20 Miles per Hour
B) Railroad Crossing
C) No Turns
D) Dangerous Intersection   --
                              (Write your answer for question 9 here.)

The first line says "Speed Limit—20 Miles." Line A says "Do Not Exceed 20 Miles per Hour." B says "Railroad Crossing." C says "No Turns." D says "Dangerous Intersection." The line that says almost the same thing as the first line is line A. That is, the one that means most nearly "Speed Limit—20 Miles" is "Do Not Exceed 20 Miles per Hour." The answer to question 9 is A. You should have marked A on the answer line for question 9.

Here is another example.
10. Dead End
A) Merging Traffic
B) No U-Turns
D) Turn on Red
D) No Through Traffic   --
                         (Write your answer for question 10 here.)

After you answer questions like the ones you have just finished, you will be asked other questions to see how well you understand what you have written. To answer the next questions, you will use the information that you wrote for the first 10 questions. Mark your answers to the next questions on the Sample Answer Sheet on page 6.

The Sample Answer Sheet has spaces that look like these:

If you wanted to mark D for your answer to question 1, you would mark it like this:

If you wanted to mark C for your answer to question 2, you would mark it like this:

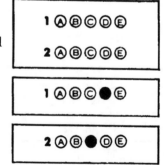

GO ON TO THE NEXT PAGE.

Each of the questions in the next part is about something you should have written on your answer lines.

In answering the next questions in this booklet, you may look back to what you have already written as often as you wish. You may look back while you are marking the Sample Answer Sheet. In the actual test, the pictures and their questions will be taken away from you before you mark the answer sheet, but you will keep what you wrote about the pictures while marking your answer sheet. So, for this practice, try not to look at the pictures but look at what you wrote about them.

Answer each of the following questions by darkening completely space A, B, C, D, or E beside the number that you are told in the question. Mark all your answers on the Sample Answer Sheet.

Question 11 is about question 1. Use what you wrote under question 1 to answer question 11. Mark your answer on the Sample Answer Sheet at the foot of the next page.

11. For number 11 on the Sample Answer Sheet,
       mark space A if only one vehicle is shown in the picture
       mark space B if only two vehicles are shown in the picture
       mark space c if only three vehicles are shown in the picture
       mark space D if only four vehicles are shown in the picture
       mark space E if only five vehicles are shown in the picture

If you look at the answer you gave for question 1, you will see that you wrote that three vehicles were shown in the picture. The question above tells you to mark space C on the Sample Answer Sheet if only three vehicles are shown. So you should have marked space C for number 11 on the Sample Answer Sheet.

Question 12 below is about question 2, and question 13 below is about question 3.
12. For number 12 on the Sample Answer Sheet, mark space
       A if a policeman is sitting on the motorcycle
       B if a man in overall is sitting on the motorcycle
       C if a boy in a sport shirt is sitting on the motorcycle
       D if a nurse is sitting on the motorcycle
       E if a man with a white beard is setting on the motorcycle

Be sure to mark your answer on the Sample Answer Sheet.
13. For number 13 on the Sample Answer Sheet, mark space
       A if the policeman is probably fixing a tire
       B if the policeman is probably using a telephone
       C if the policeman is probably taking off his cap
       D if the policeman is probably blowing a whistle
       E if the policeman is probably writing a "ticket"

Question 14 below is about question 4, and question 15 below is about question 5.
14. For number 14 on the Sample Answer Sheet, mark space
       A if a bus is passing a fire truck
       B if a motorcycle is hitting a fence
       C if a truck is backing up to a platform
       D if a passenger car is getting gas
       E if a passenger car is hitting a truck

GO ON TO THE NEXT PAGE.

15. Look at the boxes you drew for question 5. For number 15 on the Sample Answer Sheet, mark space

    A if a truck is on a ramp and a passenger car is on the street

    B if a truck is to the rear of a passenger car

    C if the front bumpers of a passenger car and a truck are in line

    D if a passenger car is to the rear of a truck

    E if a motorcycle is between a truck and a passenger car

Question 16 below is about question 6 under picture X, and question 17 below is about question 7 under picture Y.

16. For number 16 on the Sample Answer Sheet, mark space

    A if there is only one oilcan in picture X

    B if there are only two oilcans in picture X

    C if there are only three oilcans in picture X

    D if there are only four oilcans in picture X

    E if there are only five oilcans in picture X

17. For number 17 on the Sample Answer Sheet, mark space

    A if there is only one oilcan in picture Y

    B if there are only two oilcans in picture Y

    C if there are only three oilcans in picture Y

    D if there are only four oilcans in picture Y

    E if there are only five oilcans in picture Y

Question 18 below is about the chart you filled in. For this question, mark on the Sample Answer Sheet the letter of the suggested answer—A, B, C, or D—that best answers the question.

18. What is the license number of the truck that was greased? (Look at what you wrote on the chart. Don't answer from memory.)

    A) 89,564   C) 858-232

    B) 48 - 7128   D) 96,005

For number 19 on the Sample Answer Sheet, mark the space that has the same letter as the letter you wrote on the answer line for question 9.

For number 20 on the Sample Answer Sheet, mark the space that has the same letter as the letter you wrote on the answer line for question 10.

Now see if the answers you have marked on the Sample Answer Sheet are the same as the answers marked in Correct Answers to Sample Questions. If the answers you have picked are the same as the answers in Correct Answers to Sample Questions, you are showing that you can pick right answers. If the answers you have picked are not the same as the answers in Correct Answers to Sample Questions, go back to the questions to see why your answers are wrong.

EXAM 710 - Clerical Abilities Exam
(Data Conversion Operator, Clerk-Typist, Clerk Stenographer)

The sample exam that follows illustrates the types of questions that will be used in Examination 710. The samples will also show how the questions in the test are to be answered. Job descriptions for these occupations are included in Chapter Nine.

SAMPLE QUESTIONS FOR EXAMINATION 710
CLERICAL ABILITIES

The following questions are samples of the types of questions that will be used on Examination 710. Study these questions carefully. Each question has several suggested answers. You are to decide which one is the best answer. Next, on the Sample Answer Sheet below, find the answer space that is numbered the same number as the question, then darken the space that is lettered the same as the answer you have selected. After you have answered all the questions, compare your answers with the ones given in the Correct Answers to Sample Questions below the Sample Answer Sheets

Sample Questions 1 through 14 - Clerical Aptitude

In Sample Questions 1 through 3 below, there is a name or code in a box at the left, and four other names or codes in alphabetical or numerical order at the right. Find the correct space for the boxed name or number so that it will be in alphabetical and/or numerical order with the others and mark the letter of that space as your answer on your Sample Answer Sheet below.

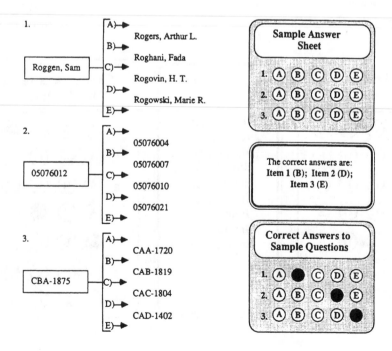

Sample Questions 4 through 8 require you to compare names, addresses, or codes. Ln each line across the page, there are three names, addresses or codes that are much alike. Compare the three and decide which ones are exactly alike. On the Sample Answer Sheet at the bottom, mark the answers:

A   if **ALL THREE** names, addresses, or codes are exactly **ALIKE**
B   if only the **FIRST** and **SECOND** names, addresses, or codes are exactly **ALIKE**
C   if only the **FIRST** and **THIRD** names, addresses, or codes are exactly **ALIKE**
D   if only the **SECOND** and **THIRD** names, addresses, or codes are exactly **ALIKE**
E   if **ALL THREE** names, addresses, or codes are **DIFFERENT**

4. Helene Bedell	Helene Beddell	Helene Beddell
5. F. T. Wedemeyer	F. T. Wedemeyer	F. T. Wedmeyer
6. 3214 W. Beaumont St.3214	Beaumount St.	3214 Beaumont St.
7. BC 3105T-5	BC 3015T-5	BC 3105T-5
8. 4460327	4460327	4460327

For the next two questions, find the correct spelling of the word and darken the appropriate answer space on your Sample Answer Sheet. If none of the alternatives are correct, darken Space D.

9.   A) accomodate
      B) acommodate
      C) accommadate
      D) none of the above

10.   A) manageble
      B) manageable
      C) manageable
      D) none of the above

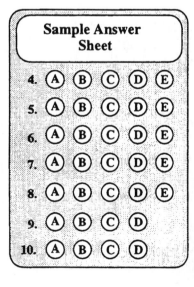
Sample Answer Sheet

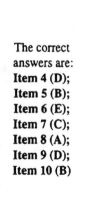
The correct answers are:
Item 4 (D);
Item 5 (B);
Item 6 (E);
Item 7 (C);
Item 8 (A);
Item 9 (D);
Item 10 (B)

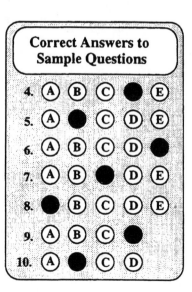
Correct Answers to Sample Questions

For Questions 11 through 14, perform the computation as indicated in the question and find the answer among the list of alternative responses. Mark your Sample Answer Sheet A, B, C, or D for the correct answer; or, if your answer is not among these, mark E for that question.

11. 32+26 =

A) 69
B) 59
C) 58
D) 54
E) none of the above

12. 57- 15=

A) 72
B) 62
C) 54
D) 44
E) none of the above

13. 23 x 7 =

A) 164
B) 161
C) 154
D) 141
E) none of the above

14. 160 / 5 =

A) 32
B) 30
C) 25
D) 21
E) none of the above

Sample Answer Sheet

11. (A) (B) (C) (D) (E)
12. (A) (B) (C) (D) (E)
13. (A) (B) (C) (D) (E)
14. (A) (B) (C) (D) (E)

The correct answers are:
Item 11 (C); Item 12 (E);
Item 13 (B); Item 14 (A)

Correct Answers to Sample Questions

11. (A) (B) ● (D) (E)
12. (A) (B) (C) (D) ●
13. (A) ● (C) (D) (E)
14. ● (B) (C) (D) (E)

Sample Questions 15 through 22 - Verbal Abilities

Sample items 15 through 17 below test the ability to follow instructions. They direct you to mark a specific number and letter combination on your Sample Answer Sheet. The answers that you are instructed to mark are, for the most part, NOT in numerical sequence (i.e., you would not use Number 1 on your answer sheet to answer Question 1; Number 2 for Question 2, etc.). Instead, you must mark the number and space specifically designated in each test question.

Sample Answer Sheet

15. Ⓐ Ⓑ Ⓒ Ⓓ Ⓔ
16. Ⓐ Ⓑ Ⓒ Ⓓ Ⓔ
17. Ⓐ Ⓑ Ⓒ Ⓓ Ⓔ

15. Look at the letters below. Draw a circle around the middle letter. Now, on your Sample Answer Sheet, find Number 16 and darken the space for the letter you just circled.

R   C   H

16. Draw a line under the number shown below that is more than 10 but less than 20. Find that number on your Sample Answer Sheet, and darken Space A.

5   9   17   22

The correct answers are:
Item 15 (B); Item 16 (C); Item 17 (A)

17. Add the numbers 11 and 4 and write your answer on the blank line below. Now find this number on your Sample Answer Sheet and darken the space for the second letter in the alphabet.

Correct Answers to Sample Questions

15. Ⓐ ● Ⓒ Ⓓ Ⓔ
16. Ⓐ Ⓑ ● Ⓓ Ⓔ
17. ● Ⓑ Ⓒ Ⓓ Ⓔ

Answer the remaining Sample Test Questions on
the Sample Answer Sheet in numerical sequence
(i.e., Number 18 on the Sample Answer Sheet for
Question 18; Number 19 for Question 19, etc.).

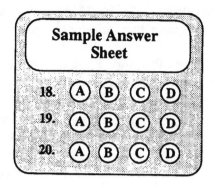

Select the sentence below which is most appropriate
with respect to grammar, usage, and punctuation
suitable for a formal letter or report.

18. A) He should of responded to the letter by now.
     B) A response to the letter by the end of the week.
     C) The letter required his immediate response.
     D) A response by him to the letter is necessary.

In questions 19 and 20 below, you will be asked to
decide what the highlighted word means.

19. The payment was **authorized** yesterday.
     Authorized most nearly means

     A) expected
     B) approved
     C) refunded
     D) received

The correct answers are:
Item 18 (C); Item 19 (B);
Item 20 (D)

20. Please **delete** the second paragraph. **Delete**
     most nearly means

     A) type
     B) read
     C) edit
     D) omit

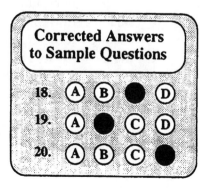

In questions 21 and 22 below, you are asked to read a paragraph, then answer the question that follows it.

21. "Window Clerks working for the Postal Service have direct financial responsibility for the selling of postage. In addition, they are expected to have a thorough knowledge concerning the acceptability of all material offered by customers for mailing. Any information provided to the public by these employees must be completely accurate."

The paragraph best supports the statement that Window Clerks

A) must account for the stamps issued to them for sale
B) have had long training in other Postal Service jobs
C) must help sort mail to be delivered by carriers
D) inspect the contents of all packages offered for mailing

22. "The most efficient method for performing a task is not always easily determined. That which is economical in terms of time must be carefully distinguished from that which is economical in terms of expended energy. In short, the quickest method may require a degree of physical effort that may be neither essential nor desirable."

The paragraph best supports the statement that

A) it is more efficient to perform a task slowly than rapidly
B) skill in performing a task should not be acquired at the expense of time
C) the most efficient execution of a task is not always the one done in the shortest time
D) energy and time cannot both be considered in the performance of a single task

Sample Answer Sheet

21. Ⓐ Ⓑ Ⓒ Ⓓ
22. Ⓐ Ⓑ Ⓒ Ⓓ

The correct answers are:
Item 21 (A); Item 22 (C);

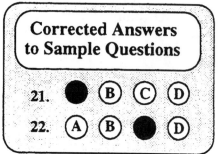

Corrected Answers to Sample Questions

21. ● Ⓑ Ⓒ Ⓓ
22. Ⓐ Ⓑ ● Ⓓ

SAMPLE ITEMS FOR COMPUTER BASED TEST 714

The CB 714 is a computer administered and scored exam. Applicants are assisted with the start-up of the exam and with the exam instructions. You do MI need prior experience on a computer terminal to take this test.

The exam contains a list of alphanumeric postal data entry items just as you see in the sample items below. Applicants must demonstrate that they can type these items on the computer terminal at the following rate(s) based on the requirements of the position. The lower level passing rate is 5 correct lines per minute. The higher level passing rate is 7 correct lines per minute. Credit is given only for correctly typed lines. Practice for the exam by typing the sample provided below.

Type each line as shown in the exercise, beginning with the first column. You may use lower-case or capital letters when typing the sample exercise. When you reach the end of a line, single space and begin typing the next line. If you reach the end of the sample items in the first column, continue with the items in the second column. If you finish both columns, simply begin again with the first column and continue to type until the five minutes have elapsed.

See whether you can copy the entire Sample Test once in a five minute timing. Now count the number of lines you typed correctly and divide this number by five to determine your per minute score. Correctly typing only the items in column 1 is approximately equal to typing 5 correct lines per minute. Correctly typing all of the items in both columns is approximately equal to typing 7 correct lines per minute.

In the exam you will have five minutes in which to type the test material. Keep in mind that in order to pass the test you must type both rapidly and accurately.

SAMPLE TEST COPY

4.90 STEERING DAMPER	18.25 DOWN SPRING
16.55 REAR DOOR LATCH	3.10 VC GASKET
23.80 TIMING CHAIN	35.45 ROCKER ARM
8721 8906	4973 5261
2013 2547	6057 7352
5972 6841	2783 4195
HANOVER RD. 600 - 699	GREENBRIAR DR. 1100 - 1399
ARKANSAS AVE. 4000 - 4199	MADISON ST. 3700 - 3799
SO. MAIN ST. 1200 - 1299	BRUNSWICK AVE. 8100 - 8199
CAPITOL DR. 500 - 599	INDUSTRIAL RD. 2300 - 2499
L ON MAPLEWOOD PL.	
RETRACE TO 421	
R ON MOHICAN TO TOWER	
4478267 LSM/LSM	
4478271 MPLSM	
4478289 EGR SECONDARY	
KNIGHT, J.R. 04/17/67	
CHARLES, S.M. 11/19/68	
JEFFERSON, W.A. 08/20/69	
SPRINGFIELD 07215	
GREENSBORO 07098	
LEXINGTON 07540	
FOURTH CLASS 363	
INTN. SECTION 27	
200 BOX 10	

EXAM 931 - Maintenance Specialists/Technicians, Engineman, Blacksmith-welder, Custodian, Building Equipment Mechanics, Carpenter, Elevator Mechanic, Fireman, General Mechanic, Machinist, Electrician, Mason, Painter, Oiler, Plumber, Stationary Engineer

Test M/N 931 covers the following Knowledge, Skills, and Abilities:

✔ *Knowledge of basic mechanics* refers to the theory of operation, terminology, usage, and characteristics of basic mechanical principles as they apply to such things as gears, pulleys, cams, pawls, power transmissions, linkages, fasteners, chains, sprockets, and belts; and including hoisting, rigging, roping, pneumatics, and hydraulic devices.

✔ *Knowledge of basic electricity* refers to the theory, terminology, usage, and characteristics of basic electrical principles such as ohm's Law, Kirchoff's Law, and magnetism, as they apply to such things as AC-DC circuitry and hardware, relays, switches, and circuit breakers.

✔ *Knowledge of basic electronics* refers to the theory, terminology, usage, and characteristics of basic electronic principles concerning such things as solid state devices, vacuum tubes, coils, capacitors, resistors, and basic logic circuitry.

✔ *Knowledge of safety procedures and equipment* refers to the knowledge of industrial hazards (e.g., mechanical, chemical, electrical, electronic) and procedures and techniques established to avoid injuries to self and others such as lock-out devices, protective clothing, and waste disposal techniques.

✔ *Knowledge of refrigeration* refers to the theory, terminology, usage, and characteristics of refrigeration principles as they apply to such things as the refrigeration cycle, compressors, condensers, receivers, evaporators, metering devices, and refrigerant oils.

✔ *Knowledge of heating, ventilation, and air conditioning (HVAC) equipment operation* refers to the knowledge of equipment operation such as safety considerations, start-up, shut-down, and mechanical and electrical operating characteristics of HVAC equipment (e.g., chillers, direct expansion units, window units, heating equipment). This does not include the knowledge of refrigeration.

✔ *Ability to perform basic mathematical computations* refers to the ability to perform basic calculations such as addition, subtraction, multiplication and division with whole numbers, fractions and decimals.

✔ *Ability to perform more complex mathematics* refers to the ability to perform calculations such as basic geometry, scientific notation, and number conversions, as applied to mechanical, electrical and electronic applications.

✔ *Ability to apply theoretical knowledge to practical applications* refers to mechanical, electrical and electronic maintenance applications such as inspection, troubleshooting equipment repair and modification, preventive maintenance, and installation of electrical equipment.

✔ *Ability to detect patterns* refers to the ability to observe and analyze qualitative factors such as number progressions, spatial relationships, and auditory and visual patterns. This includes combining information and determining how a given set of numbers, objects, or sounds are related to each other.

✔ *Ability to use written reference materials* refers to the ability to locate, read, and comprehend text material such as handbooks, manuals, bulletins, directives, checklists and route sheets.

✔ *Ability to follow instructions* refers to the ability to comprehend and execute written and oral instructions such as work orders, checklists, route sheets, and verbal directions and instructions.

✔ *Ability to use hand tools* refers to knowledge of, and proficiency with, various hand tools. This ability involves the safe and efficient use and maintenance of such tools as screwdrivers, wrenches, hammers, pliers, chisels, punches, taps, dies, rules, gauges, and alignment tools.

✔ *Ability to use technical drawings* refers to the ability to react and comprehend technical materials such as diagrams, schematics, flow charts, and blueprints.

✔ *Ability to use test equipment* refers to the knowledge of, and proficiency with, various mechanical, electrical and electronic test equipment such as VOMS, oscilloscopes, circuit tracers, amprobes, and tachometers.

✔ *Ability to solder* refers to the knowledge of, and the ability to safely and effectively apply, the appropriate soldering techniques.

The sample exam that follows illustrates the types of questions that will be used in Test M/M 931. The samples will also show how the questions in the test are to be answered. Job descriptions for these occupations are included in Chapter Nine.

UNITED STATES POSTAL SERVICE

SAMPLE QUESTIONS - TEST M/N 931

The purpose of this booklet is to illustrate the types of questions that will be used in Test M/M 931. The samples will also show how the questions in the test are to be answered.

Test M/N 931 measures 16 Knowledge, Skills, and Abilities (KSAs) used by a variety of maintenance positions. Exhibit A lists the actual KSAs that are measured, and Exhibit B lists the positions that use this examination. However, not all KSAs that are measured in this test are scored for every position listed. The qualification standard for each position lists the KSAs required for the position. Only those questions that measure KSAs required for the positions) for which you are applying will be scored for the position(s).

The suggested answers to each question are lettered A, B, C, etc. Select the BEST answer and make a heavy pencil mark in the corresponding space on the Sample Answer Sheet. Each mark must be dense black. Each mark must cover more than half the space and must not extend into neighboring spaces. If the answer to Sample 1 is B, you would mark the Sample Answer Sheet like this:

After recording your answers, compare them with those in the Correct Answers to Sample Questions. If they do not agree, carefully re-read the questions that were missed to get a clear understanding of what each question is asking.

During the test, directions for answering questions in Part I will be given orally, either by a cassette tape or by the examiner. You are to listen closely to the directions and follow them. To practice for this part of the test you might have a friend read the direction to you while you mark your answers on the Sample Answer Sheet. Directions for answering questions in Part II will be completely described in the test booklet.

STUDY CAREFULLY BEFORE YOU GO TO THE EXAMINATION ROOM

PART I

In Part I of the test, you will be told to follow directions by writing in a test booklet and then on an answer sheet. The test booklet will have lines of material like the following five samples:

SAMPLE   1.   5 _____

SAMPLE   2.   1   6   4   3   7

SAMPLE   3.   D   B   A   E   C

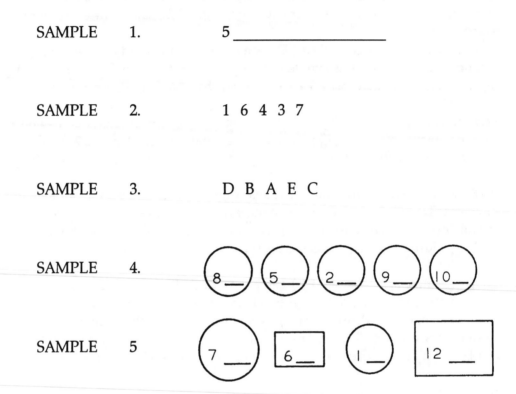

SAMPLE   4.

SAMPLE   5

To practice this test, have someone read the instructions on the **next page** to you and you follow the instructions. When they tell you to darken the space on the Sample Answer Sheet, use the one on this page.

```
                    SAMPLE ANSWER SHEET
1  Ⓐ Ⓑ Ⓒ Ⓓ Ⓔ      5  Ⓐ Ⓑ Ⓒ Ⓓ Ⓔ      9  Ⓐ Ⓑ Ⓒ Ⓓ Ⓔ
2  Ⓐ Ⓑ Ⓒ Ⓓ Ⓔ      6  Ⓐ Ⓑ Ⓒ Ⓓ Ⓔ     10  Ⓐ Ⓑ Ⓒ Ⓓ Ⓔ
3  Ⓐ Ⓑ Ⓒ Ⓓ Ⓔ      7  Ⓐ Ⓑ Ⓒ Ⓓ Ⓔ     11  Ⓐ Ⓑ Ⓒ Ⓓ Ⓔ
4  Ⓐ Ⓑ Ⓒ Ⓓ Ⓔ      8  Ⓐ Ⓑ Ⓒ Ⓓ Ⓔ     12  Ⓐ Ⓑ Ⓒ Ⓓ Ⓔ
```

Instructions to be read (the words in parentheses should not be read aloud).

You are to follow the instructions that I shall read to you. I cannot repeat them.

Look at the samples. Sample 1 has a number and a line beside it. On the line write an A. (Pause 2 seconds.) Now on the Sample Answer Sheet, find number 5 (pause 2 seconds) and darken the space for the letter you just wrote on the line. (Pause 2 seconds.)

Look at Sample 2. (Pause slightly.) Draw a line under the third number. (Pause 2 seconds.) Now look on the Sample Answer Sheet, find the number under which you just drew a line and darken space B as in baker for that number. (Pause 5 seconds.)

Look at Sample 3. (Pause slightly.) Draw a line under the third letter in the line. (Pause 2 seconds.) Now on your Sample Answer Sheet, find number 9 (pause 2 seconds) and darken the space for the letter under which you drew a line. (Pause 5 seconds.)

Look at the five circles in Sample 4. (Pause slightly.) Each circle has a number and a line in it. write D as in dog on the blank in the last circle. (Pause 2 seconds.) Now on the Sample Answer Sheet, darken the space for the number-letter combination that is in the circle you just wrote in. (Pause 5 seconds.)

Look at Sample 5. (Pause slightly.) There are two circles and two boxes of different sizes with numbers in them. (Pause slightly.) If 4 is more than 2 and if 5 is less than 3, write A in the smaller circle. (Pause slightly.) Otherwise write C in the larger box. (Pause 2 seconds.) Now on the Sample Answer Sheet, darken the space for the number-letter combination in the circle or box in which you just wrote. (Pause 5 seconds.)

Now look at the Sample Answer Sheet. (Pause slightly.) You should have darkened spaces 4B, 5A, 9A, 10D, and 12C on the Sample Answer Sheet. (If the person preparing to take the examination made any mistakes, try to help him or her understand why the mistakes are wrong.)

SAMPLE ANSWER QUESTIONS

1 Ⓐ Ⓑ Ⓒ Ⓓ Ⓔ   18 Ⓐ Ⓑ Ⓒ Ⓓ Ⓔ

2 Ⓐ Ⓑ Ⓒ Ⓓ Ⓔ   19 Ⓐ Ⓑ Ⓒ Ⓓ Ⓔ

3 Ⓐ Ⓑ Ⓒ Ⓓ Ⓔ   20 Ⓐ Ⓑ Ⓒ Ⓓ Ⓔ

4 Ⓐ Ⓑ Ⓒ Ⓓ Ⓔ   21 Ⓐ Ⓑ Ⓒ Ⓓ Ⓔ

5 Ⓐ Ⓑ Ⓒ Ⓓ Ⓔ   22 Ⓐ Ⓑ Ⓒ Ⓓ Ⓔ

6 Ⓐ Ⓑ Ⓒ Ⓓ Ⓔ   23 Ⓐ Ⓑ Ⓒ Ⓓ Ⓔ

7 Ⓐ Ⓑ Ⓒ Ⓓ Ⓔ   24 Ⓐ Ⓑ Ⓒ Ⓓ Ⓔ

8 Ⓐ Ⓑ Ⓒ Ⓓ Ⓔ   25 Ⓐ Ⓑ Ⓒ Ⓓ Ⓔ

9 Ⓐ Ⓑ Ⓒ Ⓓ Ⓔ   26 Ⓐ Ⓑ Ⓒ Ⓓ Ⓔ

10 Ⓐ Ⓑ Ⓒ Ⓓ Ⓔ   27 Ⓐ Ⓑ Ⓒ Ⓓ Ⓔ

11 Ⓐ Ⓑ Ⓒ Ⓓ Ⓔ   28 Ⓐ Ⓑ Ⓒ Ⓓ Ⓔ

12 Ⓐ Ⓑ Ⓒ Ⓓ Ⓔ   29 Ⓐ Ⓑ Ⓒ Ⓓ Ⓔ

13 Ⓐ Ⓑ Ⓒ Ⓓ Ⓔ   30 Ⓐ Ⓑ Ⓒ Ⓓ Ⓔ

14 Ⓐ Ⓑ Ⓒ Ⓓ Ⓔ   31 Ⓐ Ⓑ Ⓒ Ⓓ Ⓔ

15 Ⓐ Ⓑ Ⓒ Ⓓ Ⓔ   32 Ⓐ Ⓑ Ⓒ Ⓓ Ⓔ

16 Ⓐ Ⓑ Ⓒ Ⓓ Ⓔ   33 Ⓐ Ⓑ Ⓒ Ⓓ Ⓔ

17 Ⓐ Ⓑ Ⓒ Ⓓ Ⓔ   34 Ⓐ Ⓑ Ⓒ Ⓓ Ⓔ

PART II

1. Which device is used to transfer power and rotary mechanical motion from one shaft to another?

    A) Bearing
    B) Lever
    C) Idler roller
    D) Gear
    E) Bushing

2. Lead anchors are usually mounted in

    A) steel paneling.
    B) drywall construction.
    C) masonry construction.
    D) wood construction.
    E) gypsum board.

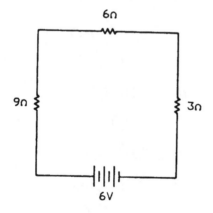

Figure III-A-22

3. Which of the following circuits is shown in Figure III-A-22?

    A) Series circuit
    B) Parallel circuit
    C) Series, parallel circuit
    D) Solid state circuit
    E) None of the above

4. Which component would BEST simulate the actions of the photocell in Figure 24-3-1?

    A) Variable resistor
    B) Variable capacitor
    C) Variable inductor
    D) Auto transformer
    E) Battery

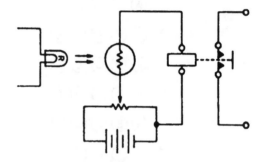

Figure 24-3-1

5. The semi-conductor materials contained in a transistor are designated by the letter(s)

    A) Q
    B) N, P
    C) CR
    D) M, P, M
    E) None of the above

6. Which of the following circuits or devices always has inductance?

    A) Rectifier
    B) Coil
    C) Current limiter
    D) Condenser
    E) Filter

7. Crowbars, light bulbs and
    vacuumbags are to be stored in the
    cabinet shown in Figure 75-25-1.
    Considering the balance of weight,
    what would be the safest
    arrangement?

    A) Top Drawer - Crowbars
        Middle Drawer - Light Bulbs
        Bottom Drawer - Vacuum bags
    B) Top Drawer - Crowbars
        Middle Drawer - Vacuum bags
        Bottom Drawer - Light Bulbs
    C) Top Drawer - Vacuum Bags
        Middle Drawer - Crowbars
        Bottom Drawer - Light Bulbs
    D) Top Drawer - Vacuum Bags
        Middle Drawer - Light Bulbs
        Bottom Drawer - Crowbars
    E) Top Drawer - Light Bulbs
        Middle Drawer - Vacuum Bags
        Bottom Drawer - Crowbars

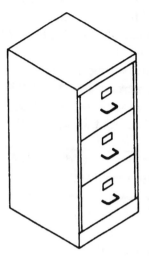

Figure 75-25-1

8. Which is most appropriate for pulling
a heavy load?

    A) Electric lift
    B) Fork lift
    C) Tow Conveyor
    D) Dolly
    E) Pallet truck

9. What measuring device is illustrated
in Figure 75-26-1?

    A) Screw pitch gage
    B) Vernier calipers
    C) Inside calipers
    D) Outside calipers
    E) Outside micrometer

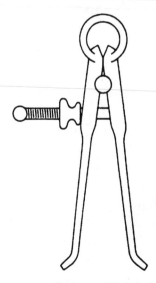

Figure 75-26-1

10. A screw pitch gauge can be used for

A) determining the pitch and number of internal threads.
B) measuring the number of gages available for use.
C) measuring the depth of a screw hole.
D) checking the thread angle.
E) cleaning the external threads.

11. What measuring device is illustrated in Figure 75-20-17?

A) Screw pitch gage
B) Vernier caliper
C) Inside calipers
D) Outside calipers
E) Outside micrometer

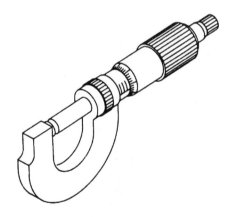

Figure 75-20-17

12. One characteristic of the breast drill is that it

A) is gearless.
B) is hand operated.
C) has a 3 and 1/4 hp motor.
D) has 4 speeds.
E) is steam powered.

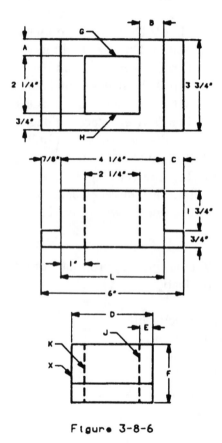

Figure 3-8-6

13. In Figure 3-8-6, what is the measurement of dimension F?

A) 1 3/4 inches
B) 2 1/4 inches
C) 2 ½ inches
D) 3 3/4 inches
E) None of the above

14. The device pictured in Figure 36 is in a rest position. Which position, if any, is the normal closed?

   A) A
   B) B
   C) C
   D) Devices of this sort have no normal closed position
   E) The normal closed is not shown in this diagram

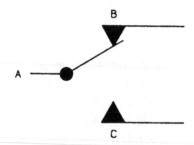

Figure 36

15. Which of the following test equipment would most likely be used in determining amplifier band width?

   A) Clamp-on ammeter
   B) Tube tester
   C) Watt meter
   D) Frequency analyzer
   E) Sweep frequency generator

16. Which instrument is used to test insulation breakdown of a conductor?

   A) Ohmmeter
   B) Ammeter
   C) Megger
   D) Wheatstone bridge
   E) Woltmeter

17. The primary purpose of soldering is to

   A) melt solder to a molten state.
   B) heat metal parts to the right temperature to be joined.
   C) join metal parts by melting the parts.
   D) harden metal.
   E) join metal parts.

18. Which of the following statements is correct of a soldering gun?

   A) Tip is not replaceable
   B) Cannot be used in cramped places
   C) Heats only when trigger is pressed
   D) Not rated by the number of watts they use
   E) Has no light

19. Contaminants have caused bearings to fail prematurely. Which pair of the items listed below should be kept away from bearings?

   A) Dirt and oil
   B) Grease and water
   C) Oil and grease
   D) Dirt and moisture
   E) Water and oil

20. The electrical circuit term "open circuit" refers to a closed loop being opened. When an ohmmeter is connected into this type of circuit, one can expect the meter to

   A) read infinity.
   B) read infinity and slowly return to ZERO.
   C) read ZERO.
   D) read ZERO and slowly return to infinity.
   E) none of the above

21. A change from refrigerant vapor to liquid while the temperature stays constant results in a

A) latent pressure loss.
B) sensible heat loss.
C) sensible pressure loss.
D) latent heat loss.
E) super heat loss.

22. The mediums normally used in condensing refrigerants are

A) air and water.
B) air and vapor.
C) water and gas.
D) liquid and vapor.
E) vapor and gas.

23. Most condenser problems are caused by

A) high head pressure.
B) high suction pressure.
C) low head pressure.
D) low suction pressure.
E) line leaks.

24. Most air conditioners with motors of 1 horsepower, or less, operate on which type of source?

A) 110-volt, single-phase
B) 110-volt, three-phase
C) 220-volt, single-phase
D) 220-volt, three-phase
E) 220-440-volt, three-phase

25. $2.6 - .5 =$

A) 2.0
B) 2.1
C) 3.1
D) 3.3
E) None of the above

26. ½ of 1/4 is

A) 1/12
B) 1/8
C) 1/4
D) ½
E) 8

27. A drawing of a certain large building is 10 inches by 15 inches. On this drawing, 1 inch represents 5 feet. If the same drawing had been made 20 inches by 30 inches, 1 inch on the drawing would represent

A) 2 ½ feet.
B) 3 1/3 feet.
C) 5 feet.
D) 7 ½ feet.
E) 10 feet.

28. In a shipment of bearings, 51 were defective. This is 30 percent of the total number of bearings ordered. What was the total number of bearings ordered?

A) 125
B) 130
C) 153
D) 171
E) None of the above

In sample question 29 below, select the statement which is most nearly correct according to the paragraph.

"Without accurate position descriptions, it is difficult to have proper understanding of who is to do what and when. As the organization obtains newer and different equipment and as more and more data are accumulated to help establish proper preventive maintenance routines, the organization will change. When changes occur, it is important that the organization chart and the position descriptions are updated to reflect them."

29. According to the above paragraph, which of the following statements is most nearly correct?

    A) Job descriptions should be general in nature to encourage job flexibility.

    B) The organizational structure is not dependent upon changes in preventive maintenance routines.

    C) As long as supervisory personnel are aware of organizational changes, there is no need to constantly update the organization chart

    D) Organizational changes can result from procurement of new, advanced equipment.

    E) Formal job descriptions are not needed for an office to function on a day-to-day basis. The supervisor knows who is to do what and when.

30. A small crane was used to raise the heavy part. Raise MOST nearly means

    A) lift
    B) drag
    C) drop
    D) deliver
    E) guide

31. Short MOST nearly means

    A) tall
    B) wide
    C) brief
    D) heavy
    E) dark

In each of the sample questions below, look at the symbols in the first two boxes. Something about the three symbols in the first box makes them alike; something about the two symbols in the other box with the question mark makes them alike. Look for some characteristic that is common to all symbols in the same box, yet makes them different from the symbols in the other box. Among the five answer choices, find the symbol that can best be substituted for the question mark, because it is <u>like</u> the symbols in the second box, and, <u>for the same reason</u>, different from those in the first box.

32.

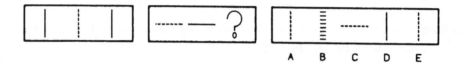

In the sample question above, all the symbols in the first box are vertical lines. The second box has two lines, one broken and one solid. Their <u>likeness</u> to each other consists in their being horizontal; and their being horizontal makes them <u>different</u> from the vertical lines in the other box. The answer must be the only one of the five lettered choices that is a horizontal line, either broken or solid. NOTE: There is not supposed to be a series or progression in these symbol questions. If you look for a progression in the first box and the second box, you will be wasting time. Remember, look for a <u>likeness</u> within each box and a <u>difference</u> between the two boxes. Now do sample question 33.

33.

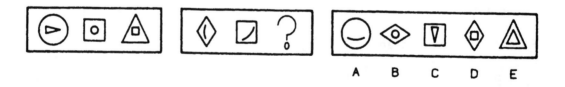

In sample question 34 below, there is at the left a drawing of a flat piece of paper and at the right, four figures labeled A, B, C, and D. When the paper is rolled, it will form one of the figures at its right. Decide which figure can be formed from the flat piece. Then on the Answer Sheet darken the space which has the same letter as your answer.

34.

         A   B   C   D

CORRECT ANSWERS TO
SAMPLE QUESTIONS

1.	D		18.	C
2.	C		19.	D
3.	A		20.	A
4.	A		21.	D
5.	B		22.	A
6.	B		23.	A
7.	E		24.	A
8.	E		25.	B
9.	C		26.	B
10.	A		27.	A
11.	E		28.	E
12.	B		29.	D
13.	C		30.	A
14.	B		31.	C
15.	D		32.	A
16.	C		33.	A
17.	E		34.	B

EXHIBIT B

The following positions use Test M/N 931:

Position Title	Register Number
Area Maintenance Specialist	M11
Area Maintenance Technician	M12
Assistant Engineman	M01
Blacksmith-Welder	M36
Building Maintenance Custodian	M13
Building Equipment Mechanic	M02
Carpenter	M14
Elevator Mechanic	M37
Engineman	M03
Fireman	M04
Fireman-Laborer	M05
General Mechanic	M38
Industrial Equipment Mechanic	M39
Letter Box Mechanic (Shop)	M40
Machinist	M41
Maintenance Electrician	M15
Mason	M21
Mechanic Helper	M42
Oiler, MPE	M43
Painter	M22
Painter/Finisher	M23
Plumber	M24
Postal Machines Mechanic	M44
Postal Maintenance Trainee A&B	M45
Scale Mechanic	M46
Stationary Engineer	M06

EXAM 932 - Electronic Technician Positions

Test M/N 932 covers the following Knowledge, Skills, and Abilities:

✔ *Knowledge of basic mechanics* refers to the theory of operation, terminology, usage, and characteristics of basic mechanical principles as they apply to such things as gears, pulleys, cams, pawls, power transmissions, linkages, fasteners, chains, sprockets, and belts; and including hoisting, rigging, roping, pneumatics, and hydraulic devices.

✔ *Knowledge of basic electricity* refers to the theory, terminology, usage, and characteristics of basic electrical principles such as ohm's Law, Kirchoff's Law, and magnetism, as they apply to such things as AC-DC circuitry and hardware, relays, switches, and circuit breakers.

✔ *Knowledge of basic electronics* refers to the theory, terminology, usage, and characteristics of basic electronic principles concerning such things as solid state devices, vacuum tubes, coils, capacitors, resistors, and basic logic circuitry.

✔ *Knowledge of digital electronics* refers to the terminology, characteristics, symbology, and operation of digital components as used in such things as logic gates, registers, adders, counters, memories, encoders and decoders.

✔ *Knowledge of safety procedures and equipment* refers to the knowledge of industrial hazards (e.g., mechanical, chemical, electrical, electronic) and procedures and techniques established to avoid injuries to self and others such as lock-out devices, protective clothing, and waste disposal techniques.

✔ Knowledge of basic computer concepts refers to the terminology, usage, and characteristics of digital memory storage/processing devices such as internal memory, input-output peripherals, and familiarity with programming concepts.

✔ *Ability to perform basic mathematical computations* refers to the ability to perform basic calculations such as addition, subtraction, multiplication and division with whole numbers, fractions and decimals.

✔ *Ability to perform more complex mathematics* refers to the ability to perform calculations such as basic geometry, scientific notation, and number conversions, as applied to mechanical, electrical and electronic applications.

✔ *Ability to apply theoretical knowledge to practical applications* refers to mechanical, electrical and electronic maintenance applications such as inspection, troubleshooting equipment repair and modification, preventive maintenance, and installation of electrical equipment.

✔ *Ability to detect patterns* refers to the ability to observe and analyze qualitative factors such as number progressions, spatial relationships, and auditory and visual patterns. This includes combining information and determining how a given set of numbers, objects, or sounds are related to each other.

✔ *Ability to use written reference materials* refers to the ability to locate, read, and comprehend text material such as handbooks, manuals, bulletins, directives, checklists and route sheets.

✔ *Ability to follow instructions* refers to the ability to comprehend and execute written and oral instructions such as work orders, checklists, route sheets, and verbal directions and instructions.

✔ *Ability to use hand tools* refers to knowledge of, and proficiency with, various hand tools. This ability involves the safe and efficient use and maintenance of such tools as screwdrivers, wrenches, hammers, pliers, chisels, punches, taps, dies, rules, gauges, and alignment tools.

✔ *Ability to use technical drawings* refers to the ability to react and comprehend technical materials such as diagrams, schematics, flow charts, and blueprints.

✔ *Ability to use test equipment* refers to the knowledge of, and proficiency with, various mechanical, electrical and electronic test equipment such as VOMS, oscilloscopes, circuit tracers, amprobes, and tachometers.

✔ *Ability to solder* refers to the knowledge of, and the ability to safely and effectively apply, the appropriate soldering techniques.

The sample exam that follows illustrates the types of questions that will be used in Test M/M 932. The samples will also show how the questions in the test are to be answered. Job descriptions for these occupations are included in Chapter Nine.

UNITED STATES POSTAL SERVICE

SAMPLE QUESTIONS - TEST M/N 932

The purpose of this booklet is to illustrate the types of questions that will be used in Test M/M 932. The samples will also show how the questions in the test are to be answered.

Test M/N 931 measures 16 Knowledge, Skills, and Abilities (KSAs) used by a variety of maintenance positions. Exhibit A lists the actual KSAs that are measured, and Exhibit B lists the positions that use this examination. However, not all KSAs that are measured in this test are scored for every position listed. The qualification standard for each position lists the KSAs required for the position. Only those questions that measure KSAs required for the position(s) for which you are applying will be scored for the position(s).

The suggested answers to each question are lettered A, B, C, etc. Select the BEST answer and make a heavy pencil mark in the corresponding space on the Sample Answer Sheet. Each mark must be dense black. Each mark must cover more than half the space and must not extend into neighboring spaces. If the answer to Sample 1 is B, you would mark the Sample Answer Sheet like this:

After recording your answers, compare them with those in the Correct Answers to Sample Questions. If they do not agree, carefully re-read the questions that were missed to get a clear understanding of what each question is asking.

During the test, directions for answering questions in Part I will be given orally, either by a cassette tape or by the examiner. You are to listen closely to the directions and follow them. To practice for this part of the test you might have a friend read the direction to you while you mark your answers on the Sample Answer Sheet. Directions for answering questions in Part II will be completely described in the test booklet.

STUDY CAREFULLY BEFORE YOU GO TO THE EXAMINATION ROOM

PART I

In Part I of the test, you will be told to follow directions by writing in a test booklet and then on an answer sheet. The test booklet will have lines of material like the following five samples:

SAMPLE   1.   5 _____

SAMPLE   2.   1 6 4 3 7

SAMPLE   3.   D B A E C

SAMPLE   4.

SAMPLE   5

To practice this test, have someone read the instructions on the **next page** to you and you follow the instructions. When they tell you to darken the space on the Sample Answer Sheet, use the one on this page.

SAMPLE ANSWER SHEET

1 Ⓐ Ⓑ Ⓒ Ⓓ Ⓔ	5 Ⓐ Ⓑ Ⓒ Ⓓ Ⓔ	9 Ⓐ Ⓑ Ⓒ Ⓓ Ⓔ
2 Ⓐ Ⓑ Ⓒ Ⓓ Ⓔ	6 Ⓐ Ⓑ Ⓒ Ⓓ Ⓔ	10 Ⓐ Ⓑ Ⓒ Ⓓ Ⓔ
3 Ⓐ Ⓑ Ⓒ Ⓓ Ⓔ	7 Ⓐ Ⓑ Ⓒ Ⓓ Ⓔ	11 Ⓐ Ⓑ Ⓒ Ⓓ Ⓔ
4 Ⓐ Ⓑ Ⓒ Ⓓ Ⓔ	8 Ⓐ Ⓑ Ⓒ Ⓓ Ⓔ	12 Ⓐ Ⓑ Ⓒ Ⓓ Ⓔ

Instructions to be read (the words in parentheses should not be read aloud).

You are to follow the instructions that I shall read to you. I cannot repeat them.

Look at the samples. Sample 1 has a number and a line beside it. On the line write an A. (Pause 2 seconds.) Now on the Sample Answer Sheet, find number 5 (pause 2 seconds) and darken the space for the letter you just wrote on the line. (Pause 2 seconds.)

Look at Sample 2. (Pause slightly.) Draw a line under the third number. (Pause 2 seconds.) Now look on the Sample Answer Sheet, find the number under which you just drew a line and darken space B as in baker for that number. (Pause 5 seconds.)

Look at Sample 3. (Pause slightly.) Draw a line under the third letter in the line. (Pause 2 seconds.) Now on your Sample Answer Sheet, find number 9 (pause 2 seconds) and darken the space for the letter under which you drew a line. (Pause 5 seconds.)

Look at the five circles in Sample 4. (Pause slightly.) Each circle has a number and a line in it. write D as in dog on the blank in the last circle. (Pause 2 seconds.) Now on the Sample Answer Sheet, darken the space for the number-letter combination that is in the circle you just wrote in. (Pause 5 seconds.)

Look at Sample 5. (Pause slightly.) There are two circles and two boxes of different sizes with numbers in them. (Pause slightly.) If 4 is more than 2 and if 5 is less than 3, write A in the smaller circle. (Pause slightly.) Otherwise write C in the larger box. (Pause 2 seconds.) Now on the Sample Answer Sheet, darken the space for the number-letter combination in the circle or box in which you just wrote. (Pause 5 seconds.)

Now look at the Sample Answer Sheet. (Pause slightly.) You should have darkened spaces 4B, 5A, 9A, 10D, and 12C on the Sample Answer Sheet. (If the person preparing to take the examination made any mistakes, try to help him or her understand why the mistakes are wrong.)

SAMPLE ANSWER QUESTIONS

1 Ⓐ Ⓑ Ⓒ Ⓓ Ⓔ   18 Ⓐ Ⓑ Ⓒ Ⓓ Ⓔ
2 Ⓐ Ⓑ Ⓒ Ⓓ Ⓔ   19 Ⓐ Ⓑ Ⓒ Ⓓ Ⓔ
3 Ⓐ Ⓑ Ⓒ Ⓓ Ⓔ   20 Ⓐ Ⓑ Ⓒ Ⓓ Ⓔ
4 Ⓐ Ⓑ Ⓒ Ⓓ Ⓔ   21 Ⓐ Ⓑ Ⓒ Ⓓ Ⓔ
5 Ⓐ Ⓑ Ⓒ Ⓓ Ⓔ   22 Ⓐ Ⓑ Ⓒ Ⓓ Ⓔ
6 Ⓐ Ⓑ Ⓒ Ⓓ Ⓔ   23 Ⓐ Ⓑ Ⓒ Ⓓ Ⓔ
7 Ⓐ Ⓑ Ⓒ Ⓓ Ⓔ   24 Ⓐ Ⓑ Ⓒ Ⓓ Ⓔ
8 Ⓐ Ⓑ Ⓒ Ⓓ Ⓔ   25 Ⓐ Ⓑ Ⓒ Ⓓ Ⓔ
9 Ⓐ Ⓑ Ⓒ Ⓓ Ⓔ   26 Ⓐ Ⓑ Ⓒ Ⓓ Ⓔ
10 Ⓐ Ⓑ Ⓒ Ⓓ Ⓔ   27 Ⓐ Ⓑ Ⓒ Ⓓ Ⓔ
11 Ⓐ Ⓑ Ⓒ Ⓓ Ⓔ   28 Ⓐ Ⓑ Ⓒ Ⓓ Ⓔ
12 Ⓐ Ⓑ Ⓒ Ⓓ Ⓔ   29 Ⓐ Ⓑ Ⓒ Ⓓ Ⓔ
13 Ⓐ Ⓑ Ⓒ Ⓓ Ⓔ   30 Ⓐ Ⓑ Ⓒ Ⓓ Ⓔ
14 Ⓐ Ⓑ Ⓒ Ⓓ Ⓔ   31 Ⓐ Ⓑ Ⓒ Ⓓ Ⓔ
15 Ⓐ Ⓑ Ⓒ Ⓓ Ⓔ   32 Ⓐ Ⓑ Ⓒ Ⓓ Ⓔ
16 Ⓐ Ⓑ Ⓒ Ⓓ Ⓔ   33 Ⓐ Ⓑ Ⓒ Ⓓ Ⓔ
17 Ⓐ Ⓑ Ⓒ Ⓓ Ⓔ   34 Ⓐ Ⓑ Ⓒ Ⓓ Ⓔ

PART II

1. The primary function of a take-up pulley in a belt conveyor is to
   A) carry the belt on the return trip.
   B) track the belt.
   C) maintain proper belt tension
   D) change the direction of the belt

2. Which device is used to transfer power and rotary mechanical motion from one shaft to another?

   A) Bearing
   B) Lever
   C) Idler roller
   D) Gear
   E) Bushing

See Figure III-A-22 on Page 66

3. Which of the following circuits is shown in Figure III-A-22?

   A) Series circuit
   B) Parallel circuit
   C) Series, parallel circuit
   D) Solid state circuit
   E) None of the above

4. A circuit has two resistors of equal value in series. The voltage and current in the circuit are 20 volts and 2 amps respectively. What is the value of EACH resistor?

   A) 5 ohms
   B) 10 ohms
   C) 20 ohms

D) Not enough information given

5. What is the total net capacitance of two 60-farad capacitors connected in series?

   A) 30 farads
   B) 60 farads
   C) 90 farads
   D) 120 farads
   E) 360 farads

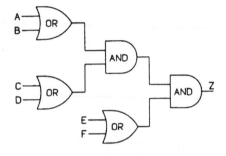

Figure 79-4-17B

6. Select the Boolean equation that matches the circuit diagram in Figure 79-4-17B.

   A) Z = AB+CD+EF
   B) Z z (A+B) (C+D) (E+F)
   C) Z = A+B+C+D+EF
   D) Z = ABCD(E+F)

7. If two 30-mH inductors are connected in series, what is the total net inductance of the combination?

   A) 15 mH
   B) 20 mH
   C) 30 mH
   D) 45 mH
   E) 60 mH

8.   In pure number 6 binary the
decimal would be expressed as

A) 001
B) 011
C) 110
D) 111

**File Cabinet Picture
See Figure 75-25-1 on
Page 67**

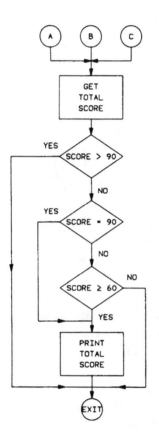

FIGURE 75-8-1 1

9.   In Figure 75-8-11, which of the
following scores will be printed?

A) All scores > 90 and < 60
B) All scores < 90
C) All scores ≤ 90 and ≥ 60
D) All scores < 60

10.   Crowbars, light bulbs and vacuum
bags are to be stored in the cabinet
shown in Figure 75-25-1. Considering the balance of weight, what
would be the safest arrangement?

A) Top Drawer - Crowbars
Middle Drawer - Light Bulbs
Bottom Drawer - Vacuum bags
B) Top Drawer - Crowbars
Middle Drawer - Vacuum bags
Bottom Drawer - Light Bulbs
C) Top Drawer - Vacuum Bags
Middle Drawer - Crowbars
Bottom Drawer - Light Bulbs
D) Top Drawer - Vacuum Bags
Middle Drawer - Light Bulbs
Bottom Drawer - Crowbars
E) Top Drawer - Light Bulbs
Middle Drawer - Vacuum Bags
Bottom Drawer - Crowbars

11.   Which is most appropriate for
pulling a heavy load?

A) Electric lift
B) Fork lift
C) Tow Conveyor
D) Dolly
E) Pallet truck

12. The electrical circuit term "open circuit" refers to a closed loop being opened. When an ohmmeter is connected into this type of circuit, one can expect the meter to

A) Read infinity
B) Read infinity and slowly return to ZERO
C) Read ZERO
D) Read ZERO and slowly return to infinity
E) None of the above

13. Contaminants have caused bearings to fail prematurely. Which pair of the items listed below should be kept away from bearings?

A) Dirt and oil
B) Grease and water
C) Oil and grease
D) Dirt and moisture
E) Water and oil

14. In order to operate a breast drill, which direction should you turn it?

A) Clockwise
B) Counterclockwise
C) Up and down
D) Back and forth
E) Right, then left

15. Which is the correct tool for tightening or loosening a water pipe?

A) Slip joint pliers
B) Household pliers
C) Monkey wrench
D) Water pump pliers
E) Pipe wrench

16. What is one purpose of a chuck key?

A) Open doors
B) Remove drill bits
C) Remove screws
D) Remove set screws
E) Unlock chucks

17. When smoke is generated as a result of using a portable electric drill for cutting holes into a piece of angle iron, one should

A) use a fire watch.
B) cease the drilling operation.
C) use an exhaust fan to remove smoke.
D) use a prescribed coolant solution to reduce friction.
E) call the Fire Department.

18. The primary purpose of soldering is to

A) melt solder to a molten state.
B) heat metal parts to the right temperature to be joined.
C) join metal parts by melting the parts.
D) harden metal.
E) join metal parts.

19. Which of the following statements is correct of a soldering gun?

A) Tip is not replaceable
B) Cannot be used in cramped places
C) Heats only when trigger is pressed
D) Not rated by the number of watts they use
E) Has no light

20. What unit of measurement is read on a dial torque wrench?

A) Pounds
B) Inches
C) Centimeters
D) Foot-pounds
E) Degrees

21.   Which instrument is used to test insulation breakdown of a conductor?

A) Ohmmeter
B) Ammeter
C) Megger
D) Wheatstone bridge
E) Voltmeter

22.   ½ of 1/4 =

A) 1/12
B) 1/8
C) 1/4
D) ½
E) 8

23.   2.6 - .5 =

A) 2.0
B) 2.1
C) 3.1
D) 3.3
E) None of the above

24.   Simplify the following expression in terms of amps:

563×10^{-6}

A) 563,000,000 amps
B) 563,000 amps
C) .563 amps
D) .000563 amps
E) .000000563 amps

25.   Solve the power equation

$P = I^2 R$ for R

A) $R = EI$
B) $R = I^2 P$
C) $R = PI$
D) $R = P/I^2$
E) $R = E/I$

26.   The product of 3 kilo ohms times 3 micro ohms is

A) 6×10^{-9} ohms
B) 6×10^{-3} ohms
C) 9×10^{3} ohms
D) 9×10^{-6} ohms
E) 9×10^{-3} ohms

In sample question 25 below, select the statement which is most nearly correct according to the paragraph.

"Prior to 1870, a conveyor that made use of rollers was developed for transporting clay. This construction substituted rolling friction at the idler bearing points for the sliding friction of the slider bed. A primitive type of "roughing belt conveyor was developed about the same time for the handling of grain. This design was improved during the latter part of the century when the "roughing idler was developed."

27.   <u>According to the above paragraph</u>, which of the following statements is most nearly correct?

A) The "roughing belt conveyor was developed about 1870 to handle clay and grain.

B) Rolling friction construction was replaced by sliding friction construction prior to 1870.

C) In the late nineteenth century, conveyors were improved with the development of the "roughing idler.

D) The "roughing idler, a significant design improvement for conveyors, was developed in the early nineteenth century.

E) Conveyor belts were invented and developed in the 1800's.

For sample question 28 below, select from the drawings of objects on the right labeled A, B, C, and D, the one that would have the TOP, FRONT, and RIGHT views shown in the drawing at the left

28.

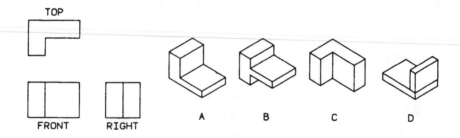

In sample question 29 below, there is, on the left, a drawing of a flat piece of paper and, on the right, four figures labeled A, B, C, and D. When the paper is bent on the dotted lines it will form one of the figures on the right. Decide which alternative can be formed from the flat piece.

29

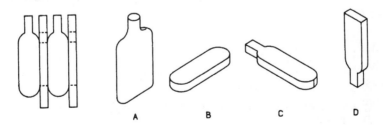

In each of the sample questions below, look at the symbols in the first two boxes. Something about the three symbols in the first box makes them alike; something about the two symbols in the other box with the question mark makes them alike. Look for some characteristic that is common to all symbols in the same box, yet makes them different from the symbols in the other box. Among the five answer choices, find the symbol that can best be substituted for the question mark, because it is <u>like</u> the symbols in the second box, and, for the same reason, different from those in the first box.

30.

USE DIAGRAM ON PAGE 72 QUESTION 32

In sample question 30 above, all the symbols in the first box are vertical lines. The second box has two lines, one broken and one solid. Their <u>likeness</u> to each other consists in their being horizontal; and their being horizontal makes them <u>different</u> from the vertical lines in the other box. The answer must be the only one of the five lettered choices that is a horizontal line, either broken or solid. NOTE: There is not supposed to be a series or progression in these symbol questions. If you look for a progression in the first box and the second box, you will be wasting time. Remember, look for a <u>likeness</u> within each box and a <u>difference</u> between the two boxes.

Now do sample questions 31 and 32.

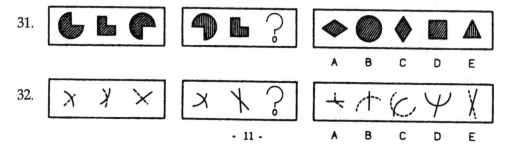

33.   In Figure 3-8-6 below, what is the measurement of Dimension F? Drawing is not actual size.

A) 1 3/4 inches
B) 2 1/4 inches
C) 2 ½ inches
D) 3 3/4 inches
E) None of the above

Use Figure 3-8-6 on page 68

34.   In Figure 160-57 below, what is the current flow through R when:

V = 50 volts
R1 = 25 ohms
R2 = 25 ohms
R3 = 50 ohms
R4 = 50 ohms
R5 = 50 ohms

and the current through the entire
circuit totals one amp?

A   0.5 amp
B) 5.0 amps
C) 5.0 milliamps
D) 50.0 milliamps
E) None of the above

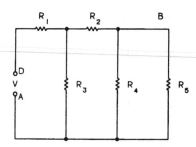

Figure 160-57

EXHIBIT B

The following positions use Test M/N 932:

Position Title	Register
Electronic Technician 8	M26
Electronic Technician 9	M27
Electronic Technician 10	M28

CORRECT ANSWERS TO
SAMPLE QUESTIONS

1.	C		18.	E
2.	D		19.	C
3.	A		20.	D
4.	A		21.	C
5.	A		22.	B
6.	B		23.	B
7.	D		24.	D
8.	C		25.	D
9.	C		26.	E
10.	E		27.	C
11.	E		28.	C
12.	A		29.	C
13.	D		30.	C
14.	A		31.	E
15.	E		32.	D
16.	B		33.	C
17.	D		34.	A

EXAM 933 - Measures 16 knowledge, skills, and abilities used by a variety of maintenance positions including Maintenance Mechanic and Overhaul Specialist.

Test M/N 933 covers the following Knowledge, Skills, and Abilities:

✔ *Knowledge of basic mechanics* refers to the theory of operation, terminology, usage, and characteristics of basic mechanical principles as they apply to such things as gears, pulleys, cams, pawls, power transmissions, linkages, fasteners, chains, sprockets, and belts; and including hoisting, rigging, roping, pneumatics, and hydraulic devices.

✔ *Knowledge of basic electricity* refers to the theory, terminology, usage, and characteristics of basic electrical principles such as ohm's Law, Kirchoff's Law, and magnetism, as they apply to such things as AC-DC circuitry and hardware, relays, switches, and circuit breakers.

✔ *Knowledge of basic electronics* refers to the theory, terminology, usage, and characteristics of basic electronic principles concerning such things as solid state devices, vacuum tubes, coils, capacitors, resistors, and basic logic circuitry.

✔ *Knowledge of safety procedures and equipment* refers to the knowledge of industrial hazards (e.g., mechanical, chemical, electrical, electronic) and procedures and techniques established to avoid injuries to self and others such as lock-out devices, protective clothing, and waste disposal techniques.

✔ *Knowledge of lubrication materials and procedures* refers to the terminology, characteristics, storage, preparation, disposal, and usage techniques involved with lubrication materials such as oils, greases, and other types of lubricants.

✔ *Ability to perform basic mathematical computations* refers to the ability to perform basic calculations such as addition, subtraction, multiplication and division with whole numbers, fractions and decimals.

✔ *Ability to perform more complex mathematics* refers to the ability to perform calculations such as basic geometry, scientific notation, and number conversions, as applied to mechanical, electrical and electronic applications.

✔ *Ability to apply theoretical knowledge to practical applications* refers to mechanical, electrical and electronic maintenance applications such as inspection, troubleshooting equipment repair and modification, preventive maintenance, and installation of electrical equipment.

✔ *Ability to detect patterns* refers to the ability to observe and analyze qualitative factors such as number progressions, spatial relationships, and auditory and visual patterns. This includes combining information and determining how a given set of numbers, objects, or sounds are related to each other.

✔   *Ability to use written reference materials* refers to the ability to locate, read, and comprehend text material such as handbooks, manuals, bulletins, directives, checklists and route sheets.

✔   *Ability to follow instructions* refers to the ability to comprehend and execute written and oral instructions such as work orders, checklists, route sheets, and verbal directions and instructions.

✔   *Ability to use hand tools* refers to knowledge of, and proficiency with, various hand tools. This ability involves the safe and efficient use and maintenance of such tools as screwdrivers, wrenches, hammers, pliers, chisels, punches, taps, dies, rules, gauges, and alignment tools.

✔   *Ability to use technical drawings* refers to the ability to react and comprehend technical materials such as diagrams, schematics, flow charts, and blueprints.

✔   *Ability to use test equipment* refers to the knowledge of, and proficiency with, various mechanical, electrical and electronic test equipment such as VOMS, oscilloscopes, circuit tracers, amprobes, and tachometers.

✔   *Ability to solder* refers to the knowledge of, and the ability to safely and effectively apply, the appropriate soldering techniques.

The sample exam that follows illustrates the types of questions that will be used in Test M/N 933. The samples will also show how the questions in the test are to be answered. Job descriptions for these occupations are included in Chapter Nine.

UNITED STATES POSTAL SERVICE

SAMPLE QUESTIONS - TEST M/N 933

The purpose of this booklet is to illustrate the types of questions that will be used in Test M/M 933. The samples will also show how the questions in the test are to be answered.

Test M/N 933 measures 16 Knowledge, Skills, and Abilities (KSAs) used by a variety of maintenance positions. Exhibit A lists the actual KSAs that are measured, and Exhibit B lists the positions that use this examination. However, not all KSAs that are measured in this test are scored for every position listed. The qualification standard for each position lists the KSAs required for the position. Only those questions that measure KSAs required for the position(s) for which you are applying will be scored for the position(s).

The suggested answers to each question are lettered A, B, C, etc. Select the BEST answer and make a heavy pencil mark in the corresponding space on the Sample Answer Sheet. Each mark must be dense black. Each mark must cover more than half the space and must not extend into neighboring spaces. If the answer to Sample 1 is B, you would mark the Sample Answer Sheet like this:

After recording your answers, compare them with those in the Correct Answers to Sample Questions. If they do not agree, carefully re-read the questions that were missed to get a clear understanding of what each question is asking.

During the test, directions for answering questions in Part I will be given orally, either by a cassette tape or by the examiner. You are to listen closely to the directions and follow them. To practice for this part of the test you might have a friend read the direction to you while you mark your answers on the Sample Answer Sheet. Directions for answering questions in Part II will be completely described in the test booklet.

STUDY CAREFULLY BEFORE YOU GO TO THE EXAMINATION ROOM

PART I

In Part I of the test, you will be told to follow directions by writing in a test booklet and then on an answer sheet. The test booklet will have lines of material like the following five samples:

SAMPLE   1.   5 _____

SAMPLE   2.   1 6 4 3 7

SAMPLE   3.   D B A E C

SAMPLE   4.

SAMPLE   5

To practice this test, have someone read the instructions on the **next page** to you and you follow the instructions. When they tell you to darken the space on the Sample Answer Sheet, use the one on this page.

SAMPLE ANSWER SHEET

1 Ⓐ Ⓑ Ⓒ Ⓓ Ⓔ	5 Ⓐ Ⓑ Ⓒ Ⓓ Ⓔ	9 Ⓐ Ⓑ Ⓒ Ⓓ Ⓔ
2 Ⓐ Ⓑ Ⓒ Ⓓ Ⓔ	6 Ⓐ Ⓑ Ⓒ Ⓓ Ⓔ	10 Ⓐ Ⓑ Ⓒ Ⓓ Ⓔ
3 Ⓐ Ⓑ Ⓒ Ⓓ Ⓔ	7 Ⓐ Ⓑ Ⓒ Ⓓ Ⓔ	11 Ⓐ Ⓑ Ⓒ Ⓓ Ⓔ
4 Ⓐ Ⓑ Ⓒ Ⓓ Ⓔ	8 Ⓐ Ⓑ Ⓒ Ⓓ Ⓔ	12 Ⓐ Ⓑ Ⓒ Ⓓ Ⓔ

<u>Instructions to be read</u> (the words in parentheses should not be read aloud).

You are to follow the instructions that I shall read to you. I cannot repeat them.

Look at the samples. Sample 1 has a number and a line beside it. On the line write an A. (Pause 2 seconds.) Now on the Sample Answer Sheet, find number 5 (pause 2 seconds) and darken the space for the letter you just wrote on the line. (Pause 2 seconds.)

Look at Sample 2. (Pause slightly.) Draw a line under the third number. (Pause 2 seconds.) Now look on the Sample Answer Sheet, find the number under which you just drew a line and darken space B as in baker for that number. (Pause 5 seconds.)

Look at Sample 3. (Pause slightly.) Draw a line under the third letter in the line. (Pause 2 seconds.) Now on your Sample Answer Sheet, find number 9 (pause 2 seconds) and darken the space for the letter under which you drew a line. (Pause 5 seconds.)

Look at the five circles in Sample 4. (Pause slightly.) Each circle has a number and a line in it. write D as in dog on the blank in the last circle. (Pause 2 seconds.) Now on the Sample Answer Sheet, darken the space for the number-letter combination that is in the circle you just wrote in. (Pause 5 seconds.)

Look at Sample 5. (Pause slightly.) There are two circles and two boxes of different sizes with numbers in them. (Pause slightly.) If 4 is more than 2 and if 5 is less than 3, write A in the smaller circle. (Pause slightly.) Otherwise write C in the larger box. (Pause 2 seconds.) Now on the Sample Answer Sheet, darken the space for the number-letter combination in the circle or box in which you just wrote. (Pause 5 seconds.)

Now look at the Sample Answer Sheet. (Pause slightly.) You should have darkened spaces 4B, 5A, 9A, 10D, and 12C on the Sample Answer Sheet. (If the person preparing to take the examination made any mistakes, try to help him or her understand why the mistakes are wrong.)

SAMPLE ANSWER QUESTIONS

1 Ⓐ Ⓑ Ⓒ Ⓓ Ⓔ   18 Ⓐ Ⓑ Ⓒ Ⓓ Ⓔ

2 Ⓐ Ⓑ Ⓒ Ⓓ Ⓔ   19 Ⓐ Ⓑ Ⓒ Ⓓ Ⓔ

3 Ⓐ Ⓑ Ⓒ Ⓓ Ⓔ   20 Ⓐ Ⓑ Ⓒ Ⓓ Ⓔ

4 Ⓐ Ⓑ Ⓒ Ⓓ Ⓔ   21 Ⓐ Ⓑ Ⓒ Ⓓ Ⓔ

5 Ⓐ Ⓑ Ⓒ Ⓓ Ⓔ   22 Ⓐ Ⓑ Ⓒ Ⓓ Ⓔ

6 Ⓐ Ⓑ Ⓒ Ⓓ Ⓔ   23 Ⓐ Ⓑ Ⓒ Ⓓ Ⓔ

7 Ⓐ Ⓑ Ⓒ Ⓓ Ⓔ   24 Ⓐ Ⓑ Ⓒ Ⓓ Ⓔ

8 Ⓐ Ⓑ Ⓒ Ⓓ Ⓔ   25 Ⓐ Ⓑ Ⓒ Ⓓ Ⓔ

9 Ⓐ Ⓑ Ⓒ Ⓓ Ⓔ   26 Ⓐ Ⓑ Ⓒ Ⓓ Ⓔ

10 Ⓐ Ⓑ Ⓒ Ⓓ Ⓔ   27 Ⓐ Ⓑ Ⓒ Ⓓ Ⓔ

11 Ⓐ Ⓑ Ⓒ Ⓓ Ⓔ   28 Ⓐ Ⓑ Ⓒ Ⓓ Ⓔ

12 Ⓐ Ⓑ Ⓒ Ⓓ Ⓔ   29 Ⓐ Ⓑ Ⓒ Ⓓ Ⓔ

13 Ⓐ Ⓑ Ⓒ Ⓓ Ⓔ   30 Ⓐ Ⓑ Ⓒ Ⓓ Ⓔ

14 Ⓐ Ⓑ Ⓒ Ⓓ Ⓔ   31 Ⓐ Ⓑ Ⓒ Ⓓ Ⓔ

15 Ⓐ Ⓑ Ⓒ Ⓓ Ⓔ   32 Ⓐ Ⓑ Ⓒ Ⓓ Ⓔ

16 Ⓐ Ⓑ Ⓒ Ⓓ Ⓔ   33 Ⓐ Ⓑ Ⓒ Ⓓ Ⓔ

17 Ⓐ Ⓑ Ⓒ Ⓓ Ⓔ   34 Ⓐ Ⓑ Ⓒ Ⓓ Ⓔ

PART II

1. The primary function of a take-up pulley in a belt conveyor is to

    A) carry the belt on the return trip.
    B) track the belt.
    C) maintain proper belt tension.
    D) change the direction of the belt.
    E) regulate the speed of the belt.

2. Which device is used to transfer power and rotary mechanical motion from one shaft to another?

    A) Bearing
    B) Lever
    C) Idler roller
    D) Gear
    E) Bushing

3. What special care is required in the storage of hard steel roller bearings? They should be

    A) cleaned and spun dry with compressed air.
    B) oiled once a month.
    C) stored in a humid place.
    D) wrapped in oiled paper.
    E) stored at temperatures below 90 degrees Fahrenheit.

4. Which is the correct method to lubricate a roller chain?

    A) Use brush to apply lubricant while chain is in motion
    B) Use squirt can to apply lubricant while chain is in motion
    C) Use brush to apply lubricant while chain is not in motion
    D) Soak chain in pan of lubricant and hang to allow excess to drain
    E) Chains do not need lubrication

5. A circuit has two resistors of equal value in series. The voltage and current in the circuit are 20 volts and 2 amps respectively. What is the value of EACH resistor?

    A) 5 ohms
    B) 10 ohms
    C) 15 ohms
    D) 20 ohms
    E) Not enough given

**See Figure III-A-22 on
Page 66**

6. Which of the following circuits is shown in Figure III-A-22?

    A) Series circuit
    B) Parallel circuit
    C) Series, parallel circuit
    D) Solid state circuit
    E) None of the above

7. What is the total net capacitance of two 60 farad capacitors connected in series?

    A) 30 F
    B) 60 F
    C) 90 F
    D) 120 F
    E) 360 F

8. If two 30 mH inductors are connected in series, what is the total net inductance of the combination?

    A) 15 mH
    B) 20 mH
    C) 30 mH
    D) 45 mH
    E) 60 mH

**File Cabinet Picture
See Figure 75-25-1 on
Page 67**

connected into this type of circuit, one
can expect the meter to

A) read infinity.
B) read infinity and slowly return to
   ZERO.
C) read ZERO.
D) read ZERO and slowly return to
   infinity.
E) None of the above

9. Crowbars, light bulbs and vacuum
   bags are to be stored in the cabinet
   shown in Figure 75-25-1. Considering
   the balance of weight, what would be
   the safest arrangement?

   A) Top Drawer - Crowbars
      Middle Drawer - Light Bulbs
      Bottom Drawer - Vacuum bags
   B) Top Drawer - Crowbars
      Middle Drawer - Vacuum bags
      Bottom Drawer - Light Bulbs
   C) Top Drawer - Vacuum Bags
      Middle Drawer - Crowbars
      Bottom Drawer - Light Bulbs
   D) Top Drawer - Vacuum Bags
      Middle Drawer - Light Bulbs
      Bottom Drawer - Crowbars
   E) Top Drawer - Light Bulbs
      Middle Drawer - Vacuum Bags
      Bottom Drawer - Crowbars

10. Contaminants have caused bearings
    to fail prematurely. Which pair of the
    items listed below should be kept
    away from bearings?

    A) Dirt and oil
    B) Grease and water
    C) Oil and grease
    D) Dirt and moisture
    E) Water and oil

11. The electrical circuit term "open
    circuit" refers to a closed loop being
    opened. When an ohmmeter is

12. Which is most appropriate for pulling
    a heavy load?

    A) Electric lift
    B) Fork lift
    C) Tow conveyor
    D) Dolly
    E) Pallet truck

13. In order to operate a breast drill,
    which direction should you turn it?

    A) Clockwise
    B) Counterclockwise
    C) Up and down
    D) Back and forth
    E) Right, then left

14. Which is the correct tool for
    tightening or loosening a water pipe?

    A) Slip joint pliers
    B) Household pliers
    C) Monkey wrench
    D) water pump pliers
    E) Pipe wrench

15. What is one purpose of a chuck key?

    A) Open doors
    B) Remove drill bits
    C) Remove screws
    D) Remove set screws
    E) Unlock chucks

16. When smoke is generated as a result of using a portable electric drill for cutting holes into a piece of angle iron. One should

A) use a fire watch.
B) cease the drilling operation.
C) use an exhaust fan to remove smoke.
D) use a prescribed coolant solution to reduce friction.
E) call the Fire Department.

17. The primary purpose of soldering is to

A) melt solder to a molten state.
B) heat metal parts to the right temperature be joined.
C) join metal parts by melting the parts.
D) harden metal.
E) join metal carts.

18. Which of the following statements is correct concerning a soldering gun?

A) Tip is not replaceable
B) Cannot be used in cramped places
C) Heats only when trigger is pressed
D) Not rated by the number of watts it uses
E) Has no light

19. What unit of measurement is read on a dial torque wrench?

A) Pounds
B) Inches
C) Centimeters
D) Foot-pounds
E) Degrees

20. Which instrument is used to test insulation breakdown of a conductor?

A) Ohmmeter
B) Ammeter
C) Megger
D) Wheatstone bridge
E) Voltmeter

21. ½ of 1/4 =

A) 1/12
B) 1/8
C) 1/4
D) ½
E) 8

22. 2.6 - .5 =

A) 2.0
B) 2.1
C) 3.1
D) 3.3
E) None of the above

23. Solve the power equation

$P = I^2R$ for R

A) $R = EI$
B) $R = I^2P$
C) $R = PI$
D) $R = P/I^2$
E) $R = E/I$

24. The product of 3 kilo ohms times 3 micro ohms is

A) 6×10^{-9} ohms
B) 6×10^{-3} ohms
C) 9×10^{3} ohms
D) 9×10^{-6} ohms
E) 9×10^{-3} ohms

In sample question 25 below, select the statement which is most nearly correct according to the paragraph.

"Prior to 1870, a conveyor that made use of rollers was developed for transporting clay. This construction substituted rolling friction at the idler bearing points for the sliding friction of the slider bed. A primitive type of roughing belt conveyor was developed about the same time for the handling of grain. This design was improved during the latter part of the century when the roughing idler was developed."

25. According to the above paragraph, which of the following statements is most nearly correct?

    A) The troughing belt conveyor was developed about 1870 to handle clay and grain.

    B) Rolling friction construction was replaced by sliding friction construction prior to 1870.

    C) In the late nineteenth century, conveyors were improved with the development of the roughing idler.

    D) The roughing idler, a significant design improvement for conveyors, was developed in the early nineteenth century.

    E) Conveyor belts were invented and developed in the 1800's.

26. A small crane was used to <u>raise</u> the heavy part. <u>Raise</u> MOST nearly means

    A) lift
    B) drag
    C) drop
    D) deliver
    E) guide

27. <u>Short</u> MOST nearly means

    A) tall
    B) wide
    C) brief
    D) heavy
    E) dark

For sample question 28 below, select from the drawings of objects on the right labeled A, B, C, and D, the one that would have the TOP, FRONT, and RIGHT views shown in the drawing at the left

28.

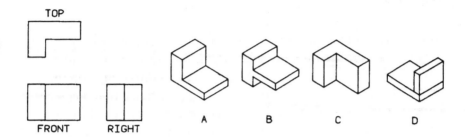

In sample question 29 below, there is, on the left, a drawing of a flat piece of paper and, on the right, four figures labeled A, B, C, and D. When the paper is bent on the dotted lines it will form one of the figures on the right. Decide which alternative can be formed from the flat piece.

29

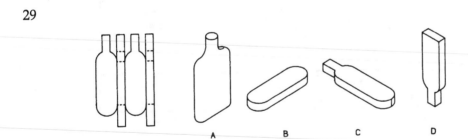

In each of the sample questions below, look at the symbols in the first two boxes. Something about the three symbols in the first box makes them alike; something about the two symbols in the other box with the question mark makes them alike. Look for some characteristic that is common to all symbols in the same box, yet makes them different from the symbols in the other box. Among the five answer choices, find the symbol that can best be substituted for the question mark, because it is like the symbols in the second box, and, for the same reason, different from those in the first box.

30.

USE DIAGRAM ON PAGE 72 QUESTION 32

In sample question 30 above, all the symbols in the first box are vertical lines. The second box has two lines, one broken and one solid. Their <u>likeness</u> to each other consists in their being horizontal; and their being horizontal makes them <u>different</u> from the vertical lines in the other box. The answer must be the only one of the five lettered choices that is a horizontal line, either broken or solid. NOTE: There is not supposed to be a series or progression in these symbol questions. If you look for a progression in the first box and the second box, you will be wasting time. Remember, look for a <u>likeness</u> within each box and a <u>difference</u> between the two bo xes.

Now do sample questions 31 and 32.

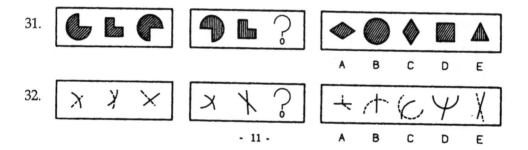

33. In Figure 3-8-6 below, what is the
measurement of Dimension F?
Drawing is not actual size.

A) 1 3/4 inches
B) 2 1/4 inches
C) 2 ½ inches
D) 3 3/4 inches
E) None of the above

R3 = 50 ohms
R4 = 50 ohms
R5 = 50 ohms

and the current through the entire circuit
totals one amp?

A   0.5 amp
B)   5.0 amps
C)   5.0 milliamps
D)   50.0 milliamps
E) None of the above

```
Use Figure 3-8-6 on page 68
```

34. In Figure 160-57 below, what is the
current flow through R when:

V = 50 volts
R1 = 25 ohms
R2 = 25 ohms

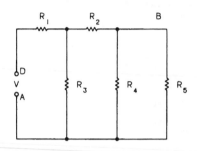

Figure 160-57

EXHIBIT B

The following positions use test M/N 933:

Position Title	Register Number
Maintenance Mechanic, MPE/06	M32
Maintenance Mechanic, MPE/07	M33
Overhaul Specialist	M34

CORRECT ANSWERS TO
SAMPLE QUESTIONS

1.	C		18.	C
2.	D		19.	D
3.	D		20.	C
4.	D		21.	B
5.	A		22.	B
6.	A		23.	D
7.	A		24.	E
8.	E		25.	C
9.	E		26.	A
10.	D		27.	C
11.	A		28.	C
12.	E		29.	C
13.	A		30.	C
14.	E		31.	E
15.	B		32.	D
16.	D		33.	C
17.	E		34.	A

Chapter Six
The 473 & 473-C Postal Exam

This chapter includes a study guide with sample test questions for the 473 and 473-C Postal Exam. You will also find helpful test taking tips and strategies that you can use for the practice and official exams.

The Postal Service hires workers for major entry-level jobs from applicants who successfully pass the 473 exam with a score of 70 or higher. You will be notified of your eligibility or ineligible rating shortly after taking the exam. Applicants who pass the exam are placed on the hiring register according to score. The highest scoring applicants will be the first to be called for an interview when a position is filled in your area. The Postal Service continues to work through the list of qualified applicants until the list is depleted. Disabled veterans who pass the exam are placed at the top of the register by law, ahead of all other applicants who took the exam. The higher your score the better chance you have of being called for an interview and hired.

In addition to exam results, the Postal Service will review your employment history, military background if applicable, and check for criminal records.

CAUTION

You don't have to pay anyone to take a postal exam. Exams are administered at no cost to the applicant. Locate exam announcements for your area online, at local, state, and federal buildings, and in your local newspaper. Direct links to the Postal Service's exam schedules are listed on the following web site:

http://postofficejobs.info/

ENTRY LEVEL JOBS COVERED BY THE 473 EXAM

City Carrier

Mail delivery and collection in the city and suburban areas by foot or vehicle. Must be able to carry 35 pound mail bags and containers or parcels weighing up to 70 pounds. Mail carriers work standing, reaching, and walking most of their workday.

Mail Processing Clerk

Sorts mail manually or by operating and monitoring automated equipment. Clerks transport processed mail in the work area, and bundle and collate mail as necessary. Heavy lifting of mail and containers may be required.

Mail handler

Responsible for transporting, unloading and loading mail containers and equipment in their facility. They frequently carry equipment and packages that weigh 70 pounds or less and push heavy wheeled containers.

Sales, Services, and Distribution Associate

Responsible for retail sales, customer support and mail distribution. All associates must also complete on-the-job training.

The **473 Major Entry Level Jobs Exam** is also referred to as the 473 Battery Exam. This exam measures an applicant's general aptitude and personal characteristics, not factual knowledge. The main difference between the 473 and 473-C exam is the target audience. The 473-C exam is announced primarily when the Postal Service is recruiting large numbers of City Letter Carriers, and the 473 exam is used to cover all of the job categories listed above. The two exams are essentially the same.

Review this chapter to improve your test scores and to become familiar with the test taking process and strategies, application forms, answer sheets, and sample questions. The 473 examination and completion of forms will require approximately two hours and fifteen minutes.

EXAM CONTENT

The five sections of the test are listed in Table 6-1 on page 105. You will only be allowed to work on one section of the test at a time. If you finish a part early you aren't permitted to proceed to the next part or to return to a part that you previously completed. The test proctor will explain each part in turn and you must follow his instructions.

Table 6-1 Entry-level Battery 473			
Test Unit	**# of Questions**	**Time Allowed**	**Covered Subjects**
Part A Address Checking	60	11 min.	Determine if two addresses are identical.
Part B Forms Completion	30	15 min.	Information identification for completing forms correctly.
Part C Section 1 - Coding	36	6 min	Using proper code to assign to addresses
Part C Section 3 - Memory	36	7 min	Memorize assigned codes for addresses
Part D Inventory of Personal Experience and Characteristics	236	90 min	Assess applicant's experience and characteristics related to the job.

Address Cross Comparison (Part A)

Part A includes 60 questions and you have 11 minutes to complete this section. You will be tested on how fast and accurately you can compare two address lists. Postal workers must be able to differentiate between two addresses to determine if they are the same or different destinations. Address differences include different spelling or transposed numbers. The questions are multiple choice.

- A is selected if there are no errors.
- B is selected if only the addresses are different.
- C is selected if only the Zip Codes are different.
- D is selected if both the address and Zip Code are different.

Forms Completion (Part B)

Part B includes 30 questions and you will have 15 minutes to complete this section. You will be provided with various sample forms and asked questions about what is to be entered on the form. For example, you might be given a form with 9 blocks, and block 5 may be the Zip Code block. A possible question would be where you would enter the zip code. The answer would be "block 5." You could also be asked what type of data goes in a specified box such as a number, check mark or name. All 30 questions are multiple choice A, B, C, or D.

Coding (Part C Section 1)

The coding section includes 36 questions and you have 6 minutes to complete this section. You will be given four delivery routes, A through D, with street addresses. The questions list an address and you have to assign the correct delivery route for the address. The delivery routes will be given to you for the Coding exam and you will have to memorize the routes for the Memory section.

Memory (Part C Section 2)

The memory section includes 36 questions that are similar to the coding section questions. You have to select the correct delivery route, A, B, C, or D, without looking at the chart. You will be given time to memorize the addresses and routes before the exam starts.

Personal Characteristics and Experience

This section takes 90 minutes to complete and has 236 questions. The Postal Service will evaluate your personal experience, characteristics and tendencies. For example, you will be asked your likes and dislikes and whether you have experience in certain areas. You really can't prepare for this section; it's your personal profile. If you answer the questions honestly the Postal Service will be able to identify the job that is best suited to your characteristics. The answers are multiple choice. The question *"Do you like to work in groups?"* would have the answers (A) Strongly Agree, (B) Agree, (C), Disagree, (D) Strongly Disagree. A question similar to *"Are you willing to work rotating shifts?"* would have the answers (A) Very Often, (B) Often, (C) Sometimes, (D) Rarely. We do include some helpful hints on how to prepare for this section later in this chapter.

Exam Answer Sheets

All exams are multiple choice and the answers are typically A, B, C or D. However, in Part D there may be up to seven answers, A through G, to choose from. All sample exams in this book are printed in black ink. Actual Postal Exam answer sheets may be printed in different colors. The following example shows the typical answer grid that we use throughout this guide. You just fill in the oval of the correct answer on the answer sheet. The actual answer grid is computer graded and much smaller in size. A sample of a realistic exam answer sheet is provided at the end of this chapter.

Sample Answer Grid			
1	Ⓐ	Ⓑ	Ⓒ Ⓓ
2	Ⓐ	Ⓑ	Ⓒ Ⓓ
3	Ⓐ	Ⓑ	Ⓒ Ⓓ
4	Ⓐ	Ⓑ	Ⓒ Ⓓ

GENERAL INFORMATION

The 473 exams are scored at the National Test Administration Center. However, all hiring for the Postal Service is decentralized. When you apply for a Postal job in Pittsburgh, PA you are only eligible for job vacancies in the local metropolitan area. Your exam results are limited to job vacancies in the area you test for and if you pass the exam you are put on the local list in rank order. The applicants with the highest grade are higher on the list. If you want to be considered for jobs in Columbus, Ohio you have to apply for and take the exam there.

I frequently counsel job hunters who are frustrated by this fact and most don't understand why they have to take the same test for each location. The reason is simply that jobs with the Postal Service — just like all federal civil service jobs — are highly competitive and it would be almost impossible to maintain a national competitive list. The goal is to get hired. After you start working for the Postal Service you can request transfers to other locations and current employees are eligible to bid on higher paying jobs through the agencies Merit Promotion System.

The Postal Service usually allows applicants taking the 473 exam to select any or all of the four available job categories; City Carrier, Mail Processing Clerk, Mail Handler and/or Sales, Services, and Distribution Associate. I suggest that you select all four if given the opportunity. The more options you select the greater chance you have of being called for an interview when they fill vacancies. After you get your foot in the door you can bid internally for more desirable positions.

Another option that you may have is the ability to select several, usually up to three, locations in the general vicinity. The more selections you make the better your chances of landing a job. In some cases when you take the exam you will be considered for all locations in the metropolitan area and you won't have an option to select your preferences.

EXAM OVERVIEW

The Postal Service will send you a scheduling notice approximately two weeks prior to the exam test date. The notice will specify the exam location, time, and date of the exam along with a booklet and an exam admission pass. The booklet provides general test information and several sample test questions for each part of the exam. You can also download a more extensive exam package, publication 60-A, a 32 page 473 Orientation Guide, directly from the Postal Service's web site at http://usps.com/employment. If you have trouble finding the link on this page go to http://postofficejobs.info/ and click on the Postal Exam button in the upper left hand corner of the page. You will find direct links to this study guide and to their exam scheduling page on this site.

The exam package that you receive instructs you to bring the following items with you to the exam:

- Your admission pass
- A picture ID (Generally your photo drivers license)
- Two #2 lead pencils (Required to mark the answer sheets)

> The items listed above are **REQUIRED**. If you neglect to bring a valid photo ID or your admission pass you will not be allowed to take the exam. You may find extra pencils at testing sites but if they don't have any it's your responsivblity to bring them with you.

You are allowed to take notes during the exam except for the memory tests in Part C. Notes are not permitted on any of the answer sheets. The only marks permitted on the answer sheets are the marks you make to identify your answer for each question. The answer sheets are electronically scanned for grading and any other marks could cause your answer sheet to be rejected. **Typically, for the scanner to read your answers you must darken over half of the circle/oval on your answer sheet and don't let your mark reach outside the oval boundaries to another circle.**

TEST TAKING STRATEGIES

The following strategies will help you improve your grades and complete more answers on the timed exams. Use these techniques on the practice tests in this book and when you take your actual Postal Service exam. If you practice these techniques now, when you take the postal exam they will become second nature.

➢ Get plenty of rest the night before the exam.

➢ Eliminate the answers in multiple choice questions that make no sense at all. You can often eliminate half of the answers through this method. If you have to guess an answer, you improve your chances through the process of elimination.

➢ You will be penalized for guessing on Part A, Address Checking, and for Part C, Coding and Memory, due to the methods that the Postal Service uses to grade these sections. It is also unwise to guess or try and manipulate your answers for Section D, Personal Characteristics. Guessing on Part B, Forms Checking, will not adversely effect your scores.

➤ Don't forget your eyeglasses, hearing aid or anything else that you may need for the exam.

➤ Review the directions to the testing facility and arrive early. You don't need the additional stress of getting lost on the way to the exam and arriving late. Arriving early will also give you time to get familiar with the testing facility. You can locate directions to the testing site on any of the Internet search engine mapping sites such the one at http://Yahoo.com.

➤ The test will take 3 hours or more including initial introductions and the time the proctors use to brief the group on each new section. Breaks are not scheduled and if you have to take a break to go to the bathroom you may lose valuable time and points. Some locations don't allow any breaks so be sure to use the bathroom facilities before the test starts, and limit your fluid intake.

➤ Be skeptical when an answer includes the words like, always, never, all, none, generally, or only. These words can be a trap. Only select an answer with these words in it if you are absolutely sure it is the right answer.

➤ If two answers have opposite meanings, take your time and look closer. Many times one of the two is correct.

➤ Be careful not to lose your place on the exam answer sheet and mark the wrong question. This is especially important if you skip a question. Make sure you mark the answer to a specific question on the answer sheet correctly. You may want to keep your pencil pointed over the answer sheet's question number that you are working on and move it to the next question as you progress through the exam. You can also use your second pencil to mark your place as you progress through the exam.

➤ One word can dramatically change the meaning of a sentence. Read each question word-for-word before answering.

➤ Don't dwell on the exam to the point that it upsets you. Answer the questions that you know first. If you have problems with the first question, skip it and go to the next test question. If time permits, after you complete the section, you can return to the unanswered questions and give them more thought.

     ✎ **One word of caution**. Once you finish a section and are directed to go on to the next part, you can't go back to previously completed sections. You can only go back within the current section that you are working on if the time isn't up.

➤ Focus on one question at a time. Don't let your mind wander back to questions you skipped or to other sections. If you stay focused on each question you will be able to concentrate better on the exam.

FOLLOW INSTRUCTIONS

Don't pick up your pencil or open your exam booklets until told to do so by an instructor. Also, when your are advised that your time is up **stop working immediately** and put your pencil down. You can be disqualified for not following instructions.

ADDRESS CHECKING - PART A

Part A includes 60 questions and you have 11 minutes to complete this section. You will be tested on how fast and accurately you can compare two lists. Postal workers must be able to differentiate between two addresses to determine if they are the same or different destinations. Address differences include different spelling or transposed numbers. The questions are multiple choice.

Questions include an address with street or P.O. Box, city, and state in the first column of each list and a ZIP Code in the second column. The example below shows the address on the left and the Zip Code on the right in each list. You will compare the *Correct List* on the left to the *List to be Checked* on the right. You are required to determine if the address to be checked is exactly the same or different as the address and Zip Code on the *Correct List*. You must determine if the address and Zip Code is exactly the same or different including the numbers, punctuation, capitalization, and spelling. You will make your selections from the list below:

- A is selected if there are no errors, everything is exactly alike.
- B is selected if only the addresses are different.
- C is selected if only the Zip Codes are different.
- D is selected if both the address and Zip Code are different.

Prior to starting the actual exam you will be given two sample exercises of several questions each to familiarize you with the process. The examiners do this to introduce you to what is expected on the exam and the answer sheets for these practice exams are in the exam booklet, not a separate page. Complete the four sample questions that follow to better understand the process.

| A. No Errors | B. Address Only | C. ZIP Code Only | D. Both |

Correct List			List to be Checked		
#	Address	Zip Code	Address	Zip Code	
S1.	1915 Park Place Fairview, TX	79411	1915 Park Place Fairview, TX	79141	
S2.	401 McAuthur Drive Benton, NC	27514-1132	401 McAuther Drive Benton, NC	27514-1132	
S3.	6915 Amber Way Pittsburgh, PA	15129-0005	6915 Amber Way Pittsburgh, PA	15129-0005	
S4.	19150 First Street Kalamazoo, MI	49007-2334	19105 First Street Kalamizoo, MI	49070-2344	

Sample Answer Grid	
S1.	(A) (B) (C) (D)
S2.	(A) (B) (C) (D)
S3.	(A) (B) (C) (D)
S4.	(A) (B) (C) (D)

Question S1

You will discover that the street, city and state are identical. However, the ZIP Code is different. The third and fourth digits in the zip code on the *List to be Checked* are reversed. Mark answer **"C"** for Zip Code Only.

Question S2

You will find the addresses have different spellings. McAuthur is spelled McAuther on the *List to be Checked*. The Zip Codes are identical. You will mark **"B"** on the sample answer sheet.

Question S3

The address and Zip Code of both lists are identical. Mark **"A"** on the answer sheet.

Question S4

You will find the street address and Zip Code numbers are different. The *Correct List* street number is 19150 and the list to be corrected street number is 19105. The last two digits of the first five Zip Code numbers are reversed. Also, the Zip Code's last 4 digits are not the same and the name Kalamazoo is misspelled. In this case you would mark **"D"** for both.

Before we start the actual practice exams for address checking there are a number of techniques you can use to improve your score and to improve your efficiency so that you will have more time to devote to the exam.

> ***Time is critical.*** You will have 11 minutes to complete 60 questions. That's only 11 seconds per question. The more you practice and prepare for the exam the more questions you will be able to answer and the greater chance you have of earning a higher score.

Lets take another look at the four sample questions on the next page. Notice that I underlined the errors. When you start the sample questions and during the test, concentrate on the address first and then move on to the Zip Code for each question. You can mark differences on the exam booklet for Part A as stated in the exam booklet on the bottom of page one. If you find an error in the address, mark it and move on to the Zip Code and do the same. Once you find an error in either the address or Zip Code don't look for additional errors. All you need to do is find one and you don't want to waste the precious time you have. You will notice that question S4 on the next page has two errors in the address. Stop after you find the first one, mark it and move on to the Zip Code.

Another helpful technique is to memorize the 4 potential answers now so that you won't waste time searching for the correct answer for each question during the exam. Memorize the answers NOW, before you take the exam.

| **A. No Errors** | **B. Address Only** | **C. ZIP Code Only** | **D. Both** |

I try to think of things in what I perceive to be logical order. When I look at the answers it makes sense that **(A)** equals **No Errors**, **(B)** is next and the first column of the *list to be corrected* is the address so I can remember that the answer for "Address Only" **(B)** is the first incorrect answer and it is in the first column of the list to be corrected. Then since the second column in the list to be corrected is the ZIP Code, if only the Zip Code is incorrect I would mark **(C).** Finally if both the address and Zip Code are incorrect I mark **(D).** To me this is logical. However we all have our own reality and you must design a scenario that makes sense to you.

Others use acronyms to remember lists. In this case you can take the first letter of each of the four answers, **NAZB** and memorize this new word.

N = No Errors = **Answer A**
A = Address Only = **Answer B**
Z = Zip Code Only = **Answer C**
B = Both = **Answer D**

	Correct List			List to be Checked	
#	**Address**	**Zip Code**		**Address**	**Zip Code**
S1.	1915 Park Place Fairview, TX	79411		1915 Park Place Fairview, TX	79<u>141</u>
S2.	401 McAuthur Drive Benton, NC	27514-1132		401 McAu<u>ther</u> Drive Benton, NC	27514-1132
S3.	6915 Amber Way Pittsburgh, PA	15129-0005		6915 Amber Way Pittsburgh, PA	15129-0005
S4.	19150 First Street Kalamazoo, MI	49007-2334		19<u>105</u> First Street Kalam<u>izoo</u>, MI	<u>49070</u>-2344

With practice you should be able to complete the 60 questions in the time allotted. If you finish early first go back and review the questions that you found to be alike. You can easily identify them because you won't have any marks on them. Check these first to see if you missed something, then go on to others if time permits. If you do find that you have to change an answer be sure to erase the incorrect answer completely. Otherwise the scanner used to grade your exam may not be able to grade that question.

It is best not to guess on answers in this section due to the way it is scored. The Postal Service adds the number of questions that you got right and then subtracts one third of the questions you got wrong. Each of the four exam parts are scored differently.

The practice exams for Part A start on the next page. The answer sheet is on the page directly following this practice exam. For your convenience you can copy the answer sheets so that your answer sheet will be next to the exam questions that you are working on. **Be sure to time yourself for this section.** The more you practice the better you score will be. Time this practice exam for 11 minutes.

— **Answer Sheet page 145, Answer Key page 149** —

PART A PRACTICE EXAM 1 (Address Checking)

A. No Errors	B. Address Only	C. ZIP Code Only	D. Both

#	Address	ZIP	Address	ZIP
1	P.O. Box 1243 Aikron, OH	44326-3452	P.O. Box 1243 Aikron, OH	44362-2352
2	6000 Buford Dr Houston, TX	77006-0001	6000 Buford Dr Houston, TX	77006-0001
3	505 SE 35th St. Portland, OR	97211-0124	505 SE 53rd St. Portland, OR	92711-0124
4	5990 Lascolinas Circle Lake Worth, FL	33463	5990 Lascolinas Circle Lake Worth, FL	33463
5	P.O. Box 5478 Hollister, FL	32147-7564	P.O. Box 5487 Hollister, FL	32147-7584
6	1767 Timber Road Vista, CA	92080	1766 Timber Road Vista, CA	92080
7	3030 Front Street Raleigh, NC	27610	3030 Front Street Raleigh, NC	27610
8	P.O. Box 10239 Camp Lejeune, NC	28547-0072	P.O. Box 12390 Camp Lejeune, NC	28547-0072
9	102 Madera Drive Eatonville, WA	98328-4461	102 Midera Drive Eatonille, WA	98328-6441
10	81000 Darting Manor Dr. Laurel, MD	29723	81000 Darting Manor Dr. Laurel, MD	29723
11	200 Rock Chain Drive Eagle River, AK	99576	200 Rock Cliff Drive Eagle River, AK	99516
12	206 Chancelor Street Suffolk, VA	23434-9802	206 Chancelor Street Sufolk, VA	24343-9802
13	1015 23rd Street Markham, IL	60427-3772	1015 23rd Street Markham, IL	80427-3772
14	900 School Brook Road Socorro, NM	87801-0212	900 School Brook Ave. Socorro, NM	87801-0121
15	4423 Potter Ave., Apt 23 Fort Wayne, IN	46835	4423 Potter Ave., Apt 23 Fort Wayne, IN	46835
16	1509 Meadow View Drive Dallas, TX	75222	1509 Meadow View Drive Fort Worth, TX	75222
17	P.O. Box 1243 Penn Hills, PA	15255-4432	P.O. Box 12433 Penn Hills, PA	15255-4432
18	3445 Sumpter Avenue Lisbon, IA	52253	3445 Sumpter Avenue Lisbon, IA	52553
19	P.O. Box 666 Ord, NE	68862	P.O. Box 666 Ord, NE	68662
20	1062 Amherst Street Moon Township, PA	15108-2601	1062 Amherst Ave. Moon Township, PA	15108-2601

A. No Errors	B. Address Only	C. ZIP Code Only	D. Both

#	Address	ZIP	Address	ZIP
21	2414 Easton Road Houston, TX	77003-8791	2414 Easton Road Houston, TX	77003-8791
22	4014 E. Belmont Chicago, IL	60614-0201	4014 E. Boumont Chicago, IL	60614-0201
23	5235 Westminster Place Portland, OR	97311-7904	5235 Westminster Place Portland, OR	97113 -7904
24	1001 Highland Avenue Needham, MA	02494	1001 Highland Place Needham, MA	04294
25	P.O. Box 1904 Hempfield, FL	32107-7543	P.O. Box 1904 Hempfield, FL	32107-7543
26	878 N 41 2nd Street Tacoma, WA	98418-2194	878 N 41 2nd Street Tacoma, WA	98418-2004
27	143 North Avenue Outreach, NC	27310	143 South Avenue Outreach, NC	27310
28	P.O. Box 432 Pendalton, SC	29708-1092	P.O. Box 325 Pendalton, SC	29709-1092
29	987 Fifth Avenue Delray, WA	97318-4298	987 Forbes Avenue Delray, WA	97318-4298
30	1208 Elm Street South Park, PA	15244-2787	1208 Elm Street South Park, PA	15244-2787
31	4520 River Road Eagles Nest, AK	99326	4520 River Road Eagles Nest, AK	99326
32	1309 Chambers Lane Wilton, VA	24389-8276	1390 Chambers Lane Wilton, VA	24389-8276
33	P.O. Box 1998 Willshier, IN	70398-0989	P.O. Box 1998 Willshier, IN	70399-0989
34	1902 Stanley Road Saddlebrook, TX	71342-0853	1902 Stanley Road Saddlebrook, TX	71344-0835
35	116 East 9th St. Torrington, CT	06790-2314	116 West 9th St. Torrington, CT	06791-2314
36	142 Midland Drive Dallas, TX	75122-2134	142 Midway Drive Dallas, TX	75122-2134
37	P.O. Box 232 Hershey, PA	18752-2790	P.O. Box 322 Hershey, PA	18752-2790
38	7675 Sharon Street Trusville, AL	35173-8312	7675 Sharon Street Trusville, AL	53573-8312
39	P.O. Box 1546 Erie, PA	16842-1978	P.O. Box 1546 Erie, PA	16842-1978
40	150 Mission Avenue Godfrey, VA	22689	160 Mission Avenue Godfrey, VA	22589

A. No Errors	B. Address Only	C. ZIP Code Only	D. Both

#	Address	ZIP	Address	ZIP
41	52 Saratoga Street Gloversville, NY	12078	52 Saratoga Street Gloversville, NY	12068-2310
42	244 North Adams Ave Eldridge, IL	61534-2101	244 South Adams Ave Eldridge, IL	61534-2101
43	6543 Marcie St. Labrook, LA	70013-2345	6543 Marty St. Labrook, LA	70113-2345
44	P.O. Box 1567 Falstaff, AZ	85287-9436	P.O. Box 1567 Falstaff, AZ	85287-9436
45	348 Park Place Harlenton, NY	12044-2107	348 Park Place Harlenton, NY	12045-2107
46	1414 16th St., Apt. 345 Tacoma, WA	98433-2224	1414 17th St., Apt. 345 Tacoma, WA	98433-2224
47	78 Lake Rd. Woodbury, NY	11779-0124	78 Lakefront Rd. Woodbury, NY	11799-0124
48	P.O. Box 1990 Randolph, NC	28649-9089	P.O. Box 1990 Randolph, NC	28649-9089
49	987 Atlantic Ave. Ocean City, NY	07200-0989	987 Atlantic Ave. Ocean City, NY	07201-0989
50	229 Westover Terrace Oklahoma, City, OK	74022-1524	229 Westover Place Oklahoma, City, OK	74022-1524
51	5120 Trenton Blvd. Wilkinsburg, PA	15219-0236	5120 Trenton Blvd. Wilkinsburg, PA	15219-0236
52	145 River Rd. Pittsburgh, PA	15222-3245	144 River Rd. Pittsburgh, PA	15221-3245
53	Manor Hall East, #456 York, PA	17404-5645	Manor Hall East, #456 York, PA	17440-5645
54	4545 S. Beacon Chicago, IL	60676-4253	4545 N. Beacon Chicago, IL	60676-4253
55	1990 Westend Dr. Boston, MA	10846-9056	1990 Westward Dr. Boston, MA	10845-9056
56	124 South Park Ave. Sandford, FL	33354-0967	124 South Park Ave. Sandford, FL	33354-0967
57	P.O. Box 1987 Seaward, LA	70124	P.O. Box 1987 Seaward, LA	70224
58	653 Northwood St. Trenton, MI	46798-2354	653 Northview St. Trenton, MI	46798-2354
59	P.O. Box 516 Chicago, IL	60654-9176	P.O. Box 515 Chicago, IL	60654-9176
60	1911 Macie St. Bradbury, NY	11687-7658	1911 Macie St. Bradbury, NY	11687-7658

FORMS CHECKING - PART B

This section includes 30 questions that have to be completed in 15 minutes. There will be 6 questions for each of five different forms on the exam. Before starting the actual test the examiners will give you a 2 minute exercise with several questions that you will answer. These questions are not graded. After the introductory exercise you will start the actual exam.

Refer to the Domestic Return Receipt form on the next page to answer the first two sample questions for practice and use the same for the first six questions of the timed exam.

Sample Questions

S1. Where do you enter the sender's address on this form?
A. Box 3 (Front)
B. Box 10 (Back)
C. Box 3 and 10
C. None of the above

ANSWER: The sender's address is entered in Box 3 and the correct answer is A.

S2. The letter will be sent certified. Each certified letter has an article number. What two blocks must be filled out to designate a certified mailing?
A. Box 1 and 2
B. Box 10 and 1
C. Box 4 and 5
D. Box 3 only

ANSWER: The correct answer is C. Questions can be tricky if you read more into the question than what is presented. In this example, all certified mailings are assigned an article number that is listed in block 4 and you would check the certified box in block 5. Even though the remainder of the form must be filled out before it can be processed, the question is only asking about what must be filled out to designate a certified mailing. Focus on what they give you in the question, the known facts.

PRACTICE EXAM PART B

Use the **Domestic Return Receipt** form on the next page for the first 6 questions of the exam. You have 15 minutes for the 30 questions or 30 second per question. Set your timer for 3 minutes for each 6 question segment. The questions are on the opposite page so that you can easily refer to the forms as needed. Take a few seconds after you set the timer to familiarize yourself with the form. Copy the answer sheet in the back of this section and have the answer sheet next to the questions so you can easily mark your answers and not lose time.

— Answer Sheet page 145, Answer Key page 149 —

DOMESTIC RETURN RECEIPT (Back)

SENDER INSTRUCTIONS

Print your name, address, and ZIP Code in the space provided.
- Complete items 1,2,3, and 4 on the reverse.
- Attach to front of article if space permits, otherwise affix to back of article.
- Endorse article "Return Receipt Requested" adjacent to number.

RETURN

TO ➡

Print Sender's name, address, and ZIP Code in the space below.

10. _____

_____

_____

DOMESTIC RETURN RECEIPT (Front)

● **SENDER:** Compare items 1 and 2 when additional services are desired, and complete 3 and 4.
Put your address in the "RETURN TO" Space on the reverse side. Failure to do this will prevent this card from being returned to you. <u>The return receipt fee will provide you the name of the person delivered to and the date of delivery.</u> For additional fees the following services are available. Consult postmaster for fees and check box(es) for additional services(s) requested.

1. ☐ Show to whom delivered, date, and addresses's address.   **2.** ☐ Restricted Delivery
↑ *(Extra charge)* ↑   ↑ *(Extra charge)* ↑

3. Article Addressed to:	**4.** Article Number:
	5. Type of Service:
	☐ Registered ☐ Insured
	☐ Certified ☐ COD
	☐ Express Mail
	Always obtain signature of addresses or agent and <u>DATE DELIVERED</u>.
6. Signature - Addressee	9. Addressee's Address *(ONLY if requested and fee paid)*
7. Signature - Agent	
8. Date of Delivery	

Start section 1 of your timed exercise, set your timer for 3 minutes. There are five sections with 6 questions each.

1. Where would you enter the article number for a certified mailing on this form?

   A. Box 10
   B. Box 4
   C. Box 3 and 9
   D. Box 3 only

2. The person sending a certified letter wants to receive the return receipt at his home address. Where does he put his return address.

   A. Box 3
   B. Box 9
   C. Box 10
   D. The article number in Box 4 and signs in Box 7

3. Which of these would indicate restricted delivery?

   A. Box 5
   B. Box 2
   C. A signature in Box 7 and Box check mark in Box 1
   D. Box 1, 3, and 7

4. Which of these could be a correct answer for Box 8?

   A. A check mark
   B. Article number
   C. Signature
   D. March 15, 2005

5. Which one of the following could be the correct entry for Box 5?

   A. Your initials
   B. 4/19/2005
   C. A check mark
   D. None of the above

6. Which of the following should have a name entered?

   A. Box 1
   B. Box 4
   C. Box 6
   D. Box 2

Practice Exam - Section 2 of Part B

Authorization to Hold Mail

Postmaster - Please hold mail for:

1. Name(s)

2. Address

3a. Begin Holding Mail (Date)	**3b.** Resume Delivery (Date)

4. ☐ **Option A**

I will pick up all accumulated mail when I return and understand that mail delivery will not resume until I do. (This is suggested if your return date may change or if no one will be at home to receive mail)

5. ☐ **Option B**

Please deliver all accumulated mail and resume normal delivery on the ending date shown above.

6. Customer Signature

For Post Office Use Only

7. Date Received

8a. Clerk	**8b.** Bin Number
9a. Carrier	**9b.** Route Number

Customer Option A Only

Carrier: Accumulated mail has been picked up:

10a. Resume delivery on (date) _____

10b. By: _____

Start section 2 of your timed exercise, questions 7 through 12. Set your timer for 3 minutes. There are five sections with 6 questions each.

7. Joe Smith, and Bob Barker live at the same address. Bob is going on an extended vacation and will be away for two months. Joe is not leaving and wants his mail to continue. What name(s) should you enter in Box 1?

   A. Joe Smith
   B. Joe Smith and Bob Barker
   C. Bob Barker
   D. The Postmaster's name

8. If you check Option B which of the following statements is correct?

   A. The person will pick up their accumulated mail when they return.
   B. Your mail carrier will deliver your mail when you return after you contact the Post Office.
   C. Your mail carrier will restart delivery on a predetermined date.
   D. None of the above

9. What fields would the customer complete on this form?

   A. Blocks 1, 2, 3a, and 6 only
   B. Blocks 1 through 6 only
   C. Blocks 7 through 10b
   D. All of the above

10. Which of the selections specify the date to start holding mail?

    A. Box 3b
    B. Box 7
    C. Box 3a
    D. Line 10a

11. What would be a correct entry for line 10a?

    A. Jay W. Brook
    B. A check mark
    C. June 1, 2005
    D. 13547

12. Postal Clerk Jim McKee accepted Jeff Brown's Authorization to Hold Mail. Jeff's carrier is Janet Ward. What box is Jim McKees' name entered in?

    A. Box 1
    B. Box 9a
    C. Box 1 and 6
    D. None of the above

Practice Exam - Section 3 of Part B

Certificate of Bulk Mailing

MAILER: Prepare this statement in ink. Affix meter stamp or uncanceled postage stamps covering the fee in the block to the right. Present for certification.

7. Meter stamp or postage (uncanceled) stamps in payment of fee to be affixed here and canceled by postmarking, including date.

Fee for Certification

USE CURRENT RATE CHART

1. Up to 1,000 pieces (1 certificate for total number)

2. For each additional 1,000 pieces, or fraction

3. Duplicate Copy

4a. Number of identical Pieces	4.b Class of Mail	4c. Postage on Each	4d. Number of Pieces to the Pound	4e. Total Number of Pounds	4f. Total Postage Paid	4g. Fee Paid

5a. Mailed For	5b. Mailed By

Postmaster's Certificate

6. It is hereby certified that the above-described mailing has been received and number of pieces and postage verified.

(Postmaster or Designee)

Start section 3 of your timed exercise, questions 13 through 18. Set your timer for 3 minutes. There are five sections with 6 questions each.

13. ACME Int'l is mailing its annual catalog under the bulk mail rates program. The company hired Abbott Services to pick up their bulk mailing of 1,000 pounds that included 5,000 individual pieces of first class mail. What figure would be placed in block 4d.

   A. 1000
   B. 5
   C. 5000
   D. ZERO

14. Using the same example as question 13, what would be entered on Line 5a and 5b?

   A. 5a "Postmaster" and 5b "Abbott Services"
   B. 5a "Cost Reduction" and 5a "ACME Int'l"
   C. 5a "ACME Int'l" and 5b "Abbott Services"
   D. None of the above

15. Can a Designee sign this form for the Postmaster?

   A. Yes
   B. No
   C. Never
   D. Only in block 5b

16. What could be the class of mail entered in block 4b?

   A. First
   B. 15th
   C. No Class
   D. None of the above

17. The mailer has 15 identical pieces for this mailing. Where would you enter this information?

   A. Box 4e
   B. No identical pieces can be added
   C. Box 4a
   D. In the remarks in Box 6

18. Where do you attach the meter stamp or postage on this form?

   A. You affix postage to each piece of mail not to the Certificate of Bulk Mailing..
   B. To the back of the certificate
   C. In Box 7
   D. In Box 6

Practice Exam - Section 4 of Part B

			Mailing Label
Bar Code		*EXPRESS* *MAIL*	

ORIGIN (POSTAL USE ONLY)				DELIVERY (POSTAL USE ONLY)			
PO ZIP Code 1a.	Day of Delivery 1b. □ Next □ Second	Flat Rate Envelope 1c. □		Delivery Attempt 1d. Mo. Day	Time 1e. □ AM □ PM	Employee Signature 1f.	
Date In 2d.	2b. □ 12 noon □ 3 PM	Postage 2c. $		Delivery Attempt 2d. Mo. Day	Time 2e. □ AM □ PM	Employee Signature 2f.	
Time In 3a. □ AM □ PM	Military 3b. □ 2nd Day □ 3rd Day	Return Receipt Fee 3c.		Delivery Attempt 3d. Mo. Day	Time 3e. □ AM □ PM	Employee Signature 3f.	
Weight 4a. Lbs. Ozs.	Int'l Alpha Country Code 4b.	COD Fee 4c.	Insurance Fee	**CUSTOMER USE ONLY** 6. □ WAIVER OF SIGNATURE			
No Delivery 5a. □ Wknd □ Holiday	Acceptance Clerk Initials 5b.	Total Postage & Fees 5c. $		Customer Signature **NO DELIVERY** □ Weekend □ Holiday			

CUSTOMER USE ONLY

Method of Payment 7a. Express Mail Corp Acct. No.	Federal Agency Acct. No. 7b. Or Postal Service Acct. No.
8a. from: (PLEASE PRINT) PHONE :_____	8b. TO: (PLEASE PRINT) PHONE:_____
	□□□□ + □□□□ zip + 4

Start section 4 of your timed exercise, questions 19 through 24. Set your timer for 3 minutes. There are five sections with 6 questions each.

19. Which of the following answers could be a correct entry for Box 1d?

    A. $18.65
    B. 12 Noon
    C. 6/15
    D. 6/15/05

20. Joe Smith dropped a Flat Rate Express Mail package at the Post Office at 11:00 AM on 8/11/05. The Postal clerk informed Joe that his package would be delivered by noon the next day. How would the clerk note this on the form?

    A. Write the date 8/12/05 in Box 1d and the time in 1e.
    B. Check "Noon" in Box 2b and "Next" in Box 1b
    C. Write the date 8/12/05 in 3c
    D. None of the above

21. The customer requests no weekend delivery and "Waiver of Signature." How does the customer select these options?

    A. Signs Box 6
    C. Checks "Waiver of Signature in Box 6
    B. Customer signs his name and checks "Waiver of Signature" and "Weekend" in Box 6.
    D. None of the above

22. The mail carrier was unable to make delivery on his first attempt on 8/12/05 because the customer was not home. The carrier (employee) did not leave the package. Where does the carrier sign this form?

    A. Box 6
    B. Box 1f
    C. Box 2f and 3f
    D. None of the above

23. The clerk weighed the Express Mail package and advised the customer that the package would cost $17.95 to mail overnight. Where does the clerk initial the mailing label and enter the package weight?

    A. Initial in Box1f and weight in Box 2c
    B. Initial in Box 5b and weight in Box 4a
    C. Enter $17.95 in Box 2c and Initial in Box 6
    D. No initials or weight is required on this form

24. Where would you enter the recipient's ZIP code on this form?

    A. Box 8a
    B. Box 4c
    C. Box 8b
    D. Zip code not required

Practice Exam - Section 5 of Part B

Application for Post Office Box or Caller Service		
Customers: Complete white boxes	Post Office: Complete shaded boxes	
1a. Name(s) to which box number(s) is (are) assigned		1b. Box or Caller Number _____ through _____
2a. Name of person applying, Title (if representing an organization), and name of organization *(if different from name in Box 1a above)*		2b. Will this box be used for: ☐ Personal use ☐ Business use
3a. Address *(number, street, apt. no., city, state, Zip Code).* When address changes, cross out address here and put new address on back.		3b. Telephone number *(Include area code)*
4a. Data application received	4b. Box size needed	4c. ID and physical address verified by *(initials)*	4d. Dates of service _____ through _____
5a. Two types of identification are required. One must contain a photograph of the addressee(s). Social security cards, credit cards, and birth certificates are unacceptable as identification. Write in identifying information. Subject to verification.		5b. Eligibility for Carrier Delivery ☐ City ☐ Rural ☐ HCR ☐ None	5c. Service Assigned ☐ Box ☐ Caller ☐ Reserve #
		6. List name(s) of minors or names of others **receiving mail** in individual box. Other persons must present two forms of valid ID. If applicant is a firm, name each member **receiving mail**. Each member must have verifiable ID upon request. *(Continue on reverse side)*	
WARNING: *The furnishing of false or misleading information on this form or omission of information may result in criminal sanctions (including fines and imprisonment) and/or civil sanctions (including multiple damages and civil penalties) (18U.S.C. 1001)*		7. Signature of applicant (Same as item 3). I agree to comply with all Postal rules regarding Post Office box or caller services.	

Start section 5 of your timed exercises, questions 25 through 30. Set your timer for 3 minutes. This is the last set of 6 questions.

25. David Jones is applying to open a Post Office Box in Canton, Ohio. He has a his Driver's License photo ID and his Social Security card for identification. Will the Postal Service process his request?

   A. The clerk will accept his application and attach photocopies of his photo ID and Social Security Card to the application.
   B. Yes, however the customer must also supply a certified copy of his birth certificate within 15 business days.
   C. No
   D. None of the above

26. What Boxes on this form must the customer fill out?

   A. Box 1a, 1b, 2a, 2b, 3a, 6, and 7
   B. All but 1b, 4a, 4b, 4c, 4d, 5a, 5b, and 5c
   C. Box 1a, 3a, 2b, 6 and 7
   D. All of the above

27. What is required to be verified by the Postal Clerk prior to accepting your application?

   A. That you are a U.S. Citizen
   B. You are eligible for carrier delivery
   C. Two forms of ID, one being a photo ID
   D. Your age

28. What would a correct entry be for Box 3a?

   A. Your name
   B. Names of all using the Post Office Box
   C. 324 Main St., Oil City, PA 15434
   D. (123) 456-7890

29. What would a correct entry be for Box 6?

   A. 1878 Forbes Ave., Fargo, ID 25678
   B. Bob Evans and Elizabeth Tyler
   C. Your signature
   D. None of the above

30. Jane Mansfield has two small children and an invalid parent that lives with her. Where does Jane list the names of others in her household who will use this box?

   A. Box 5a
   B. Nowhere, only the primary box holders name goes on this form.
   C. All must sign box 7
   D. Box 6

CODING AND MEMORY - PART C
Coding Section

The coding and memory sections both use the same "Coding Guide." You have to assign a given address to the proper delivery route for 36 questions in 6 minutes for the coding section. The coding section is open book and you will refer to the Coding Guide while answering your questions. The Memory Section of Part C requires you to remember the coding guide you used in the Coding Section and assign delivery routes without looking at the guide.

CODING GUIDE	
Address Range	**Delivery Route**
400 – 499 Amherst Ave 101 – 190 Canton St. 1 – 29 Sutton Way	A
500 – 799 Amherst Ave 30 – 199 Sutton Way	B
2500 – 2699 University Blvd. 191 – 299 Canton St. 5 – 25 Rural Route 5	C
All mail that does not fall in one of the address ranges listed above.	D

Address Range - The Coding Guide is divided into two columns. The first column is the Address Ranges for each route. If you look at the first address range of Route A notice that all addresses from 400 through 499 Amherst Avenue are included in route A. Route B picks up the remaining Amherst Avenue addresses from 500 to 799.

Delivery Route - Each delivery route has multiple addresses assigned to that carrier. Route B includes the addresses from 500 to 799 Amherst Avenue and from 30 to 199 Sutton Way. For example, if a letter was addressed 101 Sutton Way you would select Route B for the answer.

Delivery Route D includes all addresses not assigned to a specific route. If you are given the address 332 Canton St. or 1905 Fifth Avenue you would select Delivery Route D as your answer. These addresses are not included in routes A, B, or C.

Sample Questions

	Address	**Delivery Route**			
1.	425 Amherst Ave.	A	B	C	D
2.	202 Sutton Way	A	B	C	D
3.	277 Canton St.	A	B	C	D
4.	10 Rural Route 6	A	B	C	D
5.	67 Sutton Way	A	B	C	D
6.	2601 University Blvd	A	B	C	D

You are permitted to look at the Coding Guide while answering the Coding questions in this section. Use the sample answer sheet for the practice exams. Note that the Delivery Routes are listed A through D to the right of the questions in the exam booklet. Don't get confused during the exam and mark your answers in the exam booklet. **ONLY MARK YOUR ANSWERS ON THE ANSWER SHEET.** If you neglect to use the answer sheet your answers will not be graded.

Sample Question Answers

Question 1 – The address 425 Amherst Ave. Is in the address range as noted on the Coding Guide for Delivery Route A. You would darken answer A on the answer sheet. Remember to NOT put your answers in the exam booklet. Place your answer sheet next to the questions and darken the answer "**A**" on the answer sheet.

> **CAUTION:** When you get to the memory section this will be even more critical. Note the spelling for the street address in this question. It is spelled "Amherst Ave." You will run into answers that are very similar to the street address. For example Amherst can also be spelled "Amhurst." Look at the entire address. If the street address in question 1 would have been spelled "Amhurst" the answer would have been D, not A.

Question 2 – Sutton Way is located in range A and B for street numbers from 1-199. The address in question two is 202 Sutton Way which is beyond the range of either route A or B. The answer is "**D**" (all mail that does not fall in one of the address ranges listed in A, B or C)

Question 3 – The answer for this question would be "**C**." You will find the address range from 191 - 299 Canton St. In Route C.

Question 4 – You will find a Rural Route in Route C. However, it is Rural Route 5 not Route 6. The correct answer is **"D"** (all mail that does not fall in one of the address ranges listed in A, B or C)

Question 5 – The correct answer is **"B."** 67 Sutton Way is in the address range of 30 - 199 Sutton Way in Route B.

Question 6 – 2601 University Blvd is listed in Route C and the address range is 2500 - 2699. Therefore, the correct answer is **"C."**

The Coding practice exam follows. You will have 6 minutes to complete this section. Copy the answer sheet in the back of this section and place it next to your book. Time the exam to see how many question you can answer in the time allotted. The Coding Guide was repeated on this page and on page 132 so that the questions would be next to the Coding Guide. You are permitted to use the Coding Guide for this section.

PART C
Coding Section Practice Exam
36 Questions

CODING GUIDE	
Address Range	**Delivery Route**
400 – 499 Amherst Ave 101 – 190 Canton St. 1 – 29 Sutton Way	A
500 – 799 Amherst Ave 30 – 199 Sutton Way	B
2500 – 2699 University Blvd. 191 – 299 Canton St. 5 – 25 Rural Route 5	C
All mail that does not fall in one of the address ranges listed above.	D

— **Answer Sheet page 146, Answer Key page 150** —

CODING EXAM PRACTICE QUESTIONS

START TIME: _____

	Address	Delivery Route			
1.	20 Rural Route 5	A	B	C	D
2.	104 Sutton Way	A	B	C	D
3.	401 Amhurst Ave.	A	B	C	D
4.	1901 University Blvd.	A	B	C	D
5.	587 Amherst Ave.	A	B	C	D
6.	4 Sutton Way	A	B	C	D
7.	2601 Universal Blvd.	A	B	C	D
8.	197 Canton St.	A	B	C	D
9.	145 Sutton Way	A	B	C	D
10.	188 Canton St.	A	B	C	D
11.	401 Amherst Ave.	A	B	C	D
12.	2599 University Blvd.	A	B	C	D
13.	199 Sutton Way	A	B	C	D
14.	399 Canton St.	A	B	C	D
15.	634 Amherst Ave.	A	B	C	D
16.	189 Canton St.	A	B	C	D
17.	2499 University Blvd.	A	B	C	D
18.	2589 University Blvd.	A	B	C	D

TURN PAGE
TO CONTINUE

CONTINUE EXAM

CODING GUIDE	
Address Range	**Delivery Route**
400 – 499 Amherst Ave 101 – 190 Canton St. 1 – 29 Sutton Way	A
500 – 799 Amherst Ave 30 – 199 Sutton Way	B
2500 – 2699 University Blvd. 191 – 299 Canton St. 5 – 25 Rural Route 5	C
All mail that does not fall in one of the address ranges listed above.	D

CONTINUE EXAM

	Address	Delivery Route			
19.	3 Sutton way	A	B	C	D
20.	118 Sutton Way	A	B	C	D
21.	301 Canton St.	A	B	C	D
22.	24 Rural Route 5	A	B	C	D
23.	489 Amherst Ave.	A	B	C	D
24.	2601 Universal Blvd.	A	B	C	D
25.	597 Amherst Ave.	A	B	C	D
26.	19 Rural Route 5	A	B	C	D
27.	264 Canton St.	A	B	C	D
28.	127 Canton St.	A	B	C	D
29.	29 Sutton Way	A	B	C	D
30.	125 Rural Route 5	A	B	C	D
31.	616 Amherst Ave.	A	B	C	D
32.	2695 University Blvd.	A	B	C	D
33.	114 Sutton Way	A	B	C	D
34.	3 Sutton Way	A	B	C	D
35.	29 Rural Route 5	A	B	C	D
36.	201 Canton St.	A	B	C	D

STOP

Record Time Here: _____ Minutes
(You are limited to 6 minutes)

CODING AND MEMORY - PART C
Memory Section

Now that you completed the initial coding section it's time to work on Part C, Section 2, memorization. You will use the same coding guide that was used in the previous section and during the actual exam you will be given a short practice section as noted below:

Exam Schedule.

- For the first section the examiners will give you 3 minutes to memorize the Coding Guide. Following this session you will be given 90 seconds to answer 8 practice questions without the aide of the Coding Guide. You have to answer the questions from memory.
- Immediately following the practice session the examiners will allow you to study the same Coding Guide for another 5 minutes before taking the actual 36 question test. You will be allowed 7 minutes after the study period to complete the 36 questions without the aide of the Coding Guide. You must answer the questions from memory. The questions for this section are numbered 37 to 72 because the exam for part C includes the first 36 questions that you answered in Section 1 of Part C.

The questions for the memory section are similar to the questions from the previous section. The only difference between the two sections is that in Section one you are allowed to view the Coding Guide while taking the exam. In Section two you must answer questions 37 - 72 from memory. This is considered by many to be the hardest part of the exam. However, there are techniques that you can use to help you through this section and improve your scores.

Memorization Techniques

Efficient Utilization of Time

You have several study and practice sessions prior to the memory exam. You have an initial 2 minute study period in the previous Coding Section along with a 90 second practice exam. **Remember that the same coding guide is used for both the coding and memory sections.** In the memory section you have a 3 minute study period and then a 5 minute study period prior to the 36 question exam. All of these pre-exam exercises are to familiarize you with the memorization section. This study guide provides sufficient familiarization so that you can put these sessions to much better use.

I suggest that you use the entire time to study and memorize the Coding Guide. This will give you over 11 minutes to memorize the guide.

If you decide to use the time as suggested above be sure to at least mark the sample questions associated with the two pre-exam exercises so that test monitors won't stop you to explain the process. Just mark them randomly when told to and then continue studying the Coding Guide.

Number Sequence and Address Ranges

Several memory techniques were discussed earlier in Part A for address checking. The techniques listed here will help you memorize the address ranges and delivery routes in any coding guide.

CODING GUIDE	
Address Range	Delivery Route
400 – 499 Amherst Ave 101 – 190 Canton St. 1 – 29 Sutton Way	A
500 – 799 Amherst Ave 30 – 199 Sutton Way	B
2500 – 2699 University Blvd. 191 – 299 Canton St. 5 – 25 Rural Route 5	C
All mail that does not fall in one of the address ranges listed above.	D

The goal is to simplify the Coding Guide to manageable bits that you can recall easily. To do this you have to rearrange the information into a condensed and logical order that you can recall during the exam. To master this technique you need to practice on this Coding Guide and then go on to take the memory test.

Look at the Coding Guide. You will notice that street addresses repeat in the various routes. For example, Amherst Ave. is listed in Route A and B, Sutton Way repeats in A and B, and Canton St. repeats in A and C. Rural Route 5 and University Blvd. are only in route C. The goal is to put these streets into an order and number sequence that you can remember and do it within the allotted time.

Notice that most of the address ranges run sequentially. Amherst Ave runs from 400 - 499 in Route A and from 500 - 799 in Route B. Canton St., runs from 101 - 190 in Route A and from 191 - 299 in Route C. Two addresses, University Blvd., and Rural Route 5, are only in Delivery Route C. Rewrite the addresses and routes as follows:

- Amherst Ave. 400 - 499A - 799B
- Canton St. 101 - 190A - 299C
- Sutton Way 1 - 29A - 199B
- University Blvd. 2500 - 2699C
- Rural Route 5 - 25C

Remember one key fact. **The second sequential range is actually one count higher than the highest count for that street**. For example, Amherst is listed as "Amherst Ave. 400 - 499A - 799B." Route A runs from 400 - 499, add (1) to 499 and that equals 500. Therefore, Route B Amherst Ave. addresses run from 500 to 799. You only have to remember three numbers with this technique as long as you remember that the second range starts at the very next number in the first range, 500 in this example.

Most exams have sequential routes. If you run into a Coding Guide that has a non-sequential street addresses, you will have to add the complete second address range to the quick reference memory chart. If the B Route for Amherst Ave. was 601 - 799 you would write the line as "Amherst Ave. 400 - 499A - 601 -799B.

Here are several other techniques that will help you remember the revised lists. You may also have your own memory methods that you use to recall key information. Find out what works best for you and use them to your benefit.

- Reorder the list and use an acronym to recall the list. An Acronym is an abbreviation that you can easily recall to start the process. An acronym example would be "IRS" which stands for "Internal Revenue Service." look at the list to see what abbreviation you can devise to help you remember the list. I reorganized the original list to the following:

  - Canton St. 101 - 190A - 299C
  - Amherst Ave. 400 - 499A - 799B
  - Rural Route 5 - 25C
  - University Blvd. 2500 - 2699C
  - Sutton Way 1 - 29A - 199B

The acronym that I came up with is **CARUS**. Write it out in a horizontal line on your test guide just as a memory jogger. You may not have time to write your entire list down but this can help.

C = Canton St. 101 - 190A - 299C
A = Amherst Ave. 400 - 499A - 799B
R = Rural Route 5 - 25C
U = University Blvd. 2500 - 2699C
S = Sutton Way 1 - 29A - 199B

Now let's go a little further with this and use other memory joggers to help you memorize the list. Now that you have the list rewritten and reordered, how do you remember the address ranges?

1. Use associations to remember what is on the list. First, write down the acronym on your test booklet. You have to remember that C = Canton St. Now the routes associated with Canton St. are A and C. C is the first letter of the CARUS in your mind. Let it also equal A for Route A and now the second route will be C for the C in Canton, whatever makes sense to you. Now you know that C = Canton St., and that Canton St. is in Route A and C. If words don't come to you, just take the first letter of each street in whatever order makes sense to you.

2. Look at the numbers 101-299 for Canton St. next. Where does the route separate. For C = Canton St. subtract 109 and that is were the split is. You can also just remember the three numbers. Coincidentally 109 is the first two digits of 101 and the last digit of 299. Say it over several times in your head C = Canton St. = 101 - 190A - 299C. You already know that the second route starts at 191, one count up from 190.

3. I believe the easiest way to remember the address ranges and routes is to remember the entire string. Use the acronym to jog your memory and then say C = Canton St. = 101 - 190A - 299C. Close your eyes for a second and visualize the street, numbers and routes. With the acronym **CARUS** and visualization, you should be able to remember this short list in the time offered especially if you use all of the study periods, as recommended, to your advantage.

4. Many who take the exam try to streamline the amount of information to memorize even further by abbreviating the street names. Recall our discussion earlier when you had several street names with different spellings such as "Amherst" and "Amhurst." The actual exam will also include different designators and instead of using "Sutton Way" on a question it may read "Sutton Terrace." Therefore, if you only remembered "Sut" or "Sutton" you would not know what the correct answer was for that question.

5. You are allowed to make notes on the exam booklet during the memory test. You can write the acronym that you devise in the booklet and quickly note the street names and ranges. However, you need to practice before attempting this; otherwise you may take too much time and not finish the exam.

PART C
Coding Memory Section Practice Exam

You will be given 5 minutes to study the Coding Guide. Turn to page 35 and study the Coding Guide for 5 minutes. (Time this exercise) We will use the same Coding Guide as the one used in the previous section as they do in the actual exam. A second practice exam follows this one using a different Coding Guide to give you more practice with this section.

If you don't have someone to time you enter your start time below and when you finish write down the stop time. Determine the total time used for the exam. Place a copy of the answer sheet next to your book for this section.

— Answer Sheet page 146, Answer Key page 150 —

START TIME _____

	Address	Delivery Route			
37.	22 Sutton Way	A	B	C	D
38.	27 Rural Route 5	A	B	C	D
39.	534 Amherst Ave.	A	B	C	D
40.	2601 University Blvd.	A	B	C	D
41.	189 Canton St.	A	B	C	D
42.	34 Sutton Way	A	B	C	D
43.	2701 Universal Blvd.	A	B	C	D
44.	1924 Rural Route 5	A	B	C	D
45.	299 Canyon St.	A	B	C	D
46.	168 Canton St.	A	B	C	D
47.	521 Amherst Ave.	A	B	C	D
48.	189 Sutton Way.	A	B	C	D
49.	199 Sutton Place	A	B	C	D
50.	2599 University Blvd.	A	B	C	D
51.	2501 University Blvd.	A	B	C	D
52.	29 Sutton Way	A	B	C	D
53.	45 Sutton Way.	A	B	C	D
54.	35 Rural Route 5	A	B	C	D

CONTINUE EXAM

	Address	Delivery Route			
55.	19 Sutton Way	A	B	C	D
56.	31 Sutton Way	A	B	C	D
57.	205 Canton St.	A	B	C	D
58.	2691 University Blvd.	A	B	C	D
59.	432 Amherst Ave.	A	B	C	D
60.	801 Amherst Ave.	A	B	C	D
61.	151 Canton St.	A	B	C	D
62.	45 Sexton Way	A	B	C	D
63.	19 Rural Route 5	A	B	C	D
64.	619 Amherst Ave.	A	B	C	D
65.	107 Sutton Way	A	B	C	D
66.	140 Canton St.	A	B	C	D
67.	435 Fifth Ave.	A	B	C	D
68.	1500 University Blvd.	A	B	C	D
69.	122 Sutton Way	A	B	C	D
70.	35 Smithton Place	A	B	C	D
71.	578 Amherst Ave.	A	B	C	D
72.	149 Canton St.	A	B	C	D

STOP

Record Time Here:_____ Minutes

(You are limited to 7 minutes)

The memory section is considered by many to be the most difficult. Therefore, we included several practice exams. Before going on to the next memory practice exam review pages 134 to 138. Experiment with the memory techniques offered in this study guide or use your own unique methods to memorize the following new Coding Guide.

PART C
Coding Memory Section Practice Exam 2

You will be given 5 minutes to study this new Coding Guide. (Time this exercise). If you don't have someone to time you enter your start time below and when you finish write down the stop time. Determine the total time used for the exam. Remember, in the actual exam you only have 7 minutes to complete this section. Place a copy of the answer sheet next to your book for this section.

START TIME _____

CODING GUIDE	
Address Range	**Delivery Route**
1891 – 3100 Eagle LN 25 – 40 Amberwood Hwy 200 – 499 Lemington CT	A
3101 – 3800 Eagle LN 500 – 799 Lemington CT	B
620 - 800 Trent Pkwy 6000 – 10000 Bedford Ave. 41 – 100 Amberwood Hwy	C
All mail that does not fall in one of the address ranges listed above.	D

STOP TIME _____

You are given 5 minutes to memorize
this Coding Guide before starting the next practice exam.

START TIME _____

7 Minutes to Complete Practice Memory Exam 2

— **Answer Sheet page 148, Answer Key page 150** —

	Address	Delivery Route			
37.	50 Amberwood Hwy	A	B	C	D
38.	3199 Eagle LN	A	B	C	D
39.	199 Lemington CT	A	B	C	D
40.	621 Trent Pkwy	A	B	C	D
41.	7067 Bedford Ave.	A	B	C	D
42.	1955 Eagle LN	A	B	C	D
43.	99 Amberwood Hwy	A	B	C	D
44.	501 Lemington CT	A	B	C	D
45.	899 Trent Pkwy	A	B	C	D
46.	3788 Eagle LN	A	B	C	D
47.	25 Amberwood Hwy	A	B	C	D
48.	800 Lexington CT	A	B	C	D
49.	2205 Eagle LN	A	B	C	D
50.	719 Trent Pkwy	A	B	C	D
51.	125 Amberwood Hwy	A	B	C	D
52.	6099 Bedford Ave.	A	B	C	D
53.	700 Lemington CT	A	B	C	D
54.	1898 Eagle LN	A	B	C	D

Continued on next page

CONTINUE EXAM

	Address	Delivery Route			
55.	9989 Bedford Ave.	A	B	C	D
56.	701 Lemington CT	A	B	C	D
57.	43 Amberwood Hwy	A	B	C	D
58.	2901 Eagle LN	A	B	C	D
59.	799 Trent Pkwy	A	B	C	D
60.	7001 Bedford Ave.	A	B	C	D
61.	29 Amberwood Hwy	A	B	C	D
62.	278 Lemington CT	A	B	C	D
63.	3201 Eagle LN	A	B	C	D
64.	619 Amherst Ave	A	B	C	D
65.	654 Trent Pkwy	A	B	C	D
66.	30 Amberwood Hwy	A	B	C	D
67.	775 Lemington CT	A	B	C	D
68.	2677 Eagle LN	A	B	C	D
69.	8888 Bedford Ave.	A	B	C	D
70.	700 Trent Pkwy	A	B	C	D
71.	199 Amberwood Hwy	A	B	C	D
72.	4102 Eagle LN	A	B	C	D

STOP

Record Time Here: _____ Minutes
(You are limited to 7 minutes)

PERSONAL EXPERIENCE &
CHARACTERISTICS INVENTORY
PART D

This section takes 90 minutes to complete and has 236 questions. The Postal Service evaluates your personal experience, characteristics and tendencies. You will be asked your likes and dislikes, whether you have experience in certain areas. You really can't prepare for this section, it's your personal profile. if you answer the questions honestly the Postal Service will be able to identify the job that is best suited to your characteristics.

The answers are multiple choice. The question *"Do you like to work in groups"* would have the answers (A) Strongly Agree, (B) Agree, (C), Disagree, (D) Strongly Disagree. A question similar to *"Are you willing to work rotating shifts"* would have the answers (A) Very Often, (B) Often, (C) Sometimes, (D) Rarely.

Content and Structure

Part D is divided into two groups. The first group of questions includes multiple choice questions or statements with the following possible answers:

A. Strongly Agree	OR	A. Very Often
B. Agree		B. Often
C. Disagree		C. Sometimes
D. Strongly Disagree		D. Rarely

The second group of questions can have as few as four to as many as nine answer choices. You choose the answer that best describes your personal feelings and concerns.

Several typical question/statements are listed below so that you will know what to expect:

S1.   You like to work independently without interruptions.

A. Strongly Agree
B. Agree
C. Disagree
D. Strongly Disagree

S2.   You like to carefully prepare for events or activities in advance.

A. Very Often
B. Often
C. Sometimes
D. Rarely

S3.   What type of activities do you like the most?

A. activities that require planning and attention
B. activities that require little planning
C. activities that are physical and challenging
D. activities that are done while sitting
E. activities that don't require much thought
F. outdoor activities
G. not sure

Answer the questions honestly and pick the answer that represents your thoughts. If several answers seem to fit pick the one and **ONLY ONE** reply that best represents how you feel about the question or statement. There are no right or wrong answers on this part of the exam. You can only select one answer for each question. Use your entire background, including work experience, volunteer work, school work, military service, anything from your background that will help you relate to the question.

If you complete this section early you can turn
in your booklet and leave the exam room.

You need to be careful with this section. The design of the questions can reveal if you are trying to manipulate the exam. Questions are reworded or come from a different perspective and it is impossible to remember all of your answers and then evaluate what each question may mean to the examiners. The questions were designed by professionals and the Postal Service has not released any information on how this section is evaluated and scored. These types of tests are typically used to evaluate work ethics, attitudes, team work, customer service, skills, performance, and productivity.

SAMPLE ANSWER SHEETS

The next four pages have two complete sets of answer sheets that you can use for the practice exams. You can also make up additional practice exam questions and make copies of the answer sheets for additional practice. If you don't have a copy machine handy you can remove the next two pages and use the answer sheet for the practice exams. You will still have another set of answer sheets on pages 147 and 148.

The answer sheet layout is not identical to what you will find in the exam. Both sides of the actual exam answer sheet are used. Your personal information will be placed at the top of the front and answer sheet and Part A and B answers are placed at the bottom. The back of the actual sheet is used to mark your answers for Part C and D. Our layout is different to accommodate the practice tests.

SAMPLE ANSWER SHEET (1)

Part A- Address Checking

1 Ⓐ Ⓑ Ⓒ Ⓓ	16 Ⓐ Ⓑ Ⓒ Ⓓ	31 Ⓐ Ⓑ Ⓒ Ⓓ	46 Ⓐ Ⓑ Ⓒ Ⓓ
2 Ⓐ Ⓑ Ⓒ Ⓓ	17 Ⓐ Ⓑ Ⓒ Ⓓ	32 Ⓐ Ⓑ Ⓒ Ⓓ	47 Ⓐ Ⓑ Ⓒ Ⓓ
3 Ⓐ Ⓑ Ⓒ Ⓓ	18 Ⓐ Ⓑ Ⓒ Ⓓ	33 Ⓐ Ⓑ Ⓒ Ⓓ	48 Ⓐ Ⓑ Ⓒ Ⓓ
4 Ⓐ Ⓑ Ⓒ Ⓓ	19 Ⓐ Ⓑ Ⓒ Ⓓ	34 Ⓐ Ⓑ Ⓒ Ⓓ	49 Ⓐ Ⓑ Ⓒ Ⓓ
5 Ⓐ Ⓑ Ⓒ Ⓓ	20 Ⓐ Ⓑ Ⓒ Ⓓ	35 Ⓐ Ⓑ Ⓒ Ⓓ	50 Ⓐ Ⓑ Ⓒ Ⓓ
6 Ⓐ Ⓑ Ⓒ Ⓓ	21 Ⓐ Ⓑ Ⓒ Ⓓ	36 Ⓐ Ⓑ Ⓒ Ⓓ	51 Ⓐ Ⓑ Ⓒ Ⓓ
7 Ⓐ Ⓑ Ⓒ Ⓓ	22 Ⓐ Ⓑ Ⓒ Ⓓ	37 Ⓐ Ⓑ Ⓒ Ⓓ	52 Ⓐ Ⓑ Ⓒ Ⓓ
8 Ⓐ Ⓑ Ⓒ Ⓓ	23 Ⓐ Ⓑ Ⓒ Ⓓ	38 Ⓐ Ⓑ Ⓒ Ⓓ	53 Ⓐ Ⓑ Ⓒ Ⓓ
9 Ⓐ Ⓑ Ⓒ Ⓓ	24 Ⓐ Ⓑ Ⓒ Ⓓ	39 Ⓐ Ⓑ Ⓒ Ⓓ	54 Ⓐ Ⓑ Ⓒ Ⓓ
10 Ⓐ Ⓑ Ⓒ Ⓓ	25 Ⓐ Ⓑ Ⓒ Ⓓ	40 Ⓐ Ⓑ Ⓒ Ⓓ	55 Ⓐ Ⓑ Ⓒ Ⓓ
11 Ⓐ Ⓑ Ⓒ Ⓓ	26 Ⓐ Ⓑ Ⓒ Ⓓ	41 Ⓐ Ⓑ Ⓒ Ⓓ	56 Ⓐ Ⓑ Ⓒ Ⓓ
12 Ⓐ Ⓑ Ⓒ Ⓓ	27 Ⓐ Ⓑ Ⓒ Ⓓ	42 Ⓐ Ⓑ Ⓒ Ⓓ	57 Ⓐ Ⓑ Ⓒ Ⓓ
13 Ⓐ Ⓑ Ⓒ Ⓓ	28 Ⓐ Ⓑ Ⓒ Ⓓ	43 Ⓐ Ⓑ Ⓒ Ⓓ	58 Ⓐ Ⓑ Ⓒ Ⓓ
14 Ⓐ Ⓑ Ⓒ Ⓓ	29 Ⓐ Ⓑ Ⓒ Ⓓ	44 Ⓐ Ⓑ Ⓒ Ⓓ	59 Ⓐ Ⓑ Ⓒ Ⓓ
15 Ⓐ Ⓑ Ⓒ Ⓓ	30 Ⓐ Ⓑ Ⓒ Ⓓ	45 Ⓐ Ⓑ Ⓒ Ⓓ	60 Ⓐ Ⓑ Ⓒ Ⓓ

Part B – Forms Completion

1 Ⓐ Ⓑ Ⓒ Ⓓ	16 Ⓐ Ⓑ Ⓒ Ⓓ
2 Ⓐ Ⓑ Ⓒ Ⓓ	17 Ⓐ Ⓑ Ⓒ Ⓓ
3 Ⓐ Ⓑ Ⓒ Ⓓ	18 Ⓐ Ⓑ Ⓒ Ⓓ
4 Ⓐ Ⓑ Ⓒ Ⓓ	19 Ⓐ Ⓑ Ⓒ Ⓓ
5 Ⓐ Ⓑ Ⓒ Ⓓ	20 Ⓐ Ⓑ Ⓒ Ⓓ
6 Ⓐ Ⓑ Ⓒ Ⓓ	21 Ⓐ Ⓑ Ⓒ Ⓓ
7 Ⓐ Ⓑ Ⓒ Ⓓ	22 Ⓐ Ⓑ Ⓒ Ⓓ
8 Ⓐ Ⓑ Ⓒ Ⓓ	23 Ⓐ Ⓑ Ⓒ Ⓓ
9 Ⓐ Ⓑ Ⓒ Ⓓ	24 Ⓐ Ⓑ Ⓒ Ⓓ
10 Ⓐ Ⓑ Ⓒ Ⓓ	25 Ⓐ Ⓑ Ⓒ Ⓓ
11 Ⓐ Ⓑ Ⓒ Ⓓ	26 Ⓐ Ⓑ Ⓒ Ⓓ
12 Ⓐ Ⓑ Ⓒ Ⓓ	27 Ⓐ Ⓑ Ⓒ Ⓓ
13 Ⓐ Ⓑ Ⓒ Ⓓ	28 Ⓐ Ⓑ Ⓒ Ⓓ
14 Ⓐ Ⓑ Ⓒ Ⓓ	29 Ⓐ Ⓑ Ⓒ Ⓓ
15 Ⓐ Ⓑ Ⓒ Ⓓ	30 Ⓐ Ⓑ Ⓒ Ⓓ

Part C - Coding

1 Ⓐ Ⓑ Ⓒ Ⓓ	13 Ⓐ Ⓑ Ⓒ Ⓓ	25 Ⓐ Ⓑ Ⓒ Ⓓ
2 Ⓐ Ⓑ Ⓒ Ⓓ	14 Ⓐ Ⓑ Ⓒ Ⓓ	26 Ⓐ Ⓑ Ⓒ Ⓓ
3 Ⓐ Ⓑ Ⓒ Ⓓ	15 Ⓐ Ⓑ Ⓒ Ⓓ	27 Ⓐ Ⓑ Ⓒ Ⓓ
4 Ⓐ Ⓑ Ⓒ Ⓓ	16 Ⓐ Ⓑ Ⓒ Ⓓ	28 Ⓐ Ⓑ Ⓒ Ⓓ
5 Ⓐ Ⓑ Ⓒ Ⓓ	17 Ⓐ Ⓑ Ⓒ Ⓓ	29 Ⓐ Ⓑ Ⓒ Ⓓ
6 Ⓐ Ⓑ Ⓒ Ⓓ	18 Ⓐ Ⓑ Ⓒ Ⓓ	30 Ⓐ Ⓑ Ⓒ Ⓓ
7 Ⓐ Ⓑ Ⓒ Ⓓ	19 Ⓐ Ⓑ Ⓒ Ⓓ	31 Ⓐ Ⓑ Ⓒ Ⓓ
8 Ⓐ Ⓑ Ⓒ Ⓓ	20 Ⓐ Ⓑ Ⓒ Ⓓ	32 Ⓐ Ⓑ Ⓒ Ⓓ
9 Ⓐ Ⓑ Ⓒ Ⓓ	21 Ⓐ Ⓑ Ⓒ Ⓓ	33 Ⓐ Ⓑ Ⓒ Ⓓ
10 Ⓐ Ⓑ Ⓒ Ⓓ	22 Ⓐ Ⓑ Ⓒ Ⓓ	34 Ⓐ Ⓑ Ⓒ Ⓓ
11 Ⓐ Ⓑ Ⓒ Ⓓ	23 Ⓐ Ⓑ Ⓒ Ⓓ	35 Ⓐ Ⓑ Ⓒ Ⓓ
12 Ⓐ Ⓑ Ⓒ Ⓓ	24 Ⓐ Ⓑ Ⓒ Ⓓ	36 Ⓐ Ⓑ Ⓒ Ⓓ

Part C - Memory

37 Ⓐ Ⓑ Ⓒ Ⓓ	49 Ⓐ Ⓑ Ⓒ Ⓓ	61 Ⓐ Ⓑ Ⓒ Ⓓ
38 Ⓐ Ⓑ Ⓒ Ⓓ	50 Ⓐ Ⓑ Ⓒ Ⓓ	62 Ⓐ Ⓑ Ⓒ Ⓓ
39 Ⓐ Ⓑ Ⓒ Ⓓ	51 Ⓐ Ⓑ Ⓒ Ⓓ	63 Ⓐ Ⓑ Ⓒ Ⓓ
40 Ⓐ Ⓑ Ⓒ Ⓓ	52 Ⓐ Ⓑ Ⓒ Ⓓ	64 Ⓐ Ⓑ Ⓒ Ⓓ
41 Ⓐ Ⓑ Ⓒ Ⓓ	53 Ⓐ Ⓑ Ⓒ Ⓓ	65 Ⓐ Ⓑ Ⓒ Ⓓ
42 Ⓐ Ⓑ Ⓒ Ⓓ	54 Ⓐ Ⓑ Ⓒ Ⓓ	66 Ⓐ Ⓑ Ⓒ Ⓓ
43 Ⓐ Ⓑ Ⓒ Ⓓ	55 Ⓐ Ⓑ Ⓒ Ⓓ	67 Ⓐ Ⓑ Ⓒ Ⓓ
44 Ⓐ Ⓑ Ⓒ Ⓓ	56 Ⓐ Ⓑ Ⓒ Ⓓ	68 Ⓐ Ⓑ Ⓒ Ⓓ
45 Ⓐ Ⓑ Ⓒ Ⓓ	57 Ⓐ Ⓑ Ⓒ Ⓓ	69 Ⓐ Ⓑ Ⓒ Ⓓ
46 Ⓐ Ⓑ Ⓒ Ⓓ	58 Ⓐ Ⓑ Ⓒ Ⓓ	70 Ⓐ Ⓑ Ⓒ Ⓓ
47 Ⓐ Ⓑ Ⓒ Ⓓ	59 Ⓐ Ⓑ Ⓒ Ⓓ	71 Ⓐ Ⓑ Ⓒ Ⓓ
48 Ⓐ Ⓑ Ⓒ Ⓓ	60 Ⓐ Ⓑ Ⓒ Ⓓ	72 Ⓐ Ⓑ Ⓒ Ⓓ

SAMPLE ANSWER SHEET (2)

Part A- Address Checking

1	Ⓐ Ⓑ Ⓒ Ⓓ	16	Ⓐ Ⓑ Ⓒ Ⓓ	31	Ⓐ Ⓑ Ⓒ Ⓓ	46	Ⓐ Ⓑ Ⓒ Ⓓ
2	Ⓐ Ⓑ Ⓒ Ⓓ	17	Ⓐ Ⓑ Ⓒ Ⓓ	32	Ⓐ Ⓑ Ⓒ Ⓓ	47	Ⓐ Ⓑ Ⓒ Ⓓ
3	Ⓐ Ⓑ Ⓒ Ⓓ	18	Ⓐ Ⓑ Ⓒ Ⓓ	33	Ⓐ Ⓑ Ⓒ Ⓓ	48	Ⓐ Ⓑ Ⓒ Ⓓ
4	Ⓐ Ⓑ Ⓒ Ⓓ	19	Ⓐ Ⓑ Ⓒ Ⓓ	34	Ⓐ Ⓑ Ⓒ Ⓓ	49	Ⓐ Ⓑ Ⓒ Ⓓ
5	Ⓐ Ⓑ Ⓒ Ⓓ	20	Ⓐ Ⓑ Ⓒ Ⓓ	35	Ⓐ Ⓑ Ⓒ Ⓓ	50	Ⓐ Ⓑ Ⓒ Ⓓ
6	Ⓐ Ⓑ Ⓒ Ⓓ	21	Ⓐ Ⓑ Ⓒ Ⓓ	36	Ⓐ Ⓑ Ⓒ Ⓓ	51	Ⓐ Ⓑ Ⓒ Ⓓ
7	Ⓐ Ⓑ Ⓒ Ⓓ	22	Ⓐ Ⓑ Ⓒ Ⓓ	37	Ⓐ Ⓑ Ⓒ Ⓓ	52	Ⓐ Ⓑ Ⓒ Ⓓ
8	Ⓐ Ⓑ Ⓒ Ⓓ	23	Ⓐ Ⓑ Ⓒ Ⓓ	38	Ⓐ Ⓑ Ⓒ Ⓓ	53	Ⓐ Ⓑ Ⓒ Ⓓ
9	Ⓐ Ⓑ Ⓒ Ⓓ	24	Ⓐ Ⓑ Ⓒ Ⓓ	39	Ⓐ Ⓑ Ⓒ Ⓓ	54	Ⓐ Ⓑ Ⓒ Ⓓ
10	Ⓐ Ⓑ Ⓒ Ⓓ	25	Ⓐ Ⓑ Ⓒ Ⓓ	40	Ⓐ Ⓑ Ⓒ Ⓓ	55	Ⓐ Ⓑ Ⓒ Ⓓ
11	Ⓐ Ⓑ Ⓒ Ⓓ	26	Ⓐ Ⓑ Ⓒ Ⓓ	41	Ⓐ Ⓑ Ⓒ Ⓓ	56	Ⓐ Ⓑ Ⓒ Ⓓ
12	Ⓐ Ⓑ Ⓒ Ⓓ	27	Ⓐ Ⓑ Ⓒ Ⓓ	42	Ⓐ Ⓑ Ⓒ Ⓓ	57	Ⓐ Ⓑ Ⓒ Ⓓ
13	Ⓐ Ⓑ Ⓒ Ⓓ	28	Ⓐ Ⓑ Ⓒ Ⓓ	43	Ⓐ Ⓑ Ⓒ Ⓓ	58	Ⓐ Ⓑ Ⓒ Ⓓ
14	Ⓐ Ⓑ Ⓒ Ⓓ	29	Ⓐ Ⓑ Ⓒ Ⓓ	44	Ⓐ Ⓑ Ⓒ Ⓓ	59	Ⓐ Ⓑ Ⓒ Ⓓ
15	Ⓐ Ⓑ Ⓒ Ⓓ	30	Ⓐ Ⓑ Ⓒ Ⓓ	45	Ⓐ Ⓑ Ⓒ Ⓓ	60	Ⓐ Ⓑ Ⓒ Ⓓ

Part B – Forms Completion

1	Ⓐ Ⓑ Ⓒ Ⓓ	16	Ⓐ Ⓑ Ⓒ Ⓓ
2	Ⓐ Ⓑ Ⓒ Ⓓ	17	Ⓐ Ⓑ Ⓒ Ⓓ
3	Ⓐ Ⓑ Ⓒ Ⓓ	18	Ⓐ Ⓑ Ⓒ Ⓓ
4	Ⓐ Ⓑ Ⓒ Ⓓ	19	Ⓐ Ⓑ Ⓒ Ⓓ
5	Ⓐ Ⓑ Ⓒ Ⓓ	20	Ⓐ Ⓑ Ⓒ Ⓓ
6	Ⓐ Ⓑ Ⓒ Ⓓ	21	Ⓐ Ⓑ Ⓒ Ⓓ
7	Ⓐ Ⓑ Ⓒ Ⓓ	22	Ⓐ Ⓑ Ⓒ Ⓓ
8	Ⓐ Ⓑ Ⓒ Ⓓ	23	Ⓐ Ⓑ Ⓒ Ⓓ
9	Ⓐ Ⓑ Ⓒ Ⓓ	24	Ⓐ Ⓑ Ⓒ Ⓓ
10	Ⓐ Ⓑ Ⓒ Ⓓ	25	Ⓐ Ⓑ Ⓒ Ⓓ
11	Ⓐ Ⓑ Ⓒ Ⓓ	26	Ⓐ Ⓑ Ⓒ Ⓓ
12	Ⓐ Ⓑ Ⓒ Ⓓ	27	Ⓐ Ⓑ Ⓒ Ⓓ
13	Ⓐ Ⓑ Ⓒ Ⓓ	28	Ⓐ Ⓑ Ⓒ Ⓓ
14	Ⓐ Ⓑ Ⓒ Ⓓ	29	Ⓐ Ⓑ Ⓒ Ⓓ
15	Ⓐ Ⓑ Ⓒ Ⓓ	30	Ⓐ Ⓑ Ⓒ Ⓓ

Part C - Coding

1	Ⓐ Ⓑ Ⓒ Ⓓ	13 Ⓐ Ⓑ Ⓒ Ⓓ	25 Ⓐ Ⓑ Ⓒ Ⓓ
2	Ⓐ Ⓑ Ⓒ Ⓓ	14 Ⓐ Ⓑ Ⓒ Ⓓ	26 Ⓐ Ⓑ Ⓒ Ⓓ
3	Ⓐ Ⓑ Ⓒ Ⓓ	15 Ⓐ Ⓑ Ⓒ Ⓓ	27 Ⓐ Ⓑ Ⓒ Ⓓ
4	Ⓐ Ⓑ Ⓒ Ⓓ	16 Ⓐ Ⓑ Ⓒ Ⓓ	28 Ⓐ Ⓑ Ⓒ Ⓓ
5	Ⓐ Ⓑ Ⓒ Ⓓ	17 Ⓐ Ⓑ Ⓒ Ⓓ	29 Ⓐ Ⓑ Ⓒ Ⓓ
6	Ⓐ Ⓑ Ⓒ Ⓓ	18 Ⓐ Ⓑ Ⓒ Ⓓ	30 Ⓐ Ⓑ Ⓒ Ⓓ
7	Ⓐ Ⓑ Ⓒ Ⓓ	19 Ⓐ Ⓑ Ⓒ Ⓓ	31 Ⓐ Ⓑ Ⓒ Ⓓ
8	Ⓐ Ⓑ Ⓒ Ⓓ	20 Ⓐ Ⓑ Ⓒ Ⓓ	32 Ⓐ Ⓑ Ⓒ Ⓓ
9	Ⓐ Ⓑ Ⓒ Ⓓ	21 Ⓐ Ⓑ Ⓒ Ⓓ	33 Ⓐ Ⓑ Ⓒ Ⓓ
10	Ⓐ Ⓑ Ⓒ Ⓓ	22 Ⓐ Ⓑ Ⓒ Ⓓ	34 Ⓐ Ⓑ Ⓒ Ⓓ
11	Ⓐ Ⓑ Ⓒ Ⓓ	23 Ⓐ Ⓑ Ⓒ Ⓓ	35 Ⓐ Ⓑ Ⓒ Ⓓ
12	Ⓐ Ⓑ Ⓒ Ⓓ	24 Ⓐ Ⓑ Ⓒ Ⓓ	36 Ⓐ Ⓑ Ⓒ Ⓓ

Part C - Memory

37	Ⓐ Ⓑ Ⓒ Ⓓ	49 Ⓐ Ⓑ Ⓒ Ⓓ	61 Ⓐ Ⓑ Ⓒ Ⓓ
38	Ⓐ Ⓑ Ⓒ Ⓓ	50 Ⓐ Ⓑ Ⓒ Ⓓ	62 Ⓐ Ⓑ Ⓒ Ⓓ
39	Ⓐ Ⓑ Ⓒ Ⓓ	51 Ⓐ Ⓑ Ⓒ Ⓓ	63 Ⓐ Ⓑ Ⓒ Ⓓ
40	Ⓐ Ⓑ Ⓒ Ⓓ	52 Ⓐ Ⓑ Ⓒ Ⓓ	64 Ⓐ Ⓑ Ⓒ Ⓓ
41	Ⓐ Ⓑ Ⓒ Ⓓ	53 Ⓐ Ⓑ Ⓒ Ⓓ	65 Ⓐ Ⓑ Ⓒ Ⓓ
42	Ⓐ Ⓑ Ⓒ Ⓓ	54 Ⓐ Ⓑ Ⓒ Ⓓ	66 Ⓐ Ⓑ Ⓒ Ⓓ
43	Ⓐ Ⓑ Ⓒ Ⓓ	55 Ⓐ Ⓑ Ⓒ Ⓓ	67 Ⓐ Ⓑ Ⓒ Ⓓ
44	Ⓐ Ⓑ Ⓒ Ⓓ	56 Ⓐ Ⓑ Ⓒ Ⓓ	68 Ⓐ Ⓑ Ⓒ Ⓓ
45	Ⓐ Ⓑ Ⓒ Ⓓ	57 Ⓐ Ⓑ Ⓒ Ⓓ	69 Ⓐ Ⓑ Ⓒ Ⓓ
46	Ⓐ Ⓑ Ⓒ Ⓓ	58 Ⓐ Ⓑ Ⓒ Ⓓ	70 Ⓐ Ⓑ Ⓒ Ⓓ
47	Ⓐ Ⓑ Ⓒ Ⓓ	59 Ⓐ Ⓑ Ⓒ Ⓓ	71 Ⓐ Ⓑ Ⓒ Ⓓ
48	Ⓐ Ⓑ Ⓒ Ⓓ	60 Ⓐ Ⓑ Ⓒ Ⓓ	72 Ⓐ Ⓑ Ⓒ Ⓓ

Answer Key
Practice Exams

Address Checking
Page 114 - 115

Forms Completion
Pages 118 - 127

1.	C	31.	A	1.	B
2.	A	32.	B	2.	C
3.	D	33.	C	3.	B
4.	A	34.	C	4.	D
5.	D	35.	D	5.	C
6.	B	36.	B	6.	C
7.	A	37.	B	7.	C
8.	B	38.	C	8.	C
9.	D	39.	A	9.	B
10.	A	40.	D	10.	C
11.	D	41.	C	11.	C
12.	D	42.	B	12.	D
13.	C	43.	D	13.	B
14.	D	44.	A	14.	C
15.	A	45.	C	15.	A
16.	B	46.	B	16.	A
17.	B	47.	D	17.	C
18.	C	48.	A	18.	C
19.	C	49.	C	19.	C
20.	B	50.	B	20.	B
21.	A	51.	A	21.	B
22.	B	52.	D	22.	B
23.	C	53.	C	23.	B
24.	D	54.	B	24.	C
25.	A	55.	D	25.	C
26.	C	56.	A	26.	B
27.	B	57.	C	27.	C
28.	D	58.	B	28.	C
29.	B	59.	B	29.	B
30.	A	60.	A	30.	D

Answer Key
Practice Exams
Coding & Memory   Pages 131 - 139

Coding	Memory (1)	Memory (2)
1. C	37. A	37. C
2. B	38. D	38. B
3. D	39. B	39. D
4. D	40. C	40. C
5. B	41. A	41. C
6. A	42. B	42. A
7. D	43. D	43. C
8. C	44. D	44. B
9. B	45. D	45. D
10. A	46. A	46. B
11. A	47. B	47. A
12. C	48. B	48. D
13. B	49. D	49. A
14. D	50. C	50. C
15. B	51. C	51. D
16. A	52. A	52. C
17. D	53. B	53. B
18. C	54. D	54. A
19. A	55. A	55. C
20. B	56. B	56. B
21. D	57. C	57. C
22. C	58. C	58. A
23. A	59. A	59. C
24. D	60. D	60. C
25. B	61. A	61. A
26. C	62. D	62. A
27. C	63. C	63. B
28. A	64. B	64. D
29. A	65. B	65. C
30. D	66. A	66. A
31. B	67. D	67. B
32. C	68. D	68. A
33. B	69. B	69. C
34. A	70. D	70. C
35. D	71. B	71. D
36. C	72. A	72. D

Chapter Seven
The Interview Process

There are several types of interviews which you may encounter. The most common interview is called a *Structured Interview*. Most traditional interviews are based on this format. Below are some descriptions of the different types of interviews and what you can expect in each of them.[1]

Types of Interviews

- *Screening Interview*. A preliminary interview either in person or by phone, in which an agency or company representative determines whether you have the basic qualifications to warrant a subsequent interview.

- **Structured Interview**. In a structured interview, the interviewer explores certain predetermined areas using questions which have been written in advance. The interviewer has a written description of the experience, skills and personality traits of an "ideal" candidate. Your experience and skills are compared to specific job tasks. This type of interview is very common and most traditional interviews are based on this format.

- *Unstructured Interview*. Although the interviewer is given a written description of the "ideal" candidate, in the unstructured interview the interviewer is not given instructions on what specific areas to cover.

- *Multiple Interviews*. Multiple interviews are commonly used with professional jobs. This approach involves a series of interviews in which you meet individually with various representatives of the organization.

[1] The Job Search Guide, U.S. Department of Labor.

■ *Stress Interview.* The interviewer intentionally attempts to upset you to see how you react under pressure. You may be asked questions that make you uncomfortable or you may be interrupted when you are speaking. Although it is uncommon for an entire interview to be conducted under stress conditions, it is common for the interviewer to incorporate stress questions as a part of a traditional interview. Examples of common stress questions are given later in this chapter.

■ *Targeted Interview.* Although similar to the structured interview, the areas covered are much more limited. Key qualifications for success on the job are identified and relevant questions are prepared in advance.

■ *Situational Interview.* Situations are set up which simulate common problems you may encounter on the job. Your responses to these situations are measured against pre-determined standards. This approach is often used as one part of a traditional interview rather than as an entire interview format.

■ *Group Interview.* You may be interviewed by two or more agency or company representatives simultaneously. Sometimes, one of the interviewers is designated to ask "stress" questions to see how you respond under pressure.

   NOTE: Many government agencies including the Postal Service have initiated quality of worklife and employee involvement groups to build viable labor/management teams and partnerships. In this environment agencies may require applicants to be interviewed by several groups that often include peers and subordinates.

The interview strategies discussed below can be used effectively in any type of interview you may encounter.

BEFORE THE INTERVIEW

Prepare in advance. The better prepared you are, the less anxious you will be and the greater your chances for success.

■ *Role Play.* Find someone to role play the interview with you. This person should be someone with whom you feel comfortable and with whom you can discuss your weaknesses freely. The person should be objective and knowledgeable, perhaps a business associate.

■ Use a mirror or video camera when you role play to see what kind of image you project.

Assess your interviewing skills.

- What are your strengths and weaknesses? Work on correcting your weaknesses, such as speaking rapidly, talking too loudly or softly and nervous habits such as shaking hands or inappropriate facial expressions.

- Learn the questions that are commonly asked and prepare answers to them. Examples of commonly asked interview questions are provided later in this chapter. Career centers and libraries often have books which include interview questions. Practice giving answers which are brief but thorough.

- Decide what questions you would like to ask and practice politely interjecting them at different points in the interview.

Evaluate your strengths

- Evaluate your skills, abilities and education as they relate to the type of job you are seeking.

- Practice tailoring your answers to show how you meet the Postal Service's needs, if you have details about the specific job before the interview.

Assess your overall appearance.

- Find out what clothing is appropriate for your job series. Acceptable attire for most professional positions is conservative.

- Have several sets of appropriate clothing available since you may have several interviews over a few days.

- Your clothes should be clean and pressed and your shoes polished.

- Make sure your hair is neat, your nails clean and you are generally well groomed.

Research the Postal Service. The more you know about the Postal Service and the job you are applying for, the better you will do on the interview. Get as much information as you can before the interview.

Professional applicants and applicants for positions that do not require entrance exams should have extra copies of their resume or application available to take on the interview. The interviewer may ask you for extra copies. Make sure you bring along the same version of your resume or application that you originally provided them. You can also refer to your resume to complete applications that ask for job history information (i.e., dates of employment, names of former employers and their telephone numbers, job responsibilities and accomplishments.) A blank application form is provided in Appendix B for your use.

Arrive early at the interview. Plan to arrive 10 to 15 minutes early. Give yourself time to find a restroom so you can check your appearance.

It's important to make a good impression from the moment you enter the reception area. Greet the receptionist cordially and try to appear confident. You never know what influence the receptionist has with your interviewer. With a little small talk, you may get some helpful information about the interviewer and the job opening. If you are asked to fill out an application while you're waiting, be sure to fill it out completely and print the information neatly. Prepare the sample application in Appendix C.

Don't make negative comments about anyone or anything, including former employers.

DURING THE INTERVIEW

The job interview is usually a two-way discussion between you and a prospective employer. The interviewer is attempting to determine whether you have what the Postal Service needs, and you are attempting to determine if you would accept the job if offered. Both of you will be trying to get as much information as possible in order to make those decisions.[2]

The interview that you are most likely to face is a structured interview with a traditional format. It usually consists of three phases. The introductory phase covers the greeting, small talk and an overview of which areas will be discussed during the interview. The middle phase is a question-and-answer period. The interviewer asks most of the questions, but you are given an opportunity to ask questions as well. The closing phase gives you an opportunity to ask any final questions you might have, cover any important points that haven't been discussed and get information about the next step in the process.

Introductory Phase. This phase is very important. You want to make a good first impression and, if possible, get additional information you need about the job and the company.

■ Make a good impression. You only have a few seconds to create a positive first impression which can influence the rest of the interview and even determine whether you get the job.

The interviewer's first impression of you is based mainly on non-verbal clues. The interviewer is assessing your overall appearance and demeanor. When greeting the interviewer, be certain your handshake is firm and that you make eye contact. Wait for the interviewer to signal you before you sit down.

Once seated, your body language is very important in conveying a positive impression. Find a comfortable position so that you don't appear tense. Lean forward slightly and maintain eye contact with the interviewer. This posture

---

[2] Postal Service Handbook EL-312

shows that you are interested in what is being said. Smile naturally at appropriate times. Show that you are open and receptive by keeping your arms and legs uncrossed. Avoid keeping your briefcase or your handbag on your lap. Pace your movements so that they are not too fast or too slow. Try to appear relaxed and confident.

- Get the information you need. If you weren't able to get complete information about the job in advance, you should try to get it as early as possible in the interview. Be sure to prepare your questions in advance. Knowing the following things will allow you to present those strengths and abilities that the employer wants.

    ✎ Why does the Postal Service need someone in this position?

    ✎ Exactly what would they expect of you?

    ✎ Are they looking for traditional or innovative solutions to problems?

- When to ask questions. The problem with a traditional interview structure is that your chance to ask questions occurs late in the interview. How can you get the information you need early in the process without making the interviewer feel that you are taking control?

Deciding exactly when to ask your questions is the tricky part. Timing is everything. You may have to make a decision based on intuition and your first impressions of the interviewer. Does the interviewer seem comfortable or nervous, soft spoken or forceful, formal or casual? These signals will help you to judge the best time to ask your questions.

The sooner you ask the questions, the less likely you are to disrupt the interviewer's agenda. However, if you ask questions too early, the interviewer may feel you are trying to control the interview.

Try asking questions right after the greeting and small talk. Since most interviewers like to set the tone of the interview and maintain initial control, always phrase your questions in a way that leaves control with the interviewer. Perhaps say, "Would you mind telling me a little more about the job so that I can focus on the information that would be most important to the Postal Service?" If there is no job opening but you are trying to develop one or you need more information, try saying, "Could you tell me a little more about where the Postal Service is going so I can focus in those areas of my background that are most relevant?"

You may want to wait until the interviewer has given an overview of what will be discussed. This overview may answer some of your questions or may provide some details that you can use to ask additional questions. Once the middle phase of the interview has begun, you may find it more difficult to ask questions.

Middle Phase. During this phase of the interview, you will be asked many questions about your work experience, skills, education, activities and interests, You are being assessed on how you will perform the job in relation to the agency objectives.

All your responses should be concise. Use specific examples to illustrate your point whenever possible. Although your responses should be prepared in advance so that they are well-phrased and effective, be sure they do not sound rehearsed. Remember that your responses must always be adapted to the present interview. Incorporate any information you obtained earlier in the interview with the responses you had prepared in advance and then answer in a way that is appropriate to the question.

FREQUENTLY ASKED QUESTIONS

Question: "Tell me about yourself."

Reply: Briefly describe your experience and background. If you are unsure what information the interviewer is seeking, say, "Are there any areas in particular you'd like to know about?"

Question: "What is your weakest point?" (A stress question)

Reply: Mention something that is actually a strength. Some examples are:

"I'm something of a perfectionist."

"I'm a stickler for punctuality."

"I'm tenacious."

Give a specific situation from your previous job to illustrate your point.

Question: "What is your strongest point?"

Reply: "I work well under pressure." or

"I am organized and manage my time well,"

If you have just graduated from college you might say,

"I am eager to learn, and I don't have to unlearn old techniques."

Give a specific example to illustrate your point.

Question: "What do you hope to be doing five years from now?"

Reply: "I hope I will still be working here and have increased my level of responsibility based on my performance and abilities."

Question: "Why have you been out of work for so long?" (A stress question)

Reply: "I spent some time re-evaluating my past experience and the current job market to see what direction I wanted to take." or

"I had some offers but I'm not just looking for another job; I'm looking for a career."

Question: "What do you know about the Postal Service? Why do you want to work here?'"

Reply: This is where your research will come in handy.

"The Postal Service is a leader in mail/package delivery and three of the Postal Service's six product lines would qualify as Fortune 500 companies:" (Mention one or two of the following.)

- Correspondence & transactions
- Business Advertising
- Expedited Delivery
- Publications Delivery
- Standard Package Delivery
- International Mail

"The Postal Service has a superior reputation with operating revenue exceeding $65 billion a year."[3]

You might try to get the interviewer to give you additional information about the Postal Service by saying that you are very interested in learning more about the agency objectives. This will help you to focus your response on relevant areas.

Question: "What is your greatest accomplishment?"

---

[3] USPS Financial Highlights, Annual Performance Plan 2003.

Reply: Give a specific illustration from your previous or current job where you saved the company money or helped increase their profits. If you have just graduated from college, try to find some accomplishment from your school work, part-time jobs or extra-curricular activities.

Question: "Why should we hire you?" (A stress question)

Reply: Highlight your background based on the Postal Service's current needs. Re-cap your qualifications keeping the interviewer's job description in mind. If you don't have much experience, talk about how your education and training prepared you for this job.

Question: "Why do you want to make a change now?"

Reply: "I want to develop my potential." or

"The opportunities in my present company are limited."

Question: "Tell me about a problem you had in your last job and how you resolved it."

Reply: The employer wants to assess your analytical skills and see if you are a team player. Select a problem from your last job and explain how you solved it.

Some Questions You Should Ask.

✎ "What are the Postal Service's current challenges?"

✎ "Could you give me a more detailed job description?"

✎ "Why is this position open?"

✎ "Are there opportunities for advancement?"

✎ "To whom would I report?"

Closing Phase. During the closing phase of an interview, you will be asked whether you have any other questions. Ask any relevant question that has not yet been answered. Highlight any of your strengths that have not been discussed. If another interview is to be scheduled, get the necessary information. If this is the final interview, find out when the decision is to be made and when you can call. Thank the interviewer by name and say goodbye.

ILLEGAL QUESTIONS

During an interview, you may be asked some questions that are considered illegal. It is illegal for an interviewer to ask you questions related to sex, age, race, religion, national origin or marital status, or to delve into your personal life for information that is not job-related. What can you do if you are asked an illegal question? Take a moment to evaluate the situation. Ask yourself questions like:

✎ How uncomfortable has this question made you feel?

✎ Does the interviewer seem unaware that the question is illegal?

✎ Is this interviewer going to be your boss?

Then respond in a way that is comfortable for you.

If you decide to answer the question, be succinct and try to move the conversation back to an examination of your skills and abilities as quickly as possible. For example, if asked about your age, you might reply, "I'm in my forties, and I have a wealth of experience that would be an asset to your company." If you are not sure whether you want to answer the question, first ask for a clarification of how this question relates to your qualifications for the job. You may decide to answer if there is a reasonable explanation. If you feel there is no justification for the question, you might say that you do not see the relationship between the question and your qualifications for the job and you prefer not to answer it.

AFTER THE INTERVIEW

You are not finished yet. It is important to assess the interview shortly after it is concluded. Following your interview you should:

■ Write down the name, phone number, e-mail address, and title (be sure the spelling is correct) of the interviewer.

■ Review what the job entails and record what the next step will be.

■ Note your reactions to the interview; include what went well and what went poorly.

■ Assess what you learned from the experience and how you can improve your performance in future interviews.

PHONE FOLLOW-UP

If you were not told during the interview when a hiring decision will be made, call after one week.

At that time, if you learn that the decision has not been made, find out whether you are still under consideration for the job. Ask if there are any other questions the interviewer might have about your qualifications and offer to come in for another interview if necessary. Reiterate that you are very interested in the job.

- If you learn that you did not get the job, try to find out why. You might also inquire whether the interviewer can think of anyone else who might be able to use someone with your abilities, either in another department or at another agency.

- If you are offered the job, you have to decide whether you want it. If you are not sure, thank the employer and ask for several days to think about it. Ask any other questions you might need answered to help you with the decision.

- If you know you want the job and have all the information you need, accept the job with thanks and get the details on when you start. Ask whether the Postal Service will be sending a letter of confirmation, as it is best to have the offer in writing.

Who Gets Hired?

In the final analysis, the Postal Service will hire someone who has the abilities and talents which fulfill their needs. It is up to you to demonstrate at the interview that you are the person they want.

Chapter Eight
Veterans Preference

There are several special emphasis civil service employment programs available to veterans. *Veterans Preference*[1] and the *Veterans Recruitment Act (VRA)* are two of the better known programs. Unknown to many, military dependents and spouses of active duty personnel receive hiring preference for government jobs under the *Military Spouse Preference Program and the Family Member Preference Program.*

Over 24% of all federal employees are veterans.

When vacancies are announced by an agency, the selecting official can fill the position by:

✎   Internal promotions or reassignments of existing federal workers;

✎   Reemploying former employees;

✎   Using approved special purpose noncompetitive appointments such as the VRA, Spouse Preference, and Military Dependent programs; and,

✎   Appointing a new employee who has successfully completed an examination. The examination can be either written or an extensive examination of your past work experience and education as listed on a Federal Employment Application.

VETERANS PREFERENCE

When an agency advertises job vacancies through the Office of Personnel Management or locally through direct hire authority the agency must select from the top rated eligible applicants. The official may not pass over a Veterans Preference eligible, however, and appoint a non-preference eligible lower on the list unless the reasons for passing over the veteran are sufficient.

---

[1] Authorized by Law Title 5 USC, Section 2108 and Section 3501.

Veterans preference gives special consideration to eligible veterans looking for federal employment.[2] Veterans who are disabled or who served on active duty in the United States Armed Forces during certain specified time periods or in military campaigns are entitled to preference over non-veterans both in hiring into the federal civil service and in retention during *reductions in force*. There are two classes of preference for honorably discharged veterans:

Five Point Preference

Five-point preference is given to those honorable separated veterans (this means an honorable or general discharge) who served on active duty (not active duty for training) in the Armed Forces:

- During any war (this means a war declared by Congress, the last of which was World War II); **or**
- For more than 180 consecutive days, other than for training, any part of which occurred after 1/31/55 and before 10/15/76; **or**
- During the period April 28, 1952, through July 1, 1955; **or**
- During the Gulf War from August 2, 1990, through January 2, 1992; **or**
- In a campaign or expedition for which a campaign medal has been authorized, such as El Salvador, Lebanon, Granada, Panama, Southwest Asia, Somalia, and Haiti, qualifies for preference.

A campaign medal holder or Gulf War veteran who originally enlisted after September 7, 1980, or entered on active duty on or after October 14, 1982, without having previously completed 24 months of continuous active duty, must have served continuously for 24 months or the full period called or ordered to active duty.

Effective on October 1, 1980, military retirees at or above the rank of major or equivalent, are not entitled to preference unless they qualify as disabled veterans.

Ten Point Preference

Ten-point preference is given to:

- Those honorably separated veterans who 1) qualify as disabled veterans because they have served on active duty in the Armed Forces at any time and have a present service-connected disability of 10% or more or are receiving compensation, disability retirement benefits, or pension from the military or the Department of Veterans Affairs; or 2) are Purple Heart recipients;

---

[2] Reference OPM's "Vet Info Guide" available online at http://www.opm.gov/veterans/html/vetsinfo.htm.

- The mother, widow, widowers, or spouses of a veteran who died in service or who is permanently and totally disabled. This is called "derived preference."

When applying for Federal jobs, eligible veterans should claim preference on their application or resume. Applicants claiming 10-point preference must complete **form SF-15**, Application for 10-Point Veteran Preference. Veterans who are still in the service may be granted 5 points tentative preference on the basis of information contained in their applications, but they must produce a DD Form 214 prior to appointment to document entitlement to preference.

The Veterans' Preference Advisor system allows Veterans to examine the preferences for which they might be entitled with regard to Federal jobs. This Advisor was developed by the Veterans' Employment and Training Service.

To find out whether you qualify for veterans' preference, visit America's Job Bank, operated by the Department of Labor (DOL). The Internet address for the veterans' preference program is http://www.dol.gov/elaws/vetspref.htm/.

The Department of Labor's Office of the Assistant Secretary for Policy (OASP) and Veterans' Employment and Training Service (VETS) developed this "expert system" to help veterans receive the preferences to which they are entitled. This system is designed to help veterans determine the type of preference to which they are entitled, the benefits associated with the preference and the steps necessary to file a complaint due to the failure of a Federal agency to provide those benefits. (State employment service offices have veteran representatives available to assist veterans in gaining access to this information.)

VETERANS EMPLOYMENT OPPORTUNITIES ACT

This law was passed in 1998 and it gives veterans access to Federal job opportunities that might otherwise be closed to them. The law requires that:

- Agencies allow eligible veterans to compete for vacancies advertised under the agency's merit promotion procedures when the agency is seeking applications from individuals outside its own workforce.
- All merit promotion announcements open to applicants outside an agency's workforce include a statement that these eligible veterans may apply.
- OPM create an appointing authority to permit the appointment of these individuals if they are selected.

The law also establishes a new redress system for preference eligibles and makes it a prohibited personnel practice for an agency to knowingly take or fail to take a personnel action if that action or failure to act would violate a statutory or regulatory veterans' preference requirement (more about this later).

How Preference Applies In Competitive Examination

Veterans who are eligible for preference and who meet the minimum qualification requirements of the position, have 5 or 10 points added to their passing score on a civil service examination. For scientific and professional positions in grade GS-9 or higher, names of all eligibles are listed in order of ratings, augmented by veterans' preference points, if any. For all other positions, the names of 10-point preference eligibles who have a service-connected disability of 10 percent or more are placed ahead of the names of all other eligibles. Other eligibles are then listed in order of their earned ratings, augmented by veterans' preference points. A preference eligible is listed ahead of a non-preference eligible with the same score.

WHAT DOES THIS MEAN!!!

If you apply for a federal job, your knowledge, skills and abilities will be rated on a point system. You will receive points for related education, experience, special skills, awards, and written test if required. To qualify for a position you must have a score of 70 to 100 points. If an eligible five-point preference candidate accumulates 90 points, five additional points are awarded on preference for a total score of 95. Therefore, the preference veteran, in most cases, must be hired before an agency can hire anyone with 95 points or less in this example. If that same vet accumulated 100 points their final score with preference would be 105 points. A 10-point preference vet would have a total score of 100.

Vets who ace the exam will go to the top of the list since only veteran preference veterans can exceed 100 points on the exams. For example, a disabled vet can earn a maximum score of 110 points if they accumulate 100 points on the exam.

The agency must select from the top 3 candidates (known as the Rule of 3) and may not pass over a preference eligible in favor of a lower ranking non-preference eligible without sound reasons that relate directly to the veteran's fitness for employment. The agency may, however, select a lower-ranking preference eligible over a compensably disabled veteran within the Rule of 3.

A preference eligible who is passed over on a list of eligibles is entitled, upon request, to a copy of the agency's reasons for the pass over and the examining office's response.

If the preference eligible veteran is 30 percent or more disabled, the agency must notify the veteran and OPM of the proposed passover. The veteran has 15 days from the date of notification to respond to OPM. OPM then decides whether to approve the passover based on all the facts available and notifies the agency and the veteran.

SPECIAL APPOINTING AUTHORITIES FOR VETERANS

The *Veterans Recruitment Appointment* (VRA) is a special authority by which agencies can appoint an eligible veteran without competition. The VRA is an excepted appointment to a position that is otherwise in the competitive service. After 2 years of satisfactory service, the veteran is converted to a career-conditional appointment in the competitive service. Visit the O.M.'s web site at http://opm.gov or http://federaljobs.net for more information on this program. This Chapter was excerpted from *The Book of U.S. Government Jobs*, 9ᵗʰ edition.

Chapter Nine
Job Descriptions

There are over 2,000 jobs identified in the Postal Service's Position Directory,[1] all of which are listed in Chapter Ten. This Chapter features 28 job descriptions—a cross section of Postal Service occupations, from accountants and engineers to welders and custodians.

Mail carrier and clerk occupations are presented in Chapter Three. The job descriptions provided in this chapter were included to show the tremendous diversity that the U.S. Postal Service, a Fortune 500 company, offers. Many of these jobs are first offered to qualified postal employees. Anyone interested in these jobs should consider taking the 470 Battery Test or any one of the other tests administered by the Postal Service to get their foot in the door. Over half of all Postal Service workers began their career as a mail carrier or clerk after taking and passing an entrance exam.

For the majority of jobs, Postal Service employees get the first opportunity to bid (apply for) vacancies through what is called an internal merit promotion program. If the hiring manager determines that an insufficient pool of qualified applicants exists or no qualified bidders (applicants) are selected for a vacancy, the agency advertises the job to the general public through classified ads. They also post job announcements at hiring postal facilities. Not all jobs are filled through written exams. A number of jobs, including professional positions, are advertised direct to the public. Resumes and the PS Form 2591 (Application for Employment) are accepted.

To determine the number employed and pay for the listed occupations refer to Chapter Ten for a complete list, excluding manager and supervisory positions, of over 2,000 classified jobs.

---

[1] Postal Service OMSS Report PD09

Standard position descriptions

ACCOUNTING TECHNICIAN, PS-06 Occupation Code: 0525-31XX

Ensures the proper completion of a designated major segment of accounting work in a district office; or serves as assistant to the Postmaster in performing accounting and clerical duties involved in the preparation, maintenance, and consolidation of accounts and related reports in a post office.

DUTIES AND RESPONSIBILITIES

1. Performs, with assistance of accounting clerks if needed, either duty 2 or 3, in combination with duty 3. In a smaller post office having characteristics like those in the basic function, and subject to the provisions of Postal Service directives concerning internal control and separation of duties, performs any combination of duties 5 through 8.

2. In the accounting area, receives daily cash reports from all reporting units of the post office, verifies and balances reports with supporting documents, consolidates the data in one cash report, and posts the daily financial report. Items which are questionable are taken up with the reporting unit or individual in order to determine the correct entries. Reporting units are debited or credited as necessary.

3. In the budget and cost control area, receives reports and data relating to mail volume, workload, and cost ascertainment from the various reporting units, examines reports for completeness and tabulates and posts data in accordance with daily and periodic reporting requirements. Discusses with supervisor data submitted by their units in order that further necessary information and explanation may be obtained. Documents explanatory information for subsequent analysis and inclusion in management reports.

4. In addition, works closely with the supervisor in preparing weekly, biweekly, accounting period, or other periodic reports. Gives guidance and instruction to and acts as group leader for any assigned clerical assistance. May maintain accounts, reflecting trust funds, suspense items and inventories of accountable paper, stamp stock, and fixed credits. Participates with the supervisor interpreting instructions and regulations in implementing procedures pertaining to accounting. May be required to research, compile and record data for special studies and reports on various phases of postal activities as desired by the postmaster or higher authority.

5. Receives daily cash reports from all reporting units of the post office, verifies and balances reports with supporting documents, consolidates into one cash report, and post the cashbook. Items which are questionable are taken up with the reporting unit or individual to determine the correct entries.

6. Receives reports and data relating to mail volume, workload, and cost ascertainment from the various reporting units, examines reports for completeness and accuracy, makes the necessary computations, consolidates the information in accordance with daily and periodic reporting requirements. Discusses with supervisors figures submitted by them to obtain further information and explanation as required. Prepares explanatory comments for inclusion in the reports.

7. Works closely with the postmaster in preparing required accounting period reports including operating report, financial statement, workload and mail volume reports.

8. May maintain stamp stock and fill requisitions - for window clerks, stations and branches.

ARCHITECT/ENGINEER, EAS-20 Occupation Code: 0808-3020

Performs design work and assists in administering design and construction contracts within a District office.

DUTIES AND RESPONSIBILITIES

1. Provides architect/engineering consulting services, evaluates technical problems, and surveys technical alternatives for construction projects within a District office.

2. Participates in the analysis, evaluation, and determination of feasibility, costs, and technical problems related to the planning, design, installation, test, and operation of advanced engineered systems and equipment in support of construction projects.

3. Oversees construction term contracts to ensure compliance with contract requirements and adherence to established policies and procedures.

4. Participates in the activities related to the design, construction, testing, start-up, and operation of facilities, systems, and/or equipment.

5. Participates in the preparation of requests for proposal, including specifications and drawings; participates in the evaluation of contractor bids.

6. Reviews contractor specifications and drawings for technical accuracy and compliance with contract requirements.

7. Attends preconstruction and final acceptance meetings for progress review; makes on-site inspections during installation and test, and reports discrepancies in contract work.

8. Works with architects, engineers, contractors, construction representatives, and others involved in the design and construction of postal facilities.

9. Provides technical assistance to employees and others in the development of facility projects.

AREA MAINTENANCE TECHNICIAN, PS-08 Occupation Code: 4801-20XX

Installs, maintains, repairs, removes, and disposes of postal equipment as appropriate at post offices (offices not having maintenance capability) within the geographic area served by the area maintenance office to which assigned. Installs, moves, or repairs post office screen-line equipment, lock boxes, furniture, and mechanical equipment, supervising such additional help as projects may require.

DUTIES AND RESPONSIBILITIES

1. At regional direction, moves and sets up offices in new or remodeled postal quarters; assembles, installs screen-lines, workroom, lobby, and operating equipment. Supervises carpenters and/or helpers as projects may require. Classifies or assists postmasters in classification of postal equipment for disposal or refurbishing. Under postmaster's authority, purchases materials and employs helpers as warranted.

2. Makes major and minor repairs to postal operating equipment in offices without maintenance capabilities; conducts maintenance inspections and provides operating, minor repair, and maintenance instruction to postal employees in the offices served. Whenever possible, conducts maintenance inspection and the instruction of postal employees in conjunction with emergency service trips to installations.

3. Troubleshoots, repairs, overhauls, and installs postal operating equipment such as, but not limited to, stamp vending machines, canceling machines, scales, print punch money order machines, tying machines, conveyors, safe and vault locks and other components, protective systems and devices, time clocks, and money changers. Keeps abreast of current maintenance criteria and effects service accordingly.

4. Maintains inventory of all postal operating equipment in the offices served by the area maintenance office. Makes recommendations to supervisors and/or obtains stock of operating equipment repair parts, maintaining inventories at levels prescribed by the region or the Department. Maintains record of parts in stock; ships parts to territory offices as required to meet respective office needs. Keeps records of parts used, frequency of replacements, and submits reports to the regional office at prescribed intervals.

5. Installs and maintains protective systems and devices on safes and vaults in post offices. Opens safes and vaults, changes and repairs combinations, and disarms systems and devices.

6. Provides emergency service and makes minor repairs to air conditioning systems at government owned buildings not under service contracts. Prepares report of needs for the postmaster if the lessor has maintenance responsibility or the manufacturer if the system is under warranty.

7. Initiates reports to the regional office on major work assignments, shortages of equipment, and completed screen line installations. Makes reports of unsatisfactory conditions relating to equipment damage, classification, and deficiencies. Makes written recommendations for equipment improvements, operations, and fabrication changes.

8. Drives motor vehicle to respective offices to effect on-the-scene repairs and screen line installation or modifications. Communicates with postmasters by phone, correspondence, and personal visits to investigate reports of malfunctions, disorders, or other needs within the area maintenance office territory.

9. Performs other maintenance duties as instructed by the postmaster at the area maintenance office when not engaged in area maintenance duties.

10. Uses various hand and power tools and testing devices incident to the mechanical, electrical and electronic, and carpentry trades.

11. Observes established safety practices and procedures and instructs helpers accordingly.

AUTOMOTIVE MECHANIC, PS-06 Occupation Code: 5823-03XX

Repairs vehicles, including the removal and installation of complete motors, clutches, transmissions, and other major component parts.

DUTIES AND RESPONSIBILITIES

1. Diagnoses mechanical and operating difficulties of vehicles, repairing defects, replacing worn or broken parts.

2. Adjusts and tunes up engines, cleaning fuel pumps, carburetors, and radiators; regulates timing, and makes other necessary adjustments to maintain in proper operating condition trucks that are in service.

3. Repairs or replaces automotive electrical equipment such as generators, starters, ignition systems, distributors, and wiring; installs and sets new spark plugs.

4. Conducts road tests of vehicles after repairs, noting performance of engine, clutch, transmission, brakes, and other parts.

5. Operates standard types of garage testing equipment.

6. Performs other duties as assigned, such as, removing, disassembling, reassembling, and installing entire engines; overhauling transmission, rear end assemblies, and braking systems; straightening frames and axles, welding broken parts where required; making road calls to make emergency repairs; and making required truck inspections.

BUDGET AND FINANCIAL ANALYST (DISTRICT), EAS-19 Occupation Code: 0504-5022

Performs all activities for the development and control of district operating and capital budgets; performs research and analysis of district financial operations.

DUTIES AND RESPONSIBILITIES

1. Develops, prepares, allocates, implements, monitors, and controls the district operating and capital budgets; includes current estimates of future financial performance; and integrates planning assumptions into operating budget plans.

2. Integrates all district functions into the planning process and validates budget and financial forecasts developed by managers.

3. Provides-ongoing analyses to support-operations management and improve overall financial and work hour performance, including the analysis and validation of major capital, facility, and program expenditures and packages.

4. Develops and implements business planning and forecasting techniques and monitors effectiveness; analyzes operating results to identify improvement opportunities and evaluate the effectiveness of cost reduction program implementation.

5. Develops and presents training for operating managers to increase their understanding of the budget process and the financial analysis techniques used for performance measurement.

6. Provides technical guidance to financial and operating employees in the development of capital investment strategies and operating expense budgets; maintains an effective financial planning and forecasting process for all district organizations.

BUILDING EQUIPMENT MECHANIC, PS-07 Occupation Code: 5306-07XX

Performs involved trouble shooting and complex maintenance work on Building and Building Equipment systems, and preventive maintenance and preventive maintenance inspections of building, building equipment and building systems, and maintains and operates a large automated air conditioning system and a large heating system.

DUTIES AND RESPONSIBILITIES

1. Performs, on building and building equipment, the more difficult testing, diagnosis, maintenance, adjustment and revision work, requiring a thorough knowledge of the mechanical, electrical, and electronic, pneumatic, or hydraulic control and operating mechanisms of the equipment. Performs trouble shooting and repair of complex supervisory group control panels, readout and feedback circuits and associated mechanical and electrical components throughout the installation; locates and corrects malfunctions in triggering and other electro mechanical and electronic circuits.

2. Observes the various components of the building systems in operation and applies appropriate testing methods and procedures to insure continued proper operation.

3. Locates the source of and-rectifies trouble in involved or questionable cases, or in emergency situations where expert attention is required to locate and correct the defect quickly to avoid or minimize interruptions.

4. Installs or alters building equipment and circuits as directed.

5. Reports the circumstances surrounding equipment and failures, and recommends measures for their correction.

6. Performs preventive maintenance inspections of building equipment to locate incipient mechanical malfunctions and the standard of maintenance. Initiates work orders requesting corrective actions for conditions below standard; assists in the estimating of time and materials required. Recommends changes in preventative maintenance procedures and practices to provide the proper level of maintenance; assists in the revision of preventive maintenance checklists and the frequency of performing preventive maintenance routes. In instances of serious equipment failures, conducts investigation to determine the cause of the breakdown and to recommend remedial action to prevent recurrence.

7. Uses necessary hand and power tools, specialized equipment, gauging devices, and both electrical and electronic test equipment.

8. Reads and interprets schematics, blue- prints, wiring diagrams and specifications in locating and correcting potential or existing malfunctions and failures.

9. Repairs electro mechanically operated equipment related to the building or building systems. Repairs, installs, modifies, and maintains building safety systems, support systems and equipment.

10. Works off ladders, scaffolds, and rigging within heights common to the facility. Works under various weather conditions out doors.

11. Completes duties and tasks related to building equipment maintenance as required.

12. Observes established safety practices and requirements pertaining to the type of work involved; recommends additional safety measures as required.

13. In addition, may oversee the work of lower level maintenance employees, advising and instructing them in proper and safe work methods and checking for adherence to instructions; make in-process and final operational checks and tests of work completed by lower level maintenance employees.

14. Performs other job related tasks in support of primary duties.

CARRIER (CITY), PS-05 Occupation Code: 2310-01XX

Delivers and collects mail on foot or by vehicle under varying conditions in a prescribed area within a city. Maintains pleasant and effective public relations with route customers and others, requiring a general familiarity with postal laws, regulations, and procedures commonly used, and with the geography of the city. (Refer to Chapter Three for a complete description of Clerk and Mail Carrier occupations.)

CASUAL, EAS-07 Occupation Code: 5201-1001

Performs mail handling, mail processing, mail delivery, mail collection, mail transportation, and custodial functions, or a combination of such duties on a supplemental basis. (Refer to Chapter Three for a complete description of Clerk and Mail Carrier occupations.)

CLERK STENOGRAPHER, PS-05 Occupation Code: 0312-01XX

Performs miscellaneous office clerical, stenographic, and typing work.

DUTIES AND RESPONSIBILITIES

1. Takes dictation, in shorthand or on a shorthand writing machine, of letters, memorandums, reports, and other materials and transcribes it on the typewriter or wordprocessor; sets up the material transcribed in accordance with prescribed format and assembles it for required initialing, signing, routing, and dispatch.

2. Types similar materials from handwritten and other drafts, and from dictating machine-records.

3. Makes up file folders, keeps them in prescribed order, and places in and withdraws from them papers relating to the business of the office.

4. Makes and keeps routine records of the office.

5. Composes routine memorandums and letters relating to the business of the office, such as acknowledgments and transmittals.

6. Examines the incoming and outgoing mail of the office, routes it to the appropriate persons, and controls the time allowed for preparation of replies to incoming correspondence.

7. Receipts for and delivers salary checks and fills out various personnel forms.

8. Acts as receptionist and answers telephone calls, taking and relaying messages and furnishing routine information requested.

9. Relieves office clerks, typists, clerk typists or other clerk-stenographers during periods of their absence.

10. Operates copy machine and calculators.

COMPUTER SYSTEMS ANALYST/PROGRAMMER (PDC), DCS-20 Occupation Code: 0334-3056

Analyzes and evaluates existing and proposed systems and develops computer programs, systems, and procedures to process data.

DUTIES AND RESPONSIBILITIES

1. Translates user requirements to automate problem analysis and record keeping activities into detailed program flowcharts.

2. Prepares programming specifications and diagrams and develops coding logic flowcharts.

3. Codes, tests, debugs, and installs computer programs and procedures.

4. Reviews and updates computer programs and provides the necessary documentation for the computer operations function.

5. Prepares charts and diagrams to assist in problem analysis.

6. Prepares detailed program specifications and flowcharts and coordinates the system's installation with the user.

7. Provides technical advice and guidance to programmers assigned on a project basis; provides advice and assistance to managers involved in installing an automated system.

8. Has regular contact with contract employees and computer equipment vendors

CUSTODIAN, PS-02 Occupation Code: 3566-04XX

Performs manual laboring duties in connection with custody of an office or building.

DUTIES AND RESPONSIBILITIES

1. Performs any one or a combination of the duties listed below.

2. Moves furniture and equipment.

3. Uncrates and assembles furniture and fixtures, using bolts and screws for assembly.

4. Loads and unloads supplies and equipment.

5. Removes trash from work areas, lobbies, and washrooms.

6. Tends to lawns, shrubbery, and premises of the post office and cleans ice and snow from the sidewalk s and-driveways.

7. Stacks supplies in storage rooms and on shelves, and completes forms or records as required.

8. May perform cleaning duties as assigned.

DATA COLLECTION TECHNICIAN, PS-06 Occupation Code: 0301-69XX

Collects, records, and analyzes a variety of statistical data on selected operating and financial activities. Performs relief assignments for PSDS Technicians.

DUTIES AND RESPONSIBILITIES

1. Collects, records, & analyzes statistical data under any number of national data collection systems.

2. Operates computer equipment to enter data; recognizes diagnostic messages and takes appropriate actions; and performs data transfer functions through telecommunications systems.

3. Reviews input and output data to determine accuracy and compliance with national programs. Analyzes and edits data to detect and correct errors.

4. Updates national data bases; maintains and updates records and files.

5. Participates in data collection activities in support of special studies or national programs.

6. Reads and interprets reference manuals and other written materials.

7. May drive a vehicle to other facilities when work assignments require.

8. Performs other job related tasks in support of primary duties.

DISTRIBUTION CLERK, PS-05 Occupation Code: 2315-04XX

Separates mail in a post office, terminal, airport mail facility or other postal facility in accordance with established schemes, including incoming or outgoing mail or both. (Refer to Chapter Three for a complete description of Clerk and Mail Carrier occupations.)

ELECTRONICS TECHNICIAN, PS-10 Occupation Code: 0856-01XX

Carries out all phases of maintenance, troubleshooting, and testing of electronic circuitry used in equipment and systems requiring a knowledge of solid state electronics. Instructs and provides technical support on complex systems and on combinational (hardware/software) or intermittent problems.

DUTIES AND RESPONSIBILITIES

1. Performs the testing, diagnosis, maintenance, and revision work requiring a knowledge of solid state electronics.

2. Observes the various equipment and systems in operation and applies appropriate testing and diagnostic methods and procedures to ensure proper- operation.

3. Locates source of equipment and system failures, rectifies trouble in involved cases, or provides instructions to be used by maintenance employees performing repair work.

4. Makes-or participates with contractor representative or electronic technician in installing or altering equipment and systems as required.

5. Makes reports of equipment and system failures which require corrective action by contractor and follows up to see that appropriate action is taken.

6. Makes preventive maintenance inspections to discover incipient malfunctions and to review the standards of maintenance. Recommends changes in preventive maintenance procedures and practices as found to be necessary.

7. Programs scheme and/or scheme changes into memory units as requested by management.

8. Furnishes pertinent data to superiors and contract employees on operation and testing problems.

9. Participates in training programs: classroom, on-the-job, and correspondence, at postal facilities, trade schools, and manufacturer's plants as required. May assist in developing and implementing training programs. Instructs equal or lower level employees as required.

10. Observes established safety regulations pertaining to the type of work involved.

11. May drive vehicle or utilize other available mode of transportation to work site when necessary.

12. Provides technical support to other electronic technicians to resolve complex, combinational (hardware/software), and/or intermittent failures.

13. Performs such other duties as may be assigned.

FINANCIAL SERVICES COORDINATOR, EAS-18 Occupation Code: 0510-5050

Coordinates, analyzes, and monitors district wide financial accounting programs and processes; coordinates the implementation of new accounting and timekeeping policies and procedures; provides technical guidance to post offices and field units in the resolution of daily accounting problems.

DUTIES AND RESPONSIBILITIES

1. Analyzes, evaluates, and determines the need for changes to district financial accounting programs and processes; identifies deficiencies and problems; and recommends and implements corrective actions to improve quality and reduce errors.

2. Provides guidance and training to post office and field unit employees concerning financial accounting procedures, including the proper recording of statements of accounts and adjustments of daily unit financial statements.

3. Resolves accounting problems, including those associated with banking, payables, and payroll adjustments.

4. Monitors revenue reporting and performs audits of financial activities to ensure financial integrity.

5. Coordinates district accounting programs and processes with the Postal Data Center and other functional areas.

6. Implements national, area, and district accounting and timekeeping policies and procedures.

7. Provides technical advice, guidance, assistance, and training to post offices and field units throughout the district area on the full range of accounting and timekeeping programs and processes.

FLAT SORTING MACHINE OPERATOR, PS-05 Occupation Code: 2315-20XX

Operates a single or multi-position, electro mechanical operator paced flat sorting machine in the distribution of flats requiring knowledge and application of approved machine distribution of directs, alphabetical or geographic groupings, by reading the ZIP Code on each flat. (Refer to Chapter Three for a complete description of Clerk and Mail Carrier occupations.)

HUMAN RESOURCES SPECIALIST, EAS-15 Occupation Code: 0201-5117

Performs technical staff work in support of the implementation and administration of one or more human resources programs.

OPERATIONAL REQUIREMENTS

In addition to the following program responsibilities, oversees and coordinates the activities of a small size group of lower level employees, including making assignments, monitoring and reviewing work, providing continuing technical guidance, approving leave, and taking disciplinary action.

DUTIES AND RESPONSIBILITIES

1. PERSONNEL SERVICES: Implements and administers employee compensation and benefits programs, including wage and salaries, pay procedures and rules, performance evaluations, merits, suggestions, incentive and superior accomplishment awards, quality step increases, retirements, and insurance.

2. Provides information to and processes requests from state unemployment compensation agencies for separated employees; testifies in unemployment compensation hearings.

3. Administers employment and selection policies, procedures, and processes for bargaining, initial level supervisor, non-bargaining, and postmaster positions.

4. Coordinates entrance and in-service examination programs; oversees all procedures and processes related to examination scheduling, conducting, processing, grading, notification, and forwarding of test data.

5. SAFETY AND HEALTH: Monitors compliance with safety and health standards and regulations; conducts periodic inspections; ensures accurate accident reporting; analyzes accident rates and trends; and provides for improvement of safety awareness and accident prevention through training and promotional activities.

6. Implements Wellness Program by coordinating programs, services, and activities that promote employee health efforts.

7. Administers procedures under which employees with substance abuse and other personal problems are referred to external providers contracted under the Employee Assistance Program.

8. INJURY COMPENSATION: Provides comprehensive case management in the review and processing of injury compensation claims, including authorization and control of continuation of pay; controversion of claims; identification of possible fraud and abuse; third party claims and recovery; assignment to limited duty; and referral to the rehabilitation program, or for second opinions or fitness for duty exams.

9. TRAINING: Plans, schedules, implements, administers, coordinates, evaluates, and performs employee training, career planning and development, diagnostic testing, and counseling services; conducts workshops, orientations, and demonstrations; coordinates managerial and supervisory

training; and provides guidance to employees, job trainers, and management regarding training and instructional processes.

MAINTENANCE MECHANIC, PS-05

Independently performs semiskilled preventive, corrective and predictive maintenance tasks associated with the upkeep and operation of various types of mail processing, buildings and building equipment, customer service and delivery equipment.

DUTIES AND RESPONSIBILITIES

1. Independently performs preventive maintenance and minor repairs on plumbing, heating, refrigeration, air-conditioning, low-voltage electrical systems, and other building systems and equipment.

2. Performs preventive maintenance and routine repairs on simple control circuitry, bearings, chains, sprockets, motors, belts and belting, and other moving parts or wearing surfaces of equipment.

3. Assembles, installs, replaces, repairs, modifies and adjusts all types of small operating equipment such as letter boxes, mechanical scales, stamp vending equipment, building service equipment, manhandling equipment and related equipment.

4. Under the direction of skilled maintenance employees, or clearly written instructions from either hard copy or electronic format, performs specific tasks related to disassembling equipment, replacing parts, relocating and reassembling equipment; assists higher level workers in locating and repairing equipment malfunctions.

5. Maintains an awareness of equipment operation, especially excessive heat, vibration, and noise, reporting malfunctions, hazards or wear to supervisor.

6. Uses a variety of hand and power tools, gauging devices and test equipment required, or as directed, to perform the above tasks.

7. May drive a vehicle to transport tools, equipment, employees, materials or in the normal performance of assigned duties.

8. Completes or initiates work record sheets, as required. Takes readings from meters, gauges, counters and other monitoring and measuring devices. Maintains logs and other required records; reports on breakdowns and equipment being tested.

9. Follows established safety practices and requirements while performing all duties.

10. May serve as a working leader over a group of lower level employees assigned to a specific task.

11. Performs other duties as assigned.

MECHANICAL ENGINEER, EAS-24 Occupation Code: 0830-4012

Plans, organizes, and executes the design, construction, installation, and implementation of new systems, equipment, or controls of major magnitude and scope, in support of the mail processing objectives of the Postal Service.

DUTIES AND RESPONSIBILITIES

1. Translates operating objectives for mail processing into functional requirements for facilities, or equipment, oversees the reporting, analysis, and evaluation of data from field operating units related to mail volume, productivity, or costs; integrates this information with technical data to determine functional specifications.

2. Oversees the preparation and justification of engineering proposals and alternatives for complex mechanized systems equipment; evaluates engineered systems and related costs to determine alternatives to support mail processing objectives; provides program costs estimates; develops and recommends plans for program implementation.

3. Oversees engineering activities related to the design, construction, installation, test, and start-up of mechanized systems and equipment; provides technical management of contracts; evaluates contractor bids; makes recommendations affecting the selection of contractors; determines criteria for performance evaluation of prototype equipment; controls program costs; certifies contractor requests for payment.

4. Coordinates planning and implementation of mechanization systems and equipment programs with headquarters and field employees.

5. Provides mechanical engineering consulting services, as required.

6. Has frequent contact with contractors, professional consultants, officials of government agencies, and equipment manufacturers.

NURSE, OCCUPATIONAL HEALTH PNS-01 Occupation Code: 0610-4001

Provides professional nursing services to employees under the general direction of a medical officer. Implements and participates in programs to provide preventative medical care and health maintenance services in support of Postal Service safety and health goals and objectives.

DUTIES AND RESPONSIBILITIES

1. Implements, monitors, and participates in occupational health programs and services within a postal facility.

2. Provides professional nursing care to employees; administers medications at the direction of a physician; and makes arrangements for physicians' care.

3. Provides continuous health or injury care, under physicians' instructions, to employees with prolonged illnesses or injuries.

4. Assists Medical Officer in conducting re-employment or fitness-for-duty physical examinations; performs routine examinations for items such as vision, hearing, and blood pressure; and makes recommendations regarding suitability for employment and/or referral for additional testing and evaluation.

5. Advises or counsels employees regarding general and/or mental health care; assists employees with doctor and/or community service referrals, when necessary.

6. Prepares, updates, and maintains confidential health records for employees using the health and medical unit; compiles and analyzes various medical data and reports; and prepares regular summary reports.

7. Requisitions appropriate quantities and types of medical supplies and maintains security of supplies and equipment.

8. Regularly checks first aid boxes to ensure an adequate supply of necessary items.

9. Maintains the health/medical unit in a sanitary and orderly condition.

10. Provides continuous medical monitoring of workers exposed to potentially harmful substances.

11. Reports on-the-job injuries and other safety and health matters to appropriate postal officials.

12. Maintains familiarity with Workers Compensation and safety and personnel practices and procedures relative to occupational health programs.

13. Serves as liaison with employees, supervisors, physicians, PAR and safety employees; refers employees for participation in the PAR and other health related programs.

14. Performs related clerical duties.

15. Makes frequent contact with private physicians and representatives of hospitals and health clinics. Has occasional contact with customers, contractors' employees, and representatives of emergency services and social agencies.

16. Provides professional advice and guidance to supervisors regarding administrative procedures; provides health care advice and counseling to employees.

17. Exercises a normal regard for the safety of self and others.

PERSONNEL CLERK, PS-05 Occupation Code: 0203-14XX

Performs specialized clerical work involved in providing the central personnel services of a postal installation.

DUTIES AND RESPONSIBILITIES

1. Performs any one or a combination of the duties listed below.

2. Examines, documents, and otherwise processes official personnel actions.

3. Inducts new employees by taking their fingerprints, providing them with, and instructing them in filling out forms, administering oaths, and performing related operations.

4. Examines applications for leave by employees when the type or durations of leave desired fall within the categories required to be acted on centrally; compares the justification with the criteria for approval, and drafts memorandums or notifications of the action to be taken on the applications.

5. Examines for completeness or composes reports of personnel injuries sustained by employees in the performance of their duties and examines for completeness claims by such employees for compensation due to time lost from work because of such injuries; makes these reports and claims ready for forwarding to the appropriate government agency and composes notification to the employees or their supervisors of additional information needed and of decisions made on claims.

6. Furnishes information to employees and applicants about personnel regulations and practices, including employment in the postal installation, by personal conversations, telephone conversations, and composition of letters and memorandums.

7. Maintains various personnel records by performing such operations as posting actions taken concerning employees, adding names to and removing them from registers and rosters, and filing official papers in personnel folders.

8. Compiles various recurring and special statistical reports on personnel subjects, such as numbers of actions of various types, numbers of employees of various titles and salaries, numbers of vacancies of various titles and organizational locations.

9. In addition, may perform any of the following duties: document and otherwise process official personnel actions originating on the basis of personnel records; record the receipt of employee suggestions and initiate action for their review by appropriate supervisors; assist employees in filling out applications for retirement and documenting these forms for submission to appropriate

organizations; process bids for position openings on seniority basis; and accept employment applications, and forward them to appropriate organizations.

POLICE OFFICER, POSTAL (B), PPO-06

Performs a variety of duties pertaining to the security of postal buildings, personnel, property, mail, and mail-in-transit in support of the postal security program.

DUTIES AND RESPONSIBILITIES

1. Performs a variety of duties pertaining to the security of postal buildings, personnel, property, mail, and mail-in-transit.

2. Carries a firearm and exercises standard care required by the Inspection Service on firearms and use of reasonable force. Maintains assigned firearms in good condition.

3. Maintains incidents reported and daily logs of orders and basic in formation for the security force.

4. Answers the office telephone and responds to reports and inquiries.

5. Performs patrol duty, as assigned, on foot or by motor vehicle to maintain order and safeguard the facility, property, and personnel; ensures the application of security measures in manhandling areas.

6. Maintains contact with other security force personnel; responds to emergencies and other conditions, including burglaries and hold-ups, requiring immediate attention.

7. Controls access to building at an assigned post; enforces the regulations requiring identification.

8. Makes arrests and testifies in court on law violations within assigned authority.

9. Performs other job related tasks in support of the primary duties.

POSTAL INSPECTOR (PROJECTS COORDINATOR), EAS-24

Oversees and coordinates the most complex and sensitive criminal, civil, administrative, and audit investigations, programs, projects, and studies; oversees task forces and teams of Postal Inspectors in the accomplishment of investigative objectives; oversees and coordinates the planning, development, implementation, and monitoring of projects, and studies within assigned area.

OPERATIONAL REQUIREMENTS

Carries firearms when engaged in official business and for self-defense; maintains established physical requirements necessary to perform law enforcement assignments; maintains eligibility to operate a motor vehicle when engaged in official business; and maintains mental and emotional standards necessary to perform law enforcement assignments.

DUTIES AND RESPONSIBILITIES

1. Oversees and coordinates the most complex-and sensitive criminal, civil, administrative, and audit investigations, programs, projects, and studies. Investigates violations of postal laws and apprehends and arrests postal offenders.

2. Oversees and supervises the activities of task forces and teams of Postal Inspectors, and a small group of technical and support employees. Evaluates performance and takes the necessary action to correct deficiencies, including discipline or remedial training. Provides training for new or less experienced Inspection Service employees.

3. Assists U. S. Attorneys and other criminal justice employees in preparing court cases involving postal laws. Independently prepares comprehensive case presentation letters to the U. S. Attorney. Serves as a witness in court and administrative proceedings.

4. Coordinates the development, planning, and implementation of new programs and projects to improve methods, techniques, and skills of Inspection Service employees.

5. Ensures that all regularly scheduled and standard inspections are properly monitored and carried out by assigned personnel.

6. Analyzes, reviews, and initially approves investigation reports, correspondence, case history information, and other documentation prepared for management review; prepares special reports and correspondence.

7. Maintains liaison with law enforcement agencies to coordinate record exchanges, case development, suspect apprehension, jurisdiction definition, security checks, and joint training.

8. Provides technical guidance and advice to postal management. Conducts conferences with postal management on the results of major audit projects and makes recommendations for service improvements, operational economies, and other areas included in the review.

9. Recommends policies and procedures that are not covered by established Inspection Service methods or guidelines.

10. Oversees and coordinates the investigation into the misconduct of postal employees and the presentation of evidence to Postal management for consideration in disciplinary cases.

11. Represents the Inspection Service by providing supporting information or participating in the development, implementation, and administration of technology, automation, service, operations, and training programs.

12. Reacts in emergencies to protect mail and postal assets where use of firearms and defensive techniques may be required. May work in undesirable neighborhoods and in adverse and hazardous situations.

13. Has frequent contact with the general public, witnesses, victims, complainants, suspects and offenders, informants, postal customers and contractors, federal and private attorneys, and representatives of the business community, law enforcement agencies, government agencies, armed services, and the courts. Represents the Inspection Service at law enforcement, security, and civic conferences and meetings.

14. Exercises normal protective care for the use of facilities and equipment, including vehicles, weapons, and communications and technical equipment.

15. Exercises a normal regard for the safety of self and others when investigating criminal cases and apprehending or maintaining surveillance of those suspected of violating postal laws. Exercises the standard of care required by Inspection Service policies on firearms and use of reasonable force when apprehending and restraining suspects.

RURAL CARRIER, RCS-00

Cases, delivers, and collects mail along a prescribed rural route using a vehicle; provides customers on the route with a variety of services. (Refer to Chapter Three for a complete description of Clerk and Mail Carrier occupations.)

SECRETARY, EAS-11 Occupation Code: 0318-2041

Provides secretarial support for a manager and his/her staff. Processes information in accordance with established organizational and functional area administrative practices and procedures.

DUTIES AND RESPONSIBILITIES

1. Produces reports, letters and other documentation using word processing equipment, and monitors peripheral equipment.

2. Accesses, retrieves and/or updates files and other data maintained on computers.

3. Sends and receives electronic messages, files and other documentation via the local area network.

4. Produces charts, tables and other documentation using various graphics packages.

5. Compiles information on a variety of subjects; reviews periodicals, publications, and industry related documents, bringing those of interest to manager's attention.

6. Reviews materials prepared for accuracy and proper format; ensures compliance with established collective bargaining policies.

7. Performs routine clerical duties such as, answering telephones, operating office equipment, requisitioning supplies, and coordinating printing, maintenance, and other service requests.

8. Screens, logs, and routes office mail.

9. Performs other administrative duties, such as maintaining a variety of reports, such as: time and attendance records, correspondence control, training plans, etc. , and maintains office files.

TELECOMMUNICATIONS SPECIALIST, EAS-17 Occupation Code: 0393-5001

Provides analysis, coordination, and technical support for the voice and data telecommunications activities in a district.

DUTIES AND RESPONSIBILITIES

1. Analyzes voice and data telecommunications requirements, including networks and hardware; recommends new and improved services; and coordinates acquisition/implementation.

2. Prepares recommendations for system changes to improve effectiveness and reduce telecommunications costs; coordinates with national telecommunications network program specialists, and implements approved changes.

3. Coordinates the acquisition and installation of new telecommunications hardware; performs preacceptance tests to verify proper operations; makes changes to telecommunications control systems to activate or restrict specific services to designated lines, and oversees equipment repair projects.

4. Monitors all aspects of the telecommunications system, including line traffic and overall system usage; oversees the verification and certification of monthly billings, and prepares analyses and reports for management review.

5. Prepares and implements training for telecommunications system users throughout the district.

6. Troubleshoots network & equipment problems & resolves or coordinates resolution with vendors.

7. Has regular contact with representatives of local telecommunication services vendors.

8. Provides technical guidance to employees on telecommunications system operations.

WELDER, PS-06

Fabricates or repairs metal items in forge and on anvil; performs welding and brazing operations.

DUTIES AND RESPONSIBILITIES

1. Forges and fabricates or repairs tools and metal parts for building and equipment; heats metal to proper temperature in forge, hammers and bends metal to specified size and shape; hardens and tempers metals.

2. Does acetylene and electric welding on building equipment and such items as machine parts, hand truck frames, pouch racks, and conveyor equipment; also does brazing work; sets up job to be welded or brazed; sets up and adjusts proper type of welding equipment and selects proper type of rod according to the needs of the work; performs metal cutting and burning with torch.

3. Works from drawings, sketches and general instructions.

4. Uses required hand and power tools.

5. In addition, oversees helpers as assigned & may perform work incident to other trades as required.

WINDOW CLERK, PS-05

Performs a variety of services at a public window of a post office or post office branch or station. maintains pleasant and effective public relations with customers and others requiring a general familiarity with postal laws, regulations, and procedures commonly used. (Refer to Chapter Three for a complete description of Clerk and Mail Carrier occupations.)

Chapter Ten
Occupation Directory

The Postal Service employs workers in approximately 2,000 job classifications. This USPS Position Directory will assist job seekers in several ways. First, it provides a comprehensive resource for job seekers to identify all potential occupations for which they may qualify. Second, it lists the pay (refer to the pay charts in Chapter One), the total number employed for each position, and the USPS Occupational Code (OCC-CODE). Occupations featured in Chapter Nine are marked with an arrow symbol (➤).

This directory presents a pandoras box of opportunities from custodial, maintenance, and general labor trades to accountants, engineers, and computer specialists. The majority of manager's positions were excluded from this list because they are generally not entry level positions.

After reviewing this list and identifying various occupations as potential job sources, go to the "Job Hunter's Checklist" in Appendix A. This checklist will guide you step-by-step through the USPS hiring maze.

OCCUPATION DIRECTORY

OCCUPATION	OCC-CODE	PAY	TOTAL
ACCOUNT REPRESENTATIVE	2345 5031	EAS-15	436
ACCOUNT REPRESENTATIVE	2345-5032	EAS-18	62
ACCOUNTABLE CLERK ML RECOVERY CTR	2345-69XX	PS-06	4
ACCOUNTABLE PAPER CONTROL SPECLST	2001 5008	EAS-17	2
ACCOUNTABLE PAPER CONTROL SPECLST	2001-5020	EAS-19	
ACCOUNTABLE PAPER DISTRIBUTION SPC	2003-5022	EAS-23	3
ACCOUNTABLE PAPER MANUFCTRNG SPCLS	2003-6021	EAS-25	2
ACCOUNTABLE PAPER SPEC (PFSC)	0530-2009	EAS-13	in
ACCOUNTANT	0510-4055	EAS-21	11
ACCOUNTANT	0510-4056	EAS-25	11
ACCOUNTANT	0510-4057	EAS-23	1
ACCOUNTANT JR PDC	0510-3002	DCS-16	20
ACCOUNTANT POSTAL FACILITIES (A)	0510-3020	EAS-16	3
ACCOUNTING ASSOCIATE	0540-5009		2
ACCT PPR SUPP CLK	0530-05XX	PS-05	151
ACCTG ASST	0525 6003	EAS-14	I
ACCTG CLERK PDC	0520-2020	DCS-09	21

OCCUPATION	OCC-CODE	PAY	TOTAL
ACCTG CLK	0520-01XX	PS-05	72
ACCTG SPEC SP PDC	0525-5015	DCS-17	11
➤ ACCTG TECH	0525-3iXX	PS-06	1,193
ACCTG TECH COST MES	0525-2026	EAS-13	I
ACCTG TECH PDC	0525-5019	DCS-11	46
ACCTG&BUDGET TECH	0525-3010	EAS-14	2
ACCTNG SPEC PDC	0525-5018	DCS-14	83
ACCTNT PDC	0510-3014	DCS-18	26
ACCFNT PSTL FAC C	0510-6023	EAS-20	
ACCTS PAYABLE ASST CENTER SPEC	0540-5016	DCS-14	7
ACCTS PAYABLE ASST CTR ANALYST	0540-5017	DCS-18	1
ACQUISITIONS LIBRARIAN	1411-5003	EAS-16	I
ADDRESS MANAGEMENT SYSTEMS SPCLST	2310-4014		425
ADDRESS MGMT SYSTEMS SPECIALIST	2310-4013	EAS-17	9
ADM CLK EXPRESS ML	2340-81XX	PS-05	226
ADMIN COORDINATOR - PMG OFFICE	0301-5362	EAS-19	1
ADMIN SERVICES COORDINATOR	0301-5365	EAS-14	1
ADMIN SERVICES TECH	0301-5364	EAS-11	1
ADMIN SUPPORT SPEC (IS)	2335-6011	EAS-18	6
ADMIN SUPPORT SPECIALIST	2335-6010	EAS-21	6
ADMIN SUPPORT SPECIALIST	2335-6012	EAS-16	20
ADMINISTRATIVE CLERK (NISSC)	0301-2108	EAS-07	1
ADMINISTRATIVE COORDINATOR	0301-5248	EAS-19	2
ADMINISTRATIVE JUDGE	0935-4003	EAS-30	2
ADMINISTRATIVE LAW JUDGE	0935-4004		1
ADMINISTRATIVE SPEC (LAW DEPT)	0341-5046	EAS-18	2
ADMINISTRATIVE SPECIALIST (EPD)	0341-5051	EAS 14	1
ADMINISTRATIVE SPECIALIST (MTSC)	0341-5025	EAS-15	1
ADMN CLK PDC	0301-2073	DCS-07	12
ADMN CLK VMF	0301-09XX	PS-06	135
ADMN SERVICES COORDINATOR	0342-5029	EAS-14	10
ADP PLANNING SPECIALIST	0340-4002	EAS-24	1
ADP RESOURCES ANALYST	0301-5341	EAS-23	1
ADP RESOURCES ANALYST	0301-5342	EAS-21	1
ADVERTISING SPECIALIST	1081-5032		1
ADVERTISING SPECIALIST	1081-5034	EAS-23	9
ADVERTISING SPECIALIST	1081-5046	EAS-25	1
ADVISORY RESOURCES SPECIALIST	1081-5056	EAS-23	1
AIR RECORDS PROCESSOR	2330-46XX	PS-05	504
AIR TRANSPORTATION SPECIALIST (B)	2330-6012	EAS-17	35
AIR TRANSPTN SPEC A	2330-5016	EAS-15	26
ANALYST SCHEMES&SCHD	2350-4003		24
APPEALS INFORMATION SYSTEMS SPCLST	0335-5002	EAS-19	1
APPEALS REVIEW EXAMINER/ANALYST	0954-4015	EAS-21	13
APPEALS REVIEW SPECIALIST	0954-4012	EAS-23	21
APPEALS REVIEW SPECIALIST	0954-5001	EAS-25	2
APPEALS TECHNICIAN	0301-5350	EAS-14	1
APPEALS TECHNICIAN	0335-3019		5
APPLIED TECHNOLOGY PLANNER	0334-4111	EAS-24	3
APPRAISER	1171-4003	EAS-25	1
APPRAISER	1171-4004	EAS-23	2
ARBITRATION SCHED COORD	0303-5001	EAS-13	5
ARCHITECT/ENGINEER	0808-3017	EAS-21	9
ARCHITECT/ENGINEER	0808-3018	EAS-23	46
ARCHITECT/ENGINEER	0808-3019	EAS-25	34
➤ ARCHITECT/ENGINEER	0808-3020	EAS-20	103
AREA COORD EI/QWL PROCESSES	0230-5064	EAS-18	39
AREA MAIL TRANSPORT EQUIPMENT SPEC	2330-4028	EAS-19	10
AREA MAINT SPEC	4801-21XX	PS-07	150
➤ AREA MAINT TECH	4801-20XX	PS-08	323
AREA MGR STAMP DISTRIBUTION NETWK	2003-7021	EAS-19	2
ASSIGNMENT CLK	0212-05XX	PS-06	12
ASSOC JUDICAL OFFICER	0905-5030	PCES-I	1
ASSOC MEDICAL DIRECTOR AREA OFFICE	0602-7006	EAS-26	29
ASST PSTL INSP-P-IN-CHG	2335-7032	EAS-26	19

ASST SECRETARY TO THE BOG	0301-5563	PCES-1	
ASST SUPT NGHT TOUR WHT HSE	2315-6039	EAS-16	1
ASST SUPT WHT HSE ML SEC	2305-6039	EAS-18	1
ASST SUPV REC SEC CTR WHT HSE	2340-6016	EAS-16	1
ASST TREASURER BANKING	0505-7070	PCES-I	1
ASST TREASURER FINANCING/INVESTMENT	0505-7069		1
ATTORNEY	0905-4034	APS-01	123
AUDIOVISUAL PRODUCER	1071-5014	EAS-18	5
AUDIOVISUAL TECHNICIAN	1071-3018	EAS-16	2
AUTOMATED OPRNS SOFTWARE SPEC	0334-4116	EAS-20	3
AUTOMATION INTEGRATION ANALYST	0301-5366	PCES-I	I
AUTOMATION INTEGRATION ANALYST	0301-5367	EAS-25	1
AUTOMATION INTEGRATION ANALYST	0301-5368	EAS-23	1
AUTOMOTIVE MECH	5823-03XX	PS-07	6
➤ AUTOMOTIVE MECH	5823-03XX	PS-06	2,762
AUTOMOTIVE MECHANIC JUNIOR	5823-02XX		
AUTOMOTIVE MECHANIC JUNIOR	5823-02XX	PS-05	87
AUTOMOTIVE PAINTER	415S-OIXX	PS-06	33
AUTOMOTIVE TECHNICIAN ASSOCIATE	5823-11XX	PS-05	
AUTOMOTIVE TECHNICIAN ASSOCIATE	5823-11XX		3
AUX RURAL CARRIER	2325-03XX	RAUX-05	177
BANKING OFFICER	0505-4035	EAS-23	2
BANKING SYSTEMS OFFICER	0505-4040	EAS-25	
BLDG SVC MECH	5306-OBXX	OSD-07	3
BODY AND FENDER REPAIRMAN	3809-02XX	PS-07	289
BUDGET & FINANCIAL ANALYST	0560-5022	EAS-20	3
BUDGET AND FINANCIAL ANALYST	0560-5023	EAS-23	I
BUDGET ASSOCIATE	0560-5021	EAS-16	1
BUDGET SPECIALIST	0560-4027	EAS-25	4
BUDGET SPECIALIST	0560-4028	EAS-23	7
BUDGET SPECIALIST	0560-4029	EAS-21	3
BUDGET&COST ANALYST	0560-4025	EAS-20	1
BUDGET/COST ANALYST	0560-4018	EAS-22	6
BUDGET/COST ANALYST	0560-4019	EAS-24	3
BUDGET/COST ANALYST	0560-4030	EAS-20	1
BUDGET/FINANCIAL ANALYST(AREA OFC)	0504-5019	EAS-21	56
➤ BUDGET/FINANCIAL ANALYST(DIST)	0504-5022	EAS-19	146
BUDGET/PERSONNEL COORDINATOR	0301-5346		1
BUILDING CUSTODIAN	4749-06XX	PS-04	2
➤ BUILDING EQUIPMENT MECH	5306-07XX	PS-07	1,928
BUILDING MAINTENANCE CUSTODIAN	4749-10XX	PS-04	1,004
BUILDING SERVICES SPECIALIST	1601-4004	EAS-19	2
BUILDING SERVICES SPECIALIST	1601-4026	EAS-21	I
BULK MAIL DOCK CLK	2315-99XX	PS-06	403
BULK ML CLK	2320-15XX		4
BULK ML CLK	2320-15XX	PS-05	1,350
BULK ML TECH	2320-28XX	PS-06	1,864
BUSINESS MAIL ENTRY ANALYST	2345-4019	EAS-15	76
BUSINESS PROJECT			42
LEADER	0334-4131	EAS-24	
BUSINESS REENGINEERING ANALYST	0334-4123	EAS-25	4
BUSINESS SYSTEMS ANALYST	0334-4129	EAS-23	62
BUSINESS SYSTEMS ENGINEER	0334-4132	EAS-24	9
BUSINESS SYSTEMS MANAGER	0334-6045	EAS-25	26
CABINETMAKER/CARPENTER	4605-OIXX	OSD-07	I
CAPITAL INVESTMENT SPECIALIST	0505-4037	EAS-25	2
CAPITAL INVESTMENT SPECIALIST	0505-4036	EAS-23	
CAPITAL INVESTMENT SPECIALIST	0505-4039	EAS-21	1-
CAPITAL MARKETS ASSOCIATE	0505-4033	EAS-23	1
CAREER PLANNING SPECIALIST	0212-5049	EAS-25	
CAREER PLANNING SPECIALIST	0212-5050	EAS-23	
CAREER PLANNING SPECIALIST	0212-5051	EAS-21	I
CARPENTER	4607-02XX	PS-06	145
CARRIER (CITY)	2310-2009	?Q?-05	
➤ CARRIER CITY OR SPEC	2310-01XX	PS-05	223,562
CARRIER TECH	2310-02XX	PS-06	28,240

CARRIER TECHNICIAN	2310-2010	?Q?-06	
CASH MANAGER	0505-4031	EAS-23	1
➤ CASUAL	5201-1001	EAS-07	27,854
CASUAL SEVERLY HANDICAPPED	5201-1005		1
CHAUFFEUR	5703-2010	EAS-11	5
CHF COUNS CLASS & CUSTOMER SERVICE	0905-7037	PCES-I	1
CHF COUNS CONSUMER PROTECTION LAW	0905-7038		1
CHF COUNS EMPLOYEE RELATIONS LAW	0905-7039		1
CHF COUNS LABOR RELATIONS LAW	0905-7040		1
CHF COUNS LITIGATION & PROG SUPP	0905-7042		1
CHF COUNSEL ETHICS & INFO LAW	0905-7032		1
CHF COUNSEL STATE & LOCAL POLICIES	0905-7047		1
CHIEF CAPITAL MARKETS ASSOCIATE	0505-4032	EAS-25	1
CHIEF COUNSEL APPELLATE	0905-7041	PCES-I	1
CHIEF COUNSEL CLAIMS LAW	0905-7044		1
CHIEF COUNSEL ENFORCEMENT LAW	0905-7043		1
CHIEF COUNSEL FACILITIES LAW	0905-7034		1
CHIEF COUNSEL LEGISLATIVE	0905-7035		1
CHIEF COUNSEL PURCHASING LAW	0905-7033		1
CHIEF COUNSEL RATEMAKING	0905-7036		1
CHIEF FIELD COUNSEL	0905-7045		a
CHIEF INSPECTOR	0301-7036	PCES-IL	1
CHIEF INVESTMENT OFFICER	0505-4028	EAS-25	1
CLAIMS & INQUIRY CLK	2345-15XX	PS-05	395
CLAIMS SPECIALIST	0992-5006	EAS-15	4
CLASSIFICATION SPECIALIST	2345-4016	EAS-25	3
CLASSIFICATION SPECIALIST	2345-4017	EAS-23	2
CLASSIFICATION SUPPORT SPEC SR	2345-4010		16
CLASSIFICATION SUPPORT SPEC STF	2345-4013	EAS-19	1
CLASSIFICATION SUPPORT SPECIALIST	2345-4011	EAS-21	41
CLASSIFICATION SUPPORT TECHNICIAN	2345-3002	EAS-15	1
CLEANER	3565-OIXX	PS-03	
CLEANER	3565-01XX	PS-02	2
CLEANER	3565-01XX	PS-01	48
CLEANER EXECUTIVE AREAS	3565-06XX	OSD-02	1
CLERK ADP EQUIPMENT	0301-2105	MESC-05	10
CLERK FINANCE ST	2320-05XX	PS-06	1,137
CLERK RECOVERY CENTER LETTERS	2345-07XX	PS-05	168
CLERK RECOVERY CENTER PARCELS	2345-09XX		33
➤ CLERK STENOGRAPHER	0312-01XX		673
CLERK TYPIST	0322-02XX	PS-04	313
CLK VEHICLE DISPATCHING	0301-47XX	PS-05	118
CLK-INCHG SPCLL DLVY SVC	2310-24XX	PS-06	1
CLMS&VCHER EXAM SPEC SR PDC	0540-5007	DCS-17	3
CLMS&VCHR EXAM SPEC PDC	0540-5011	DCS-14	57
CLMS&VCHR EXAM TECH PDC	0540-5012	DCS-11	34
COMMUN CNTRL TECH	0394-2003	EAS-11	1
COMMUN SPEC STAFF	0391-4006	EAS-18	4
COMMUNICATIONS ENGINEER	0855-4029	EAS-25	1
COMMUNICATIONS ENGINEER	0855-4031	EAS-23	4
COMMUNICATIONS EQUIPMENT SPEC	0392-3003	EAS-21	4
COMMUNICATIONS EQUIPMENT SPECIALST	0391-4005		22
COMMUNICATIONS PROGRAMS SPECIALIST	1081-5055	EAS-23	40
COMMUNICATIONS RESOURCES SPECIALST	1081-5057		1
COMMUNICATIONS SOFTWARE SPECIALIST	0334-4035	EAS-22	2
COMMUNICATIONS SPECIALIST	0391-4003	EAS-24	2
COMMUNICATIONS SPECIALIST	1081-5013	EAS-16	11
COMMUNICATIONS SPECIALIST	1081-5036	EAS-18	4
COMMUNICATIONS TECHNICAL COORD	0393-4001	EAS-23	I
COMMUNICATIONS TECHNOLOGY SPECLST	0801-4067	EAS-25	1
COMP PRINT LN PROD OPER	4401-02XX	MH-05	8
COMP PROGMR	0334-3023	EAS-19	1
COMP SYS OPER	0332-3009	EAS-11	1
COMP SYS OPER LEAD	0332-4002	EAS-17	3
COMPENSATION SPECIALIST	0201-5099	EAS-23	5
COMPENSATION SPECIALIST	0201-5100	EAS-21	2

COMPENSATION SPECIALIST (BENEFITS)	0201-5098	EAS-25	
COMPENSATION SPECIALIST (PAY)	0201-5097		1
COMPLAINTS & INQUIRY CLK	2345-23XX	PS-06	396
COMPUTER ANALYSIS TECHNICIAN	0301-5535	EAS-14	
COMPUTER OPERATIONS SUPPORT SPCLST	0332-3025	EAS-17	4
COMPUTER OPERATIONS SUPPORT SPEC	0332-3026	EAS-15	3
COMPUTER PERFORMANCE SPECIALIST	0334-4084	EAS-24	3
COMPUTER PROGRAMMER	0334-3021	EAS-21	4
COMPUTER PROGRAMMER	0334-3035	EAS-16	I
COMPUTER PROGRAMMER/ANALYST	0334-3026	EAS-18	1
COMPUTER PROGRAMMER/SOFTWARE SPCLS	0334-4040	EAS-23	37
COMPUTE SYS ANLST/PRGMR ASSOC PDC	0334-3061	DCS-18	84
➤ COMPUTER SYS ANLST/PRGMR PDC	0334-3056	DCS-20	125
COMPUTER SYS ANLST/PRGMR SR PDC	0334-3057	DCS-22	128
COMPUTER SYS OPR LEAD PDC	0332-3013	DCS-17	10
COMPUTER SYS OPR SR PDC	0332-3012	DCS-14	18
COMPUTER SYS SPEC (JCL) SR (PDC)	0335-4005	DCS-18	15
COMPUTER SYS SPEC JCL (PDC)	0335-4008	DCS-16	18
COMPUTER SYSTEM OPERATOR JR (PDC)	0332-3005	DCS-08	2
COMPUTER SYSTEM SCHEDULER SR (PDC)	0330-5003	DCS-20	6
COMPUTER SYSTEMS ADMIN	0334-4020	EAS-21	6
COMPUTER SYSTEMS ADMIN JR PDC	0334-3031	EAS-19	1
COMPUTER SYSTEMS ADMINISTRATOR	0334-4055	EAS-24	2
COMPUTER SYSTEMS ADMNSTR PDC	0330-4008	EAS-23	4
COMPUTER SYSTEMS ANALYST	0334-4017	EAS-22	4
COMPUTER SYSTEMS ANALYST	0334-4022	EAS-23	13
COMPUTER SYSTEMS ANALYST	0334-4026	EAS-19	24
COMPUTER SYSTEMS OPERATOR	0332-4003	EAS-14	134
COMPUTER SYSTEMS OPERATOR (MDC)	0332-3018	MESC-09	2
COMPUTER SYSTEMS OPERATOR PDC	0332-3006	DCS-11,	22
COMPUTER SYSTEMS SCHEDULER PDC	0330-4021	DCS-17	6
COMPUTER SYSTEMS SPECIALIST	0335-3010	EAS-18	12
COMPUTER SYSTMS ANALYST/PROG ASSOC	0334-3060		14
COMPUTER SYSTMS ANALYST/PROGRAM SR	0334-3045	EAS-22	20
COMPUTER SYSTMS ANALYST/PROGRAMMER	0334-3044	EAS-20	15
CONFIDENTIAL SECTRY FLD	0318-2030		
CONSOLE OPERATOR	2315-64XX	PS-07	28
CONSOLE OPERATOR	2315-64XX	PS-06	2
CONSOLE OPERATOR	2315-65XX	MH-07	4
CONSOLE OPERATOR	2315-65XX	MH-06	I
CONSUMER AFFAIRS REPRESENTATIVE	2345-6008	EAS-15	1
CONTRACT PRICE ANALYST	1102-5033	EAS-23	3
CONTRACT PRICE ANALYST	1102-5034	EAS-20	2
CONTRACT PRICE ANALYST	1102-5052	EAS-25	2
CONTRACT TECHNICIAN	1102-01XX	PS-06	346
CONTRACT TRANSPORTATION SPECIALIST	2330-4033	EAS-21	41
CONTRACT TRANSPORTATION SPECIALIST	2330-4034	EAS-19	50
CONVEYOR MECH	5343-02XX	PS-06	2
COORD TERMINAL HANDLING FACILITY	2330-2011	EAS-14	2
CORRESPONDENCE CONTROL COORD	0301-5195	EAS-16	1
COST ACCOUNTANT (MES)	0510-4058	EAS-20	
CPTR PERF SPEC	0334-4086	EAS-21	9
CPTR PERF SPEC SR	0334-4085	EAS-23	1
CPTR PROGMR SOFTWARE SPEC	0334-4019	EAS-22	25
CPTR SYS ANLST SR (MINI/MICRO)	0334-4074	EAS-23	9
CPTR SYS SPEC PDC	0335-3009	DCS-18	23
CRIMINAL ELECTRONICS ENGINEER	0802-4012	EAS-23	1
CURRICULUM DEVELOPMENT SPECIALIST	1710-5020		5
CURRICULUM DEVELOPMENT SPECIALIST	1710-5021	EAS-25	1
CURRICULUM DEVELOPMENT SPECIALIST	1710-5025	EAS-21	6
CURRICULUM PLANNING SPECIALIST	1710-5012	EAS-25	1
CURRICULUM PLANNING SPECIALIST	1710-5014	EAS-23	2
CURRICULUM PLANNING SPECIALIST	1710-5015	EAS-21	1
CURRICULUM PLNG & DEVELOP SPEC	1710-5026	EAS-23	5
CUST LABORER A	3566-05XX	OSD-01	12
CUST LABORER B	3566-06XX	OSD-02	12

CUST LABORER C	3566-07XX	OSD-03	a
CUST LABORER D	3566-08XX	OSD-04	3
CUST SUPPT SPEC PDC	0335-3008	DCS-15	26
CUST SUPPT TECH PDC	0335-3007	DCS-13	45
CUSTODIAL MGMT SPEC	3502-5001	EAS-14	1
CUSTODIAN	3566-04XX	PS-04	5
CUSTODIAN	3566-04XX	PS-03	58
➤ CUSTODIAN	3566-04XX	PS-02	1,844
CUSTOMER PROGRAMS SPECIALIST	0301-5336	EAS-25	
CUSTOMER PROGRAMS SPECIALIST	0301-5337	EAS-23	I
CUSTOMER RELATIONS COORDINATOR	2345-5035	EAS-17	198
CUSTOMER RESPONSE SPECIALIST	0301-5168	EAS-20	11
CUSTOMER RESPONSE SPECIALIST	0301-5335	EAS-23	2
CUSTOMER SERVICE ANALYST	0301-5332	EAS-25	8
CUSTOMER SERVICE ANALYST	0301-5333	EAS-23	4
CUSTOMER SERVICE ANALYST	0301-5334	EAS-21	1
CUSTOMER SERVICE REPRESENTATIVE	2345-401B	EAS-13	2B9
CUSTOMER SERVICE REPRESENTATIVE	2345-5034	EAS-16	86
CUSTOMER SERVICE SPECIALIST	0301-5352	EAS-23	1
CUSTOMER SERVICE SPECIALIST	0301-5353	EAS-20	1
CUSTOMER SERVICES ANALYST	2310-5027	EAS-16	442
CUSTOMER SERVICES CLERK (PFSC)	0530-2015	PS-06	26
CUSTOMER SUPPORT CENTER SPECIALIST	2050-5005	EAS-25	1
CUSTOMER SUPPORT PROG SPEC (NCSC)	1140-6021		2
CUSTOMER SUPPORT TECHNICIAN	0335-4081	EAS-13	
CUSTOMER SUPPT SPEC	0335-3011	EAS-15	9
CUSTOMER SVC PRGM ANALYST(AREA OF)	2340-5041	EAS-21	19
CUSTOMER SVC PRGM ANALYST(AREA OF)	2340-5042	EAS-23	19
CUSTOMER SVC SUPPORT ANLYST	1140-5042	EAS-21	9
CUSTOMER SVC SUPPORT ANLYST	1140-5043	EAS-23	23
CUSTOMER SVC SUPPORT ANLYST	1140-5044	EAS-25	20
DATA ADMINISTRATOR	0334-4094	EAS-22	4
DATA ADMINISTRATOR	0334-4095	EAS-23	1
DATA BASE MANAGEMENT SPECIALIST	0334-4110	EAS-25	4
DATA CNTRL TECH JR PDC	0335-2008	DCS-08	11
DATA CNTRL TECH SR PDC	0335-4007	OCS-13	3
➤ DATA COLL TECH	0301-69XX	PS-06	1,183
DATA CONTROL TECHNICIAN (MDC)	0335-3020	MESC-07	1
DATA CONVERSION GROUP LEADER PDC	0356-2004	DCS-09	1
DATA CONVERSION OPERATOR	0356-09XX	PS-04	8,078
DATA CONVERSION OPERATOR (MES)	0356-2019		2
DATA CONVERSION OPERATOR GROUP LDR	0356-2020	MESC-05	1
DATA CONVERSION OPERATOR PDC	0356-2003	DCS-06	16
DATA SYSTEMS TECHNICIAN SR	0335-4003	EAS-13	3
DATABASE ADMINISTRATOR	0334-4134	EAS-23	19
DATABASE SPECIALIST	0334-4089	EAS-21	5
DECISION SUPPORT SPECIALIST	0505-5018	EAS-25	1
DELIVERY AND RETAIL ANALYST	2310-5003	EAS-15	I
DELIVERY/CUSTOMER SVCS EQUIPMT SPC	0801-5020	EAS-25	3
DELIVERY/RETAIL ANALYST	2310-5026	EAS-17	74
DEPUTY CHIEF FIELD COUNSEL	0905-6014	PCES-I	7
DEPUTY CHIEF INSPECTOR	2335-7040		3
DEPUTY GENERAL COUNSEL	0905-7046	PCES-I	1
DEPUTY POSTMASTER GENERAL	0340-7011	PCES-IL	1
DIGITAL SYSTEMS SPECIALIST	0855-4024	EAS-25	I
DIRECTIVES & FORMS SPECIALIST	0343-5061	EAS-21	2
DIRECTIVES/FORMS SPECIALIST	0343-5053	EAS-23	2
DIRECTIVES/FORMS SPECIALIST	0343-5056	EAS-25	I
DIRECTORY ANALYSIS SPECIALIST	2340-5029	EAS-15	263
DISBURSING SPEC POC	0530-5007	DCS-14	3
DISBURSING SPEC SR PDC	0530-5006	DCS-17	5
DISBURSING TECH PDC	0530-5008	DCS-11	5
DIST CLK MACH MPLSM	2315-13XX	PS-06	29,851
DIST CLK MACH MPLSM TRNEE	2315-17XX		80
DIST CLK MACH MPLSM TRNEE	2315-17XX	PS-05	6,163
DIST CLK MACH SPLSM	2315-14XX	PS-06	973

DIST CLK MACH SPLSM TRNEE	2315-18XX		I
DIST CLK MACH SPLSM TRNEE	2315-18XX	PS-05	225
DIST WINDOW CLK	2340-02XX	PS-05	58,930
DISTANCE LEARNING SYSTEMS COORD	1710-4029	EAS-21	3
DISTRIBUTION CLERK	2315-04XX	PS-06	257
DISTRIBUTION CLERK	2315-04XX	PS-05	90,394
DISTRIBUTION SPECIALIST	2330-4036	EAS-21	20
DISTRIBUTION WINDOW & MARK UP CLK	2340-80XX	PS-05	5,312
DISTRICT MANAGER	0340-7118	PCES-I	16
DISTRICT MANAGER	0340-7121		14
DISTRICT MANAGER	0340-7122		53
DIVERSITY DEVELOPMENT EDUCTN PSYCH	0180-4016	EAS-23	1
DIVERSITY DEVELOPMENT INFO SYS SPC	0334-4128		1
DIVERSITY DEVELOPMENT SPEC (FLD)	0160-5056	EAS-19	38
DIVERSITY DEVELOPMENT SPECIALIST	0160-5053	EAS-25	1
DIVERSITY DEVELOPMENT SPECIALIST	0160-5054	EAS-23	8
DIVERSITY DEVELOPMENT SPECIALIST	0160-5055	EAS-21	1
DIVERSITY DEVELOPMENT SPLST(AREA)	0160-5057		17
DIVERSITY STRATEGIC PROGRAMS SPEC	0160-5061	EAS-25	I
DIVERSITY VENDOR PROGRAMS SPECLST	1102-5056		1
DRAFTING CLK	0818-01XX	PS-05	59
DRAFTING/DESIGN SPECIALIST	0802-4010	EAS-21	1
DRAFTSMAN	0818-3002	EAS-11	2
DRIVER INSTRUCTOR & EXAMINER	5752-01XX	PS-06	113
DUPLICATOR OPERATOR	0301-2089	EAS-09	3
EAP ANALYST	0301-5343	EAS-23	I
EAP COORDINATOR	0301-5363	EAS-21	83
ECONOMIST	0110-4016	EAS-25	20
ECONOMIST	0110-4017	EAS-23	8
ECONOMIST	0110-4018	EAS-21	2
EDITOR	1081-5004	EAS-25	2
EEO COMPLIANCE/APPEALS COORDINATOR	0954-4016	EAS-24	5
EEO COUNSELOR/INVESTIGATOR	0160-5050	EAS-17	1
EEO COUNSELOR/INVESTIGATOR	0160-5060		238
EEO COUNSELOR/INVESTIGATOR	1810-5001	EAS-19	4
ELCT ENGN TECHNLST	0856-3019	EAS-20	1
ELCT-MECH ENGN TECH	0802-3009	EAS-19	4
ELECTRICAL ENGINEER	0850-4007	EAS-25	3
ELECTRICAL EQUIP/POWER ENGINEER	0850-3009	EAS-21	1
ELECTRICAL LEADER	2805-05XX	OSD-08	I
ELECTRICIAN	2805-02XX	PS-07	1
ELECTRICIAN	2805-09XX	OSD-07	5
ELECTRICIAN HELPER	2805-06XX	OSD-04	
ELECTRO-OPTICS ANALYST	0855-4014	EAS-25	1
ELECTRO-OPTICS SYSTEMS SPEC	0855-4025		2
ELECTRONIC ENGINEER	0855-3005	EAS-22	I
ELECTRONIC ENGINEER	0855-4009	EAS-23	10
ELECTRONIC ENGINEER	0855-4010	EAS-24	5
ELECTRONIC ENGINEER	0855-4011	EAS-25	5
ELECTRONIC ENGINEER	0855-4034	EAS-21	
➤ ELECTRONIC TECHNICIAN	2604-01XX	PS-09	5,896
ELECTRONICS TECH	0856-01XX	PS-10	119
ELECTRONICS TECH	0856-01XX	PS-09	452
ELEVATOR & BOILER INSPECTION COORD	5401-5002	EAS-21	2
ELEVATOR ELECTRONIC TECH	5313-05XX	OSD-09	2
ELEVATOR MECH	5313-03XX	PS-07	30
ELEVATOR MECHANIC	5313-04XX	OSD-08	
ELEVATOR OPER	5438-01XX	PS-03	224
ELEVATOR/BOILER INSPECTOR	5401-3001	EAS-17	41
EMPLMT&PLACMT SPEC	0212-5025	EAS-21	4
EMPLOYEE FEEDBACK PROCESS COORD	0301-5539	EAS-18	
EMPLOYEE RELATIONS PROGRAMS SPCLST	0201-5081	EAS-23	1
EMPLOYEE RELATIONS SPECIALIST	0018-5029	EAS-23	1
EMPLOYEE TRANSPORTATION COORD	0301-5360	EAS-15	14
EMPLOYMENT & PLACEMENT SPECIALIST	0212-5023	EAS-23	2
EMPLOYMENT/PLACEMENT SPECIALIST	0212-5047	EAS-19	2

EMPLOYMENT/PLACEMENT SPECIALIST	0212-5052	EAS-25	
ENGINEERING TECHNICIAN	0802-3025	EAS-18	2
ENGINEERING TECHNICIAN	0802-4011	EAS-20	2
ENGINEMAN	5309-02XX	PS-06	1
ENGINEMAN	5309-1001	MESC-06	6
ENVIRONMENTAL COMPLIANCE COOR DIST	0819-5004	EAS-21	
ENVIRONMENTAL SPECIALIST	0819-4001	EAS-25	6
ENVIRONMENTAL COMPL COORD (DIST)	0819-5003	EAS-19	3
ENVIRONMENTAL COMPLIANCE COORD(AO)	0819-5001	EAS-25	6
ENVIRONMENTAL COMPLIANCE COORD(AO)	0819-5002	EAS-23	11
ENVIRONMENTAL PROGRAMS ANALYST	0819-4003	EAS-21	
ENVIRONMENTAL PROGRAMS ANALYST	0819-4005	EAS-25	1
ENVIRONMENTAL SPECIALIST	0819-4002	EAS-23	6
EQUIP HAND	3502-12XX	OSD-03	
EQUIP HAND TRUCK DRIVER	3502-11XX	OSD-05	1
ERGONOMIST	0896-4053	EAS-24	1
ESTIMATOR	0828-4001	EAS-23	2
EXAMINATION SPECIALIST	0203-19XX	PS-06	2
EXAMINATIONS ASST	0203-5004	EAS-14	3
EXAMINATIONS PROC CLK SR	0301-2097	EAS-11	5
EXAMINATIONS PROCESSING CLERK	0301-2060	EAS-09	5
EXAMINATIONS SUPPLY CLERK	2005-2008	EAS-08	3
EXEC DIR INTERNATIONAL POSTAL REL	0345-7051	PCES-I	1
EXECUTIVE CAREER DEVELOPMENT SPEC	0235-5059	EAS-25	1
EXECUTIVE CAREER DEVELOPMENT SPEC	0235-5060	EAS-23	2
EXECUTIVE DEVELOPMENT SPECIALIST	0235-5051	EAS-25	1
EXECUTIVE DEVELOPMENT SPECIALIST	0235-5052	EAS-23	1
EXECUTIVE DEVELOPMENT SPECIALIST	0235-5053	EAS-21	1
EXECUTIVE VICE PRESIDENT	0340-7098	PCES-IL	1
EXHIBITS SPECIALIST	1010-5003	EAS-22	2
EXPEDITED SERVICE SPECIALIST	2345-6056	EAS-15	170
EXPRESS MAIL SERVICE CLK	2330-77XX	PS-06	233
EXPRESS ML TECH	2340-82XX		73
EXTRACTION CODE CLERK	2315-63XX	PS-05	52
FACILITIES CONTRACT SPECIALIST	1102-5020	EAS-21	1
FACILITIES CONTRACT SPECIALIST	1102-5032	EAS-18	8
FACILITIES CONTRACT TECHNICIAN	1106-5005	EAS-15	34
FACILITIES ENGINEER	1601-4016	EAS-19	47
FACILITIES PLANNING SPECIALIST	0345-5085	EAS-21	
FACILITIES PLANNING SPECIALIST	0345-5086	EAS-23	1
FACILITIES PLANNING SPECIALIST	0345-5087	EAS-25	3
FACILITIES PROGRAMS ANALYST	0345-5088		2
FACILITIES PROGRAMS ANALYST	0345-5089	EAS-23	5
FACILITIES PROGRAMS ANALYST	0345-5090	EAS-21	2
FACILITIES REQUIREMENTS SPECIALIST	0801-4050	EAS-25	2
FACILITIES SPECIALIST	1601-3008	EAS-17	84
FACILITY ACTIVATION COORDINATOR	0345-5119	EAS-18	
FACILITY ACTIVATION COORDINATOR	0345-5120	EAS-20	1
FACILITY ACTIVATION COORDINATOR	0345-5121	EAS-22	1
FACILITY ACTIVATION SPECIALIST	0345-5095	EAS-25	2
FACILITY ACTIVATION SPECIALIST	0345-5096	EAS-23	4
FACILITY ACTIVATION SPECIALIST	0345-5097	EAS-21	2
FACILITY COMMUNICATIONS TECH	0332-3023	OCS-17	17
FACILITY COMMUNICATIONS TECH SR	0332-3027	DCS-19	3
FACILITY MGMT AND SERVICES COORD	0301-5240	EAS-19	1
FACILITY REQUIREMENTS SPECIALIST	0801-5015	EAS-23	2
FIELD COORDINATOR, QWL PROCESS	0230-5074	EAS-18	
FIELD HUMAN RESOURCES POLICY SPCLS	0201-5103	EAS-25	I
FIELD LIAISON COMMUNICATIONS	1081-5048		2
FILE CLERK	0305-03XX	PS-04	6
FINANCIAL ANALYST	0345-5098	EAS-25	5
FINANCIAL ANALYST	0345-5099	EAS-23	2
FINANCIAL ANALYST	0345-5100	EAS-21	1
FINANCIAL PLANNING SPECIALIST	0345-5107	EAS-25	2
FINANCIAL PLANNING SPECIALIST	0345-5108	EAS-23	2
➤ FINANCIAL SERVICES COORDINATOR	0510-5050	EAS-18	85

FINANCIAL SPECIALIST	0505-5107	EAS-25	1
FINANCIAL SVCS/SYSTEMS COORDINATOR	0510-5052	EAS-18	6
FINANCIAL SYSTEMS ANALYST	0505-4014	EAS-21	1
FINANCIAL SYSTEMS ANALYST	0505-5012	EAS-23	1
FINANCIAL SYSTEMS ANALYST	0505-5013		1
FINANCIAL SYSTEMS ANALYST	0505-5019		28
FINANCIAL SYSTEMS COORDINATOR	0505-5051	EAS-18	77
FINANCIAL SYSTEMS SPECIALIST	0505-5015	EAS-25	4
FINANCIAL SYSTEMS SPECIALIST	0505-5016	EAS-23	4
FINGERPRINT TECH	0072-3007	EAS-14	
FIREMAN	5402-01XX	PS-04	3
FIREMAN LABORER	5402-02XX		467
FLAT SORTING MACHINE OPERATOR	2315-20XX	PS-05	13,195
FLAT SORTING MACHINE OPERATOR	2315-21XX	PS-06	6,745
FORENSIC ANALYST	0802-3041	EAS-23	33
FORENSIC ANALYST	0802-3042	EAS-19	
FORENSIC ANALYST	0802-3043	EAS-17	
FORENSIC ANALYST	0802-3044	EAS-21	1
FORENSIC LATENT PRNT ANALYST IS	0072-3005		
FORENSIC LATENT PRNT ANALYST STAFF	0072-3004	EAS-19	
FORENSIC LATENT PRNT ASSOCIATE IS	0072-3003	EAS-17	
FORENSIC PHOTOGRAPHER	1060-3002		2
FORENSIC PHOTOGRPHR/EVIDENCE TECH	1060-3011	EAS-19	3
FORFEITURE PROGRAM ADMINISTRATOR	2335-5025	EAS-24	1
FORFEITURE SPECIALIST	2335-5020	EAS-16	42
FORKLIFT OPERATOR	5704-1001	MTEC-05	41
FORKLIFT OPERATOR	5704-1003	MESC-05	32
FRNSC DOC ANALYST (INSP SRV)	1397-3008	EAS-21	
FRNSC DOC ANALYST ASSOC (IS)	1397-3006	EAS-17	
FRNSC DOC ANALYST SR (INSP SRV)	1397-3009	EAS-23	4
FRNSC DOC ANALYST STAFF (IS)	1397-3007	EAS-19	
FRNSC LATENT PRT ANLST SR (INSP)	0072-3006	EAS-23	
GARAGEMAN	6955-02XX	PS-04	333
GEN CLERK	0301-2106	MESC-05	I
GEN CLK	2340-01XX	PS-06	42
GEN CLK	2340-OIXX	PS-05	3,350
GEN ENGINEER	0801-3005	EAS-23	17
GEN MECHANIC	4749-02XX	PS-05	56
GEN MECHANIC (MES)	4749-1002	MESC-05	3
GEN SERVICE MECHANIC	4749-1001	MTEC-05	3
GEN SUPV BLDG SVC	3501-6011	EAS-13	3
GEN SUPV COMPUTERIZED MARK-UP UNIT	0301-6103	EAS-17	31
GEN SUPV MTEC	6951-6003		1
GEN SUPV PSDS OPERATIONS (A)	0301-7174	EAS-15	37
GEN SUPV PSDS OPERATIONS (S)	0301-7175	EAS-17	56
GEN SUPV PSDS OPERATIONS ©	0301-7176	EAS-19	30
GEN SUPV REPAIRS (MTEC)	4801-6004	EAS-17	2
GENERAL CLERK VMF	0301-48XX	PS-05	266
GENERAL EXPEDITOR	2315-11XX	PS-06	3,747
GENERAL OFC CLK FOREIGN MAILS	2340-16XX		42
GRAPHICS PRODUCTION SPECIALIST	1084-5009	EAS-24	1
GRAPHICS PRODUCTION SPECIALIST	1084-5010	EAS-21	1
GROUP LEADER ADMINIST CLERK (PDC)	0301-5320	DCS-10	I
GROUP LEADER CUSTODIAL	3501-01XX	PS-04	497
GROUP LEADER, INTERNATIONAL ACCTS	0540-5005	DCS-16	3
GROUP LEADER, WAREHOUSING	6960-1001	MESC-05	11
GRP LDR CUSTODIAL	3501-1001	MESC-04	1
GRP LDR DATA CONVERSION OPERATOR	0356-10XX	PS-05	11
GRP LDR MAIL EQUIP REPAIR	3105-1001	MTEC-05	9
GRP LDR MAIL EQUIPMENT HANDLERS	3501-1002		8
GRP LDR MAILBAG EXAMINATION	3152-1001		1
GRP LDR ML HANDLER	2315-02XX	MH-05	1,230
GRP LDR SEWING MACHINE OPERS (MES)	3111-1004	MESC-05	I
GRP LEADER SACK SORT MCH OPER	2315-28XX	MH-06	3
HEADQUARTERS INJURY COMPENSTN ASOC	0230-5065	EAS-15	1
HEAVY TRUCK DRIVER	5755-01XX	OSD-04	2

HIGHWAY TRANSPORTATION CLK	2330-13XX	PS-06	35
HR SPECIALIST (INSPECTION SERVICE)	0201-5121	EAS-17	4
HR STRATEGIC PLANNING SPEC	0201-5125	EAS-23	
HRIS COORDINATOR	0201-5128	EAS-16	
HRIS SPECIALIST	0201-5091	EAS-19	14
HRIS SPECIALIST	0201-6054	EAS-21	4
HRIS TECHNICIAN	0201-5092	EAS-17	2
HUMAN FACTORS SPECIALIST	0896-4044	EAS-24	1
HUMAN RES ADMNR	0235-5029	EAS-16	2
HUMAN RESOURCE ASSOCIATE IS	0201-5123	EAS-11	66
HUMAN RESOURCE SPECIALIST	0201-5122	EAS-15	6
HUMAN RESOURCES ANALYST	0201-5102	EAS-25	1
HUMAN RESOURCES ANALYST (AREA OFC)	0201-5116	EAS-23	47
HUMAN RESOURCES ASSOCIATE	0201-5111	EAS-16	4
HUMAN RESOURCES ASSOCIATE	0201-5112	EAS-11	750
HUMAN RESOURCES ASSOCIATE (HFU)	0201-5109		2
HUMAN RESOURCES ASSOCIATE (HFU)	0201-5110	EAS-14	1
HUMAN RESOURCES INITIATIVES SPEC	0201-5124	EAS-21	
HUMAN RESOURCES PROGRAMS ASSISTANT	0201-5126	EAS-13	1
HUMAN RESOURCES SPECIALIST	0201-5101	EAS-23	I
HUMAN RESOURCES SPECIALIST	0201-5106	EAS-21	5
➤ HUMAN RESOURCES SPECIALIST	0201-5117	EAS-15	1,288
HUMAN RESOURCES SPECIALIST	0201-5118	EAS-17	323
HUMAN RESOURCES SPECIALIST	0201-5119	EAS-19	2
HUMAN RESOURCES SPECIALIST (HFU)	0201-5127	EAS-15	I
HUMAN RESOURCES SPECIALIST (HQ)	0201-5129	EAS-19	
ILLUSTRATOR	1020-OIXX	PS-07	25
ILLUSTRATOR TECHNICAL	1020-5010	EAS-16	2
INDUSTRIAL ENG	0896-9007	EAS-26	1
INDUSTRIAL ENGINEER (FLD)	0896-4036	EAS-19	105
INDUSTRIAL ENGINEER (HDQS)	0896-4035	EAS-23	4
INDUSTRIAL ENGINEER (HDQS)	0896-4039	EAS-25	3
INDUSTRIAL ENGINEER SR (FLD)	0896-3020		29
INDUSTRIAL EQUIPMENT MECHANIC	5828-01XX	PS-06	52
INDUSTRIAL HYGIENIST	0690-4003	EAS-24	1
INFO SYS SPEC	0334-4083	EAS-21	16
INFO SYSTEMS COORDINATOR	0334-4044	EAS-22	1
INFORMATION CLK	2320-12XX	PS-06	122
INFORMATION DEVELOPMENT COORDINATR	1529-5002	EAS-25	1
INFORMATION DISCLOSURE SPEC	0343-5036	EAS-23	1
INFORMATION DISCLUSURE TECHNICIAN	0343-5054	EAS-17	2
INFORMATION SCIENCES SPECIALIST	0330-4013	EAS-25	8
INFORMATION SERVICES SPECIALIST	0334-4118		4
INFORMATION SPECIALIST (INSP SRVC)	1081-5058	EAS-21	2
INFORMATION SPECIALIST INSP SRVC	1081-5038	EAS-19	2
INFORMATION SYSTEMS COORDINATOR	0330-5017	EAS-15	94
INFORMATION SYSTEMS COORDINATOR	0334-4043	EAS-19	6
INFORMATION SYSTEMS COORDINATOR	0334-4045	EAS-23	19
INFORMATION SYSTEMS COORDINATOR	0334-4058	EAS-16	10
INFORMATION SYSTEMS COORDINATOR	0334-4125	EAS-25	3
INFORMATION SYSTEMS COORDINATOR	0334-4127	EAS-21	17
INFORMATION SYSTEMS PROGRAMS COORD	0334-6018	EAS-25	5
INFORMATION SYSTEMS SECURITY SPEC	0334-5002	EAS-23	7
INFORMATION SYSTEMS SECURITY SPEC	0334-5003	EAS-21	2
INFORMATION SYSTEMS SECURITY SPEC	0334-5014	EAS-24	5
INFORMATION SYSTEMS SECURITY SPEC	0334-5021	EAS-16	2
INFORMATION SYSTEMS SPECIALIST	0330-5016	EAS-17	110
INFORMATION SYSTEMS SPECIALIST	0334-4082	EAS-23	14
INFORMATION SYSTEMS SPECIALIST	0334-4090	EAS-19	3
INFORMATION SYSTEMS SPECIALIST	0334-4108	EAS-25	8
INFORMATION TECHNOLOGY PLANNER	0334-4109		4
INFORMATION TECHNOLOGY SPEC	0334-3065	EAS-18	19
INFORMATION TECHNOLOGY SPEC	0334-3066	EAS-20	18
INJURY COMPENSATION SPECIALIST	0230-5066	EAS-23	2
INJURY COMPENSATION SPECIALIST	0230-5067	EAS-21	1
INJURY COMPENSATION SPECIALIST	0230-5068	EAS-25	1

INSPECTION SERVICE OPERATIONS COOR	0341-5055	EAS-14	47
INSPECTION SERVICE OPERATIONS SPEC	0345-5116	EAS-15	9
INSPECTION SERVICE PROGRAM SPEC	0345-5117	EAS-19	12
INSPECTION SERVICE PROGRAM SPEC	0345-5118	EAS-23	7
INTEGRATED SUPPORT PLANNING SPCLST	2001-5017	EAS-25	1
INTERCONNECTION/INFO SYS SPECLST	0334-4119		2
INTERN	0301-2109	EAS-17	2
INTERN HEADQUARTERS	0301-2110	EAS-07	
INTERNATIONAL POSTAL AFFAIRS SPCLS	0345-5109	EAS-21	3
INTERNATIONAL POSTAL AFFAIRS SPCLS	0345-5110	EAS-23	3
INTERNATIONAL POSTAL AFFAIRS SPCLS	0345-5111	EAS-25	4
INTERNATIONAL RECORDS UNIT COORD	2340-6030	EAS-18	1
INTL CVL/MLTRY MAIL COORD	2330-4026	EAS-21	4
INTL SURFACE ML REP	2330-4011	EAS-15	2
INTRNL CLAIMS CLK, PAY OFC	2345-16XX	PS-07	6
INVENTORY CONTROL CLERK	2040-2009	MESC-05	11
INVENTORY PROGRAMS SPECIALIST	2003-5029	EAS-25	1
INVENTORY SPECIALIST	2010-5007	EAS-23	7
INVENTORY SPECIALIST	2010-5008	EAS-20	6
IS BUSINESS AREA SPECIALIST	0334-5019	EAS-25	7
IS OPERATIONS TECH	0301-2234	EAS-11	443
JR CLERK	0301-2023	EAS-04	2
JR STENO	0312-2007	EAS-07	1
JUDICIAL OFFICER	0905-7008	PCES-II	1
LABEL MACH OPER	4401-05XX	MH-04	5
LABEL PRINTING TECH	4401-06XX	MH-05	12
LABEL PRINTING TECH (EASC)	4401-1013	PS-05	3
LABOR ECONOMIST	0110-4015	EAS-25	2
LABOR RELATIONS ANALYST IS	0230-5073	EAS-21	1
LABOR RELATIONS PROGRAMS COORD	0233-5013	EAS-19	1
LABOR RELATIONS REP PDC	0230-5030		1
LABOR RELATIONS SPEC (AREA OFFICE)	0233-5019	EAS-23	35
LABOR RELATIONS SPECIALIST	0230-5012	EAS-21	4
LABOR RELATIONS SPECIALIST	0230-5013	EAS-23	10
LABOR RELATIONS SPECIALIST	0230-5014	EAS-25	10
LABOR RELATIONS SPECIALIST	0233-5016	EAS-19	356
LABOR RELATIONS SPECIALIST	0233-5017	EAS-17	
LABOR RELATIONS SPECIALIST (FIELD)	0233-5021	EAS-24	6
LABOR RELATIONS SPECLST(AREA OFC)	0233-5018	EAS-21	32
LABOR RELATIONS SPECLST(AREA OFC)	0233-5020	EAS-25	10
LABOR RELATIONS SYSTEMS SPECIALIST	0301-5351	EAS-21	1
LABOR RELATIONS TECHNICIAN	0301-5348	EAS-16	2
LABOR RELATIONS TECHNICIAN	0301-5349	EAS-14	2
LABORATORY TECHNICIAN	2335-4001	EAS-11	1
LABORER	3502-07XX	OSD-02	3
LABORER CUSTODIAL	3502-03XX	PS-06	6
LABORER CUSTODIAL	3502-03XX	PS-05	15
LABORER CUSTODIAL	3502-03XX	PS-04	13
LABORER CUSTODIAL	3502-03XX	PS-03	13,134
LABORER CUSTODIAL	3502-03XX	PS-02	13
LABORER CUSTODIAL	3502-1019	MESC-03	12
LABORER CUSTODIAL (MES)	3502-1022		6
LABORER CUSTODIAL (MTEC)	3502-1024	MTEC-03	
LABORER LEADER	3502-08XX	OSD-06	
LABORER MATERIALS HANDLING (MES)	3502-1023	MESC-03	8
LABORER MTL HNDLNG	3502-14XX	PS-03	2
LAN SPECIALIST	0334-3063	EAS-21	
LAN SPECIALIST	0334-3064	EAS-23	1
LBR REL ASST FLD	0230-5028	EAS-16	1
LEAD AUTOMOTIVE MECHANIC	5823-10XX	PS-07	444
LEATHER WORKER (MES)	3102-1002	MESC-05	
LEGAL ADVISOR OFC OF LEGAL ADV	0905-9021	EAS-35	I
LEGAL INTERN	0301-2111	EAS-16	6
LEGAL SECRETARY	0986-3005	EAS-11	19
LEGAL SECRETARY	0986-3008	EAS-14	22
LEGAL SYS SPEC	0950-5004	EAS-18	1

LEGISLATIVE AFFAIRS ANALYST	0301-5356	EAS-17	2
LEGISLATIVE AFFAIRS ANALYST	0301-5358	EAS-21	4
LEGISLATIVE AFFAIRS ANALYST	0301-5359	EAS-23	1
LEGISLATIVE AFFAIRS REPRESENTATIVE	0301-5354		8
LETTER BOX MECHANIC (MES)	3843-02XX	PS-06	195
LIBRARIAN	1410-5009	EAS-20	3
LIBRARIAN	1410-5011	EAS-25	1
LIBRARY TECHNICIAN	1411-5002	EAS-14	2
LIBRARY TECHNICIAN	1411-5004	EAS-16	2
LOCAL AREA NETWORK ADMINISTRATION	0334-4136	EAS-21	2
LOCAL AREA NETWORK ADMINISTRATION	0334-4137	EAS-19	
LOCK AND SAFE MECHANIC	5311-06XX	PS-06	1
LOCK BOX EQUIPMENT REPAIRER (MES)	5311-1004	MESC-05	
LOCKMAKER	5311-02XX	PS-05	1
LOCKMAKER (MES)	5311-1002	MESC-05	4
LOCKSMITH CARPENTER	5311-04XX	OSD-07	2
LOGISTICS REQUIREMENTS PLANNG SPC	2003-5030	EAS-25	I
LOGISTICS SUPPORT SPECIALIST	2003-5037	EAS-16	2
LOGISTICS TECHNICAL DATA SPECIALST	2003-5034	EAS-25	I
MACHINE OPER PHILATELIC FULFILLMNT	2340-05XX	PS-05	12
MACHINE OPERATOR (MES)	3401-1002	MESC-04	44
MACHINE OPERATOR (MES)	3401-1003	MESC-03	33
MACHINE OPERATOR A (MES)	3401-1001	MESC-06	1
MACHINE OPERATOR B (MES)	3401-1004		2
MACHINIST	3414-02XX	PS-07	22
MACHINIST	3414-1002	EAS-13	I
MACHINIST HELPER	3414-1001	EAS-10	1
MAIL ACCEPTANCE SPECIALIST	2345-6057	EAS-16	103
MAIL CLASS CLK MSC	2345-52XX	PS-07	44
MAIL CLASS CLK MSC	2345-52XX	PS-06	30
MAIL CLERK	0305-2001	EAS-06	5
MAIL EQUIPMENT HANDLER	3502-01XX	MH-04	67
MAIL EQUIPMENT HANDLER	3502-1020	MTEC-04	197
MAIL EQUIPMENT SHOP TECHN (MES)	6753-1001	MESC-09	I
MAIL HANDLER	2315-0IXX	MH-05	219
➤ MAIL HANDLER	2315-01XX	MH-04	46,390
MAIL HANDLER LEADMAN	2315-8OXX	MH-05	3
MAIL MESS COORDINATOR	0305-04XX	OSD-05	1
MAIL MESS DRIVER	2340-09XX	OSD-04	1
MAIL MGMNT SPECIALIST	0305-2010	EAS-12	I
MAIL ORDER CLERK (PFSC)	0530-26XX	PS-05	12
MAIL PROCESSING MACHINE OPERATOR	2340-45XX	MH-05	1,599
MAIL PROCESSOR	2315-55XX	PS-04	22,719
MAIL REWRAPPER	2340-27XX	MH-04	32
MAILING REQUIREMENTS CLK	2345-32XX	PS-07	4
MAILING REQUIREMENTS CLK	2345-32XX	PS-06	350
MAILING REQUIREMENTS CLK	2345-32XX	PS-05	188
MAILPIECE DESIGN ANALYST	2345-5033	EAS-15	168
MAIN TECH	4749-08XX	OSD-06	4
MAINT CNTL CLK	0301-16XX	PS-06	3
MAINT CNTL CLK	0301-16XX	PS-05	560
MAINT CNTL TECH	0301-07XX	PS-06	416
MAINT ELECTRICIAN	2805-03XX		217
MAINT MECH MPE	5342-01XX	PS-07	5,482
MAINT SOFTWR SPEC	0334-3046	EAS-21	10
MAINT SUPPORT CLERK	0303-02XX	PS-06	1
MAINTENANCE CONTROL AND STOCK CLK	0301-19XX	PS-05	378
MAINTENANCE ELECTRICIAN	2805-1010	MESC-06	1
MAINTENANCE ENGINEERING ANALSYT	1670-4017	EAS-21	43
MAINTENANCE ENGINEERING SPECIALIST	1641-5004	EAS-18	108
MAINTENANCE ENGINEERING SPECIALIST	1670-4025	EAS-25	3
MAINTENANCE FIELD SUPPORT SPECLST	1641-4024		3
MAINTENANCE HELPER	4701-02XX	OSD-04	1
MAINTENANCE INFORMATION SPECIALIST	1641-4019	EAS-16	4
MAINTENANCE MAN	4749-05XX	PS-04	2
MAINTENANCE MANAGEMENT SPECIALIST	1601-4018	EAS-23	14

MAINTENANCE MECH GEN (SPLY CTR)	5301-1008	MESC-06	4
➤ MAINTENANCE MECHANIC	4749-03XX	PS-05	2,386
MAINTENANCE MECHANIC	4749-11XX	PS-04	353
MAINTENANCE MECHANIC GENERAL	5301-1007	MTEC-06	9
MAINTENANCE MECHANIC MACHINIST	3414-1003	EAS-12	1
MAINTENANCE PROGRAMS/POLICY SPCLST	1641-5003	EAS-25	1
MAINTENANCE REQUIRE/PLANNING SPCLS	1641-5002		1
MAINTENANCE SUPPORT CLERK	0303-01XX	PS-05	
MAINTENANCE SUPPORT PLANNING SPCLS	0801-4038	EAS-24	2
MANAGEMENT ANALYST	0343-3012	EAS-19	13
MANAGEMENT ANALYST	0343-3013	EAS-17	10
MANAGEMENT ANALYST	0343-5021	EAS-22	2
MANAGEMENT ANALYST PDC	0343-3014	EAS-19	6
MANAGEMENT ASSOCIATE	0301-5504	SMD-04	12
MANAGEMENT ASSOCIATION RELTNS SPEC	0341-5052	EAS-21	2
MANAGEMENT ASSOCIATION RELTNS SPEC	0341-5053	EAS-23	1
MANAGEMENT DEVELOPMENT SPECIALIST	0235-5054	EAS-25	1
MANAGEMENT DEVELOPMENT SPECIALIST	0235-5055	EAS-23	2
MANAGEMENT DEVELOPMENT SPECIALIST	0235-5056	EAS-21	I
MANAGEMENT INTERN	0301-5501	SMD-01	17
MANAGEMENT TRAINEE	0301-5505	SMD-05	5
MANAGEMENT TRAINING SPECIALIST	1710-5022	EAS-21	8
MANAGEMENT TRAINING SPECIALIST	1710-5023	EAS-23	3
MARKET RESEARCH SPECIALIST	1140-5045	EAS-25	5
MARKET RESEARCH SPECIALIST	1140-5046	EAS-23	3
MARKET RESEARCH SPECIALIST	1140-5047	EAS-21	I
MARKETING SPECIALIST	1140-5009		8
MARKETING SPECIALIST	1140-5011	EAS-23	24
MARKETING SPECIALIST	1140-5025	EAS-25	35
MARKTING SERVICES SPECIALIST (BMC)	2345-5036	EAS-19	2
MARKTING SERVICES SPECIALIST (BMC)	2345-5037	EAS-18	19
MARKUP CLK AUTOMATED	0301-41XX	PS-04	6,124
MARKUP CLK MANUAL	0301-40XX		5
MASON	3603-02XX	PS-06	1
MATERIAL CLERK	2005-2019	MESC-05	is
MATERIAL HANDLING EQUIP OPER (MES)	5704-1002		3
MATERIALS ENGINEER	0806-4001	EAS-25	2
MATERIALS ENGINEER	0806-4005	EAS-24	2
MATERIALS HANDLING SYSTEMS SPEC	0801-4044	EAS-25	I
MATERIALS HANLDING EQUIP OPER	5704-01XX	PS-04	90
MATERIALS TECHNICIAN	0802-3023	EAS-19	2
MATERIEI DISTRIBUTION SYSTEMS SPCL	2030-5003	EAS-25	1
MATERIEL LOGISTICS SPECIALIST	2003-5031	EAS-21	17
MATERIEL LOGISTICS SPECIALIST	2003-5032	EAS-23	11
MATERIEL MANAGEMENT SPEC (MES)	2003-5038	EAS-15	2
MATERIEL MANAGEMENT SPECIALIST	2003-5021	EAS-25	3
MATERIEL MANAGEMENT SPECIALIST	2003-5023	EAS-23	10
MATERIEL MANAGEMENT SPECIALIST	2003-5024	EAS-20	33
MATERIEL MANAGEMENT SPECIALIST	2003-5036	EAS-15	85
MATHEMATICAL STATISTICIAN	1529-4011	EAS-21	2
MATHEMATICAL STATISTICIAN	1529-4012	EAS-23	4
MATHEMATICAL STATISTICIAN	1529-5001	EAS-25	9
MEASUREMENT/EVALUATION SPCLST	1710-5017		1
MEASUREMENT/EVALUATION SPCLST	1710-5018	EAS-23	6
MEASUREMENT/EVALUATION SPCLST	1710-5019	EAS-21	
MECH HLPR	4701-01XX	PS-04	8
MECHANIC HELPER (MES)	4701-1001	MESC-04	
MECHANICAL'ENGINEER	0830-3008	EAS-23	10
MECHANICAL ENGINEER	0830-4010	EAS-21	3
MECHANICAL ENGINEER	0830-4011	EAS-23	3
➤ MECHANICAL ENGINEER	0830-4012	EAS-24	12
MECHANICAL ENGINEER	0830-4013	EAS-25	6
MECHANICAL EQUIP/SERVICE ENG (FLD)	0830-3016	EAS-21	1
MECHANIZATION ESTIMATE/PLAN SPCLST	0801-4056	EAS-25	1
MEDIA RELATIONS REP, INSP SRVC	1081-5045	EAS-23	1
MEDIA RELATIONS REPRESENTATIVE	1081-5001	EAS-24	4

MEDICAL DIRECTOR	0602-7004	PCES-I	1
MEDICAL OFFICER	0602-6001	EAS-26	1
MEDICAL OFFICER FIELD DIVISION	0602-6009		16
MESSENGER/WAREHOUSEMAN	5703-1013	MESC-04	
MGMT ANALYST INSPECTION SERVICE	0343-5062	EAS-21	5
MGR ACCOUNTING OPERATIONS	0510-7078	PCES-I	1
MGR ACCOUNTING SERVICE CENTER	0510-7076		3
MGR., DIST. OPRNS (CAREER LADDER)	2315-7147	EAS-22	
MGR., DIST. OPRNS (CAREER LADDER)	2315-7148	EAS-20	
MICROMATION SPEC POC	0301-3014	EAS-14	1
MICROMATION TECHNICIAN PDC	0301-3009	DCS-12	1
ML FLOW CNTLR	2315-2011	EAS-14	254
ML HANDLER TECH	2315-62XX	MH-05	1,155
MLHDLR EQUIP OPER	5704-03XX		4,620
MO ACCTG SPEC PDC	0525-5014	DCS-16	7
MODEL MAKER	3403-3001	EAS-18	
MODEL MAKER	3403-3002	EAS-17	I
MOTOR VEH OPER	5703-02XX	PS-06	14
MOTOR VEH OPER	5703-02XX	PS-05	3,475
NATIONAL ACCOUNTS REPRESENTATIVE	1101-5042		82
NATIONAL ACCOUNTS REPRESENTATIVE	1101-5043	EA'S-23	22
NATIONAL ACCOUNTS REPRESENTATIVE	1101-5044	EAS-25	21
NATIONAL LAB MAINTENANCE ENGINEER	1601-3009	EAS-15	1
NETWORK PERFORMANCE SPECIALIST	0391-4009	EAS-21	1
NETWORK PERFORMANCE SPECIALIST PR	0391-4007	EAS-24	1
NETWORK PERFORMANCE SPECIALIST SR	0391-4008	EAS-23	1
NETWORK PLANNING SPECIALIST	2330-4032	EAS-21	48
NETWORK PLANNING SPECIALIST	2330-4038	EAS-19	102
NETWORKS SPECIALIST	2150-5010	EAS-15	278
OCCUP HEALTH NURSE ADMINISTRATOR	0610-4002	EAS - 17	67
➤ OCCUP HLTH NURSE	0610-4001	PNS-01	183
OCCUPATION SAFETY/HEALTH SPECIALST	0018-5022	EAS-25	1
OCCUPATION SAFTY/HEALTH SPECIALIST	0018-5015	EAS-23	2
OFC STAFF ASST (TYPIST)	0318-07XX	PS-05	1
OFF CLK-CUSTODIAL	0301-05XX		95
OFF MACH OPER	0350-OIXX	MH-05	14
OFF MACH OPER	0350-02XX	PS-05	22
OFFICE AIDE	0001-1001	EAS-01	3
OFFICE APPLIANCE REPAIRMAN	4806-04XX	PS-05	2
OFFICE CLERK	0301-OIXX		4
OFFICE CLERK	0301-OIXX	PS-04	89
OFFICE CLERK (MTEC)	0301-2104	MTEC-05	7
OFFICE CLERK (SUPPLY CENTER)	0301-2102	MESC-05	
OFFICE CLK VEHICLE OPERATIONS	0301-04XX	PS-05	92
OFFICE MACHINE OPERATOR	0350-OIXX	MH-04	1
OFFICE SERVICES ASSISTANT (AREA)	0342-2003	EAS-10	6
OFFICE SERVICES ASSISTANT PDC	0301-2034	DCS-10	4
OFFICE SERVICES CLERK	0301-2103	MESC-04	1
OFFICE SERVICES CLERK (AREA)	0301-2100	EAS-10	9
OFFICE SYSTEMS COORDINATOR ASSOC	0342-5028	EAS-14	2
OFFSET PRESS OPER	4417-OIXX	PS-05	3
OLYMPICS SPECIALIST	2340-5047	EAS-23	5
OLYMPICS SPECIALIST, PCES	2340-5048	PCES-I	
OPERATING ENGINEER	5415-02XX	OSD-06	6
OPERATING ENGINEER HELPER	5415-03XX	OSD-04	
OPERATIONAL REQUIREMENTS SPECIALST	0345-5112	EAS-23	18
OPERATIONS PERFORMANCE ANALYST	2305-5027	EAS-25	2
OPERATIONS PERFORMANCE ANALYST	2305-5028	EAS-23	1
OPERATIONS PERFORMANCE ANALYST	2305-5029	EAS-21	4
OPERATIONS PRGMS ANALYST(AREA OFC)	2310-5023	EAS-23	20
OPERATIONS PRGMS ANALYST(AREA OFC)	2310-5024	EAS-21	18
OPERATIONS QUALITY IMPROVEMENT SPC	1910-4015	EAS-17	247
OPERATIONS QUALITY IMPROVEMENT SPC	1910-5005	EAS-25	1
OPERATIONS QUALITY IMPROVEMENT SPC	1910-5006	EAS-23	3
OPERATIONS QUALITY IMPROVEMENT SPC	1910-5007	EAS-21	2
OPERATIONS QUALITY IMPROVEMT ANLST	1910-3001	EAS-15	32

Occupation	Code	Grade	Count
OPERATIONS REDESIGN SPECIALIST	2305-5031	EAS-21	1
OPERATIONS REDESIGN SPECIALIST	2305-5032	EAS-23	4
OPERATIONS REDESIGN SPECIALIST	2305-5033	EAS-25	5
OPERATIONS REDESIGN SPECIALIST	2305-5037	EAS-19	1
OPERATIONS RESEARCH ANALYST	1515-4014	EAS-23	10
OPERAT... ANALYST	1515-4015	EAS-21	7
OPERAT...	1515-4024	EAS-25	9
OPERAT...	1515-4025	EAS-23	9
OPERA...	1515-5001	EAS-25	8
OPERA...	1515-4027		1
OPERA...	2305-5023		29
OPERA...	2305-5024	EAS-23	31
OPER...	2305-5025	EAS-21	13
OPER...	2305-5026	EAS-19	
OPER...	0345-5114	EAS-21	38
OPE...	0345-5115	EAS-23	42
OPE...	2340-5043	EAS-20	90
OP...	2340-5044	EAS-18	215
OP...	2340-5045	EAS-16	338
O...	2340-5046	EAS-14	54
O...	0801-4058	EAS-25	3
...	0801-4059	EAS-23	2
	4401-10XX	PS-05	2
	4401-1012	MESC-05	
	3111-1001	MTEC-04	4
	2305-7097	EAS-22	1
	2305-7055	EAS-21	18
	0201-5094	EAS-25	1
	0201-5095	EAS-23	1
	0201-5096	EAS-21	2
	0201-5105	EAS-14	I
	5342-11XX	PS-08	12
	7002-03XX	MH-04	14
	6907-1002	MESC-04	47
	4102-02XX	PS-06	166
	4102-03XX	OSD-06	1
	4740-OIXX	OSD-07	1
	0950-5003	EAS-16	12
	0950-5005	EAS-18	1
	2315-06XX	PS-06	59
	2315-06XX	PS-05	9,572
	0544-5003	DCS-14	36
	0544-5004	DCS-16	13
	0544-6008	EAS-20	7
	0544-5006	DCS-11	72
	0301-7141		3
	0301-7142		27
	2335-7030		3
	0201-5025	EAS-14	3
	0201-2004	EAS-11	5
PERSONNEL ...	0203-14XX	PS-05	179
PERSONNEL MANAGEMENT ...IST	0230-5069	EAS-19	2
PEST CONTROLLER	5026-01XX	PS-06	5
PHIL CLK	2345-02XX	PS-05	95
PHIL STMP STOCK EXMR	0525-4008	EAS-13	4
PHILATELIC CONTROL SPECIALIST	2003-5015	EAS-22	1
PHILATELIC DESIGN SPECIALIST	1001-5030	EAS-24	I
PHILATELIC PROCUREMENT SPECIALIST	2003-5033	EAS-23	1
PHILATELIC PROGRAM SPECIALIST	1001-5014	EAS-17	2
PHILATELIC SALES PROGRAM ANALYST	1101-5040	EAS-20	2
PHOTOGRAPHER	1060-4002	EAS-21	I
PLANT MAINTENANCE ENGINEER	601-5004	EAS-19	6
PLANT MAINTENANCE ENGINEER (HFU)	1601-5005	EAS-17	
PLUMBER	4206-02XX	PS-06	60
PLUMBER	4206-05XX	OSD-07	2
PLUMBER HELPER	4206-04XX	OSD-04	1

PLUMBER LEADER	4206-03XX	OSD-08	I
PM RELIEF/REPLCMNT	2305-6100	PMLR-55	1,905
PM RELIEF/REPLCMNT	2305-6111	PMLR-09	5,161
PM RELIEF/REPLCMNT	2305-6113	PMLR-11	4,915
PM RELIEF/REPLCMNT	2305-6115	PMLR-13	970
PM/US VIRGIN ISLANDS COORDINATOR	2301-7140	EAS-22	1
POST OFFICE CLK	2340-04XX	PS-03	844
POSTAGE DUE CLK	2340-06XX	PS-05	350
POSTAGE DUE TECHN	2340-24XX	PS-06	280
POSTAL INSPECTOR (PROGRAM MGR)	2335-5018	EAS-24	95
➤ POSTAL INSPECTOR (PROJECT COORD)	2335-3004		352
POSTAL MAINTENANCE SPECIALIST	0801-4020	EAS-25	7
POSTAL OPER ASSOC	2340-5016	EAS-15	1
POSTAL OPER TECH	2340-2010	EAS-11	2
POSTAL OPERATIONS ANALYST	2340-3001	EAS-21	4
POSTAL OPERATIONS ANALYST	2340-3002	EAS-23	24
➤ POSTAL POLICE OFFICER (8)	2335-24XX	PPO-06	1,108
POSTAL POLICE OFFICER IN CHARGE(A)	2335-6009	EAS-15	40
POSTAL POLICE OFFICER IN CHARGE(B)	2335-7008	EAS-17	12
POSTAL POLICE OFFICER IN CHARGE©	2335-7009	EAS-20	3
POSTAL POLICE SUPERVISOR	2335-6008	EAS-14	150
POSTAL SYSTEMS COORDINATOR	0525-5020	EAS-15	204
POSTMASTER	2301-5103	EPM-52	20
POSTMASTER	2301-6104	EPM-53	721
POSTMASTER	2301-6105	EPM-54	44
POSTMASTER	2301-6106	EPM-55	987
POSTMASTER	2301-6111	EAS-11	5,307
POSTMASTER	2301-6113	EAS-13	6,013
POSTMASTER	2301-6115	EAS-15	2,643
POSTMASTER	2301-6118	EAS-18	3,877
POSTMASTER	2301-6120	EAS-20	2,127
POSTMASTER	2301-6213	EAS-13	279
POSTMASTER	2301-6215	EAS-15	3,024
POSTMASTER	2301-7121	EAS-21	975
POSTMASTER	2301-7122	EAS-22	675
POSTMASTER	2301-7139	PCES-I	26
POSTMASTER (F)	2301-7004	EAS-24	224
POSTMASTER (G)	2301-7005	EAS-26	49
POSTMASTER (I)	0340-7008	PCES-I	
POSTMASTER GENERAL	0340-7010	PCES-II	1
PREFERENTIAL MAIL CLERK	0305-2011	EAS-09	1
PRESENTATION SPECIALIST	1084-4001	EAS-20	2
PRESENTATION SPECIALIST	1084-4004	EAS-22	1
PRESS OPERATOR	3803-1001	MESC-05	2
PREVENTIVE MAINT ENGINEER	0802-3017	EAS-20	1
PRGM ANLST STAFF	0345-4038	EAS-18	3
PRGM MGR TELE	0334-4060		6
PRGMG LIBRARIAN	0335-2013	EAS-10	1
PRGMG LIBRN PDC	0335-2009	DCS-10	4
PRINCIPAL STATISTICIAN	1530-5002	EAS-25	2
PRINTING CONTR SPEC SR	1654-4003	EAS-21	1
PRIVATE SECRETARY TO THE PMG	0318-2024	EAS-23	1
PROC CLERK	1106-01XX	PS-05	62
PROCUR SPEC	1105-02XX	PS-06	I
PROCUREMENT & SUPPLY ASSISTANT PDC	1105-2002	DCS-13	6
PROCUREMENT & SUPPLY ASST (SMISC)	1105-2006	DCS-15	1
PROCUREMENT & SUPPLY ASST (SMISC)	1105-2007	DCS-17	1
PROCUREMENT SPECIALIST STAFF	1102-5010	EAS-17	1
PROCUREMENT/MATERIEL MGMT ASSIST	2003-09XX	PS-06	78
PROCUREMENT/SUPPLY ASSISTANT NISSC	1105-2004	EAS-13	1
PRODUCT PUBLICITY SPECIALIST	1081-5050	EAS-24	4
PRODUCTION PLANNING COORDINATOR	1152-6002	EAS-15	23
PROF/SPEC TRAINEE A	0301-5205	DCS-14	2
PROF/SPEC TRAINEE AA	0301-5264	EAS-13	12
PROF/SPEC TRAINEE 8	0301-5206	DCS-16	
PROF/SPEC TRAINEE B	0301-5213	EAS-15	

PROF/SPEC TRAINEE C'	0301-5202	EAS-16	
PROF/SPEC TRAINEE C	0301-5207	DCS-18	
PROF/SPEC TRAINEE D	0301-5214	EAS-17	
PROF/SPEC TRAINEE E	0301-5203	EAS-18	
PROF/SPEC TRAINEE F	0301-5247	EAS-19	I
PROG DIR OPERATIONS RESEARCH	1515-4023	EAS-26	
PROGRAM ANALYST	0345-4036	EAS-22	3
PROGRAM ANALYST	0345-4037	EAS-20	3
PROGRAM EVALUATION SPECIALIST	0345-5104	EAS-25	4
PROGRAM EVALUATION SPECIALIST	0345-5105	EAS-23	4
PROGRAM EVALUATION SPECIALIST	0345-5106	EAS-21	1
PROGRAM PERFORMANCE SPECIALIST	0345-5101	EAS-25	3
PROGRAM PERFORMANCE SPECIALIST	0345-5102	EAS-23	I
PROGRAM PERFORMANCE SPECIALIST	0345-5103	EAS-21	1
PROP INVN ASST	2001-2001	EAS-11	2
PROP MAINT&INV TECH	2001-2003	EAS-14	1
PROP SUP SPEC	2003-1OXX	OSO-06	
SPECIALIST POC	2003-2001	DCS-14	
PROPERTY CONTROL 3	0301-45XX	PS-06	1,344
PSO TECH			
PSTL INSP A	2335-2002	EAS-17	
PSTL INSP B	2335-3003	EAS-19	
PSTL INSP C	2335-3006	EAS-21	
PSTL INSP D	2335-3002	EAS-23	1,674
PSTL INSP-IN-CHG B	2335-7007	PCES-I	32
PSTL MACHS MECH	4801-06XX	PS-06	118
PSYCHOLOGIST	0180-4003	EAS-23	3
PSYCHOLOGIST	0180-4007	EAS-21	3
PSYCHOLOGIST	0180-4015	EAS-25	2
PURCHASING ASSISTANT	1105-5006	EAS-13	25
PURCHASING POLICIES SPECIALIST	1102-5029	EAS-23	4
PURCHASING POLICIES SPECIALIST	1102-5040	EAS-25	9
PURCHASING SPECIALIST	1102-5012	EAS-23	61
PURCHASING SPECIALIST	1102-5026	EAS-20	199
PURCHASING SPECIALIST	1102-5041	EAS-25	21
PURCHASING SPECIALIST	1102-5047	EAS-17	89
PURCHASING SPECIALIST	1102-5059		2
PURCHASING SPECIALIST	1102-5060	EAS-16	a
PURCHASING/MATERIEL COMPLIANCE SPC	1101-5041	EAS-23	I
PURCHASING/SUPPLY SYSTEMS SPCIALST	1101-5032	EAS-21	7
PURCHASING/SUPPLY SYSTEMS SPCIALST	1101-5033	EAS-23	5
PURCHASING/SUPPLY SYSTEMS SPCIALST	1101-5035	EAS-24	2
PURCHASING/SUPPLY TECHNICIAN	0301-5294	EAS-14	1
QUAL ASSUR ANLST PDC	1910-3011	0	
QUAL ASSUR ANLST SR PDC	1910-3010	OCS-18	11
QUAL ASSUR TECH PDC	1910-3012	D	
QUAL CNTL ANLST PDC	1910-4014	EAS-17	3
QUALITY ASSURANCE SPECIALIST	1910-3009	EAS-21	11
QUALITY ASSURANCE SPECIALIST	1910-4016	EAS-19	3
QUALITY ASSURANCE SPECIALIST	1910-4017	EAS-23	10
QUALITY ASSURANCE SPECIALIST	1910-4019	EAS-21	3
QUALITY ASSURANCE SPECIALIST	1910-4021	EAS-23	7
QUALITY ASSURANCE SPECIALIST	1910-5004	EAS-25	4
QUALITY CONTROL SPECIALIST	1910-3003	EAS-19	2
QUALITY FIRST CONSULTANT	0301-5331	EAS-25	8
QUALITY FIRST CONSULTANT	0301-7210	PCES-I	7
QUALITY FIRST TRAINER AD HOC	0301-5538	EAS-25	5
QUALITY SPECIALIST	0301-5326	EAS-24	1
QUALITY SPECIALIST	0301-5338	EAS-25	
QUALITY SPECIALIST	0301-5339	EAS-23	3
QUALITY SPECIALIST	0301-7211	PCES-I	1
QUALITY SPECIALIST	0343-5064	EAS-23	
QUALITY SPECIALIST	0343-5065	EAS-21	
QUALITY SPECIALIST (HQ)	0343-5063	EAS-25	
RAMP CLK AMF	2330-42XX	PS-06	476
REAL ESTATE SPECIALIST	1170-5017	EAS-21	29

REAL ESTATE SPECIALIST	1170-5019	EAS-23	60
REAL ESTATE SPECIALIST	1170-5018	EAS-25	37
RECEIVING AND SHIPPING CLERK	2040-2012	MESC-05	12
RECEIVING CLK FOREIGN AIR MAIL	2340-18XX	PS-06	57
RECEIVING&SHIPNG CLK	2040-20XX	OSD-05	1
RECEPTIONIST	0304-2008	EAS-09	1
RECEPTIONIST CORPORATE PERSNL OPRS	0304-2007	EAS-11	1
RECEPTIONIST OFC OF PMG	0304-2001		1
RECOGNITION SYSTEMS SPECIALIST	0855-4033	EAS-25	3
RECORDER	0986-3006	EAS-17	2
RECORDS CLK-INTERNATIONAL AIR MAIL	2340-10XX	PS-06	79
RECORDS MANAGEMENT CLERK	0301-2032	EAS-07	1
RECORDS SPECIALIST	0343-5057	EAS-25	1
RECORDS SPECIALIST	0343-5058	EAS-23	1
RECORDS SPECIALIST	0343-5059	EAS-21	3
REFERENCE LIBRARIAN	1410-4011	EAS-23	1
REGISTRAR	0301-5239	EAS-20	2
RELOCATION SPECIALIST	0303-5004	EAS-14	2
REPAIR PARTS CATALOGER	2050-5001	EAS-13	2
REQUIREMENTS ANALYST	0345-5091	EAS-25	2
REQUIREMENTS ANALYST	0345-5092	EAS-23	2
REQUIREMENTS ANALYST	0345-5093	EAS-21	2
ASSOCIATE POSTAL HISTORY	0170-5001	EAS-16	2
RESEARCH HISTORIAN	0301-6057		1
RESOURCE MANAGEMENT ANALYST	0343-4022	EAS-23	7
RESOURCE MANAGEMENT ANALYST	0343-5060	EAS-21	4
RESOURCES SPECIALIST	0301-5298	EAS-19	1
RETAIL SALES CLK POSTAL STORES	2320-39XX	PS-05	31
RETAIL SPECIALIST	2345-5030	EAS-16	173
RETIREMENT SPEC PDC	0501-5009	OCS-14	10
RETIREMENT SPEC SR PDC	0501-5008	DCS-16	2
RETIREMENT TECH PDC	0501-5010	DCS-11	13
REVIEW CLK	2315-26XX	PS-06	1,005
RURAL CARR ASSOC/SRV AUX RTE	2325-09XX	RAUX-05	4,700
RURAL CARR ASSOC/SRV REG RTE	2325-07XX		46,102
RURAL CARR ASSOC/SRV VAC RTE	2325-08XX		898
➤ RURAL CARRIER	2325-01XX	RCS-00	46,471
RURAL CARRIER RELIEF	2325-06XX	RAUX-05	2,934
SACK SORTING MACHINEOPR	2315-70XX	PS-06	136
SACK SORTING MACHINE OPR	2315-72XX	MH-05	1,618
SACK SORTING MACHINE OPR	2315-72XX	MH-04	71
SAFETY AND HEALTH ASSOCIATE	0018-5023	EAS-16	1
SAFETY ENGINEER	0803-4002	EAS-24	
SAFETY SPECIALIST	0018-5028	EAS-17	65
SALES SUPPORT SPECIALIST	1140-5048	EAS-23	10
SCALE MECH	3341-02XX	PS-05	2
SCHEDULE CLERK FOREGIN MAILS	2350-06XX	PS-06	2
SCHEDULE EXAMINER VEHICLE RUNS	2330-22XX	PS-07	16
SCHEMES & SCHEDULE CLK	2350-08XX	PS-06	36
SCHEMES EXAMNR	1712-04XX		9
SECRETARY	0318-2010	EAS-11	1
➤ SECRETARY	0318-2041		959
SECRETARY	0318-2042	EAS-14	123
SECRETARY	0318-2043	EAS-16	29
SECRETARY	0318-2045	EAS-18	4
SECRETARY TO THE DPMG	0318-2013	EAS-20	
SECRETARY TO THE EXECUTIVE VP	0318-2044		
SECRETARY-STENOGRAPHER	0318-04XX	PS-05	4
SECRETARY-TYPIST	0318-OSXX		5
SECURITY ENGINEERING TECH	0856-3013	EAS-16	7
SECURITY ENGINEERING TECHNICIAN	0856-3021	EAS-19	48
SECY USPS BD OF GOV	0301-5258	PCES-I	1
SELF SERVICE POSTAL CENTER TECH	2340-48XX	PS-06	828
SENIOR LOCKMAKER	5311-03XX		1
SERVICE REQ SPEC	0345-5021	EAS-18	1
SETUP PRESSMAN (MES)	3803-1002	MESC-06	1

SEWING MACHINE MECHANIC	5312-1001	EAS-11	2
SHEET METAL WORKER	3806-01XX	PS-07	1
SHIPPING COORD	2340-5011	EA -@14	1
SIGN PAINTER-ILLSTR	1020-OSXX	PS-06	29
SIGN PAINTER/LETTERER	4104-04XX	PS-05	33
SOFTWARE PROCESS ADMINISTRATOR	0334-4133	EAS-23	5
SOFTWARE SYSTEMS ADMINISTRATOR	0334-4046	EAS-24	12
SOFTWARE TEST ENGINEER	0854-4001	EAS-25	
SOFTWARE TEST ENGINEER	0854-4002	EAS-23	
SOFTWARE TEST ENGINEER	0854-4003	EAS-21	
SORTATION SYSTEMS SPECIALIST	0801-4063	EAS-25	2
SPACE & PROCUREMENT SPEC	0301-5010	EAS-21	1
SPACE MANAGEMENT SPECIALIST	0342-5013	EAS-17	1
SPACE MGMT SPEC	0342-5010	EAS-20	2
SPEC DEL MESSGR	2310-53XX	PS-05	1,555
SPEC POSTAL CLK	2315-08XX	PS-06	181
SPEC PSTL CLK	2320-31XX		31
SPEC TRANS CLERK	2330-02XX	PS-07	12
SPECIAL ASST - BOG	0318-2047	EAS-22	1
SPECIAL EVENTS COORDINATOR	1010-5002	EAS-25	1
SPECIAL TRANSFER CLERK AMF	2330-43XX	PS-07	9
SPECL SVC CUSTODIAN	5026-02XX	OSO-03	
SPEECHWRITER	1081-5052	EAS-25	2
SPEECHWRITER	1081-5053	EAS-23	2
SR BUDGET/FINANCIAL ANALYST (AREA)	0504-5020		29
SR BUDGET/FINANCIAL ANALYST(DIST)	0504-5021	EAS-21	78
SR CLERK PDC	0301-2072	DCS-06	11
SR COUNSEL	0905-4039	PCES-I	
SR DIRECTOR TECHNOLOGY INTEGRATION	0340-7128		
SR EEO COMPLAINTS PROCESSING SPCLS	0160-5058	EAS-21	2
SR EEO COMPLAINTS PROCESSING SPCLS	0160-5059	EAS-19	62
SR INJURY COMPENSATION SPEC	0230-5071	EAS-19	54
SR INJURY COMPENSATION SPEC	0230-5072	EAS-17	20
SR LABOR RELATIONS SPEC	0233-5015	EAS-21	73
SR LOCKMAKER (MES)	5311-1003	MESC-06	2
SR MAIL PROCESSOR	2315-56XX	PS-05	239
SR MARKUP CLK AUTOM	0301-49XX		81
SR MEDICAL DIRECTOR (AREA OFFICE)	0602-7005	EAS-26	9
SR MGR DISTRIBUTION OPERATIONS	2315-7138	EAS-25	39
SR OPERATIONS ANALYST	2310-5025	EAS-20	63
SR OPERATIONS ANALYST	2310-7039	EAS-22	14
SR PERSONNEL SERVICES SPECIALIST	0201-5115	EAS-21	72
SR PERSONNEL/TRAINING SPECIALIST	0201-5113		13
SR PSDS TECHNICIAN	0301-84XX	PS-07	6
SR SAFETY/HEALTH	0018-5026	EAS-19	60
SR SAFETY/HEALTH	0018-5027	EAS-17	12
SR SAFETY/INJURY COMP SPEC	0018-5024	EAS-19	11
SR SYS ACCT PDC	0510-4046	EAS-22	8
SR TRAINING SPECIALIST	0235-5058	EAS-19	67
SR VP CORPORATE/LEGISLATIVE AFFAIR	0340-7099	PCES-II	1
SR VP FINANCE	0340-7106		1
SR VP GENERAL COUNSEL	0905-7011		1
SR VP MARKETING	0340-7123		1
STAFF COUNSEL/HEARING OFFICER	0905-4038	APS-01	1
STAFF SECRETARY	0318-2039	EAS-09	102
STAFF SECRETARY (PDC)	0318-2040	DCS-09	9
STAMP DISTRIBUTION CLERK-SDN	2345-70XX	PS-06	
STAMP DISTRIBUTION TECHNICIAN	2003-4005	EAS-11	6
STAMP SUPP CLK	2320-03XX	PS-06	99
STATIONARY ENGINEER	5415-01XX	PS-07	71
STATIONARY ENGINEER'	5415-1001	MESC-07	1
STATISTICAL PROGRAMS COORDINATOR	1530-6005	EAS-18	84
STATISTICAL PROGRMS ANALYST (SPSC)	1530-5004	EAS-20	10
STOREKEEPER	2040-21XX	OSD-05	1
STOREKEEPER A (MES)	2040-1008	MESC-05	
STOREKEEPER B (MES)	2040-1009		1

STOREKPR AUTO PARTS	2040-11XX	PS-07	74
STOREKPR AUTO PARTS	2040-11XX	PS-06	111
STRATEGIC BUSINESS SYTEMS PLANNER	0334-4135	EAS-25	1
STRATEGIC PLANNING SPECIALIST	0345-4055	EAS-25	2
SUMMER INTERN	0301-2088	EAS-07	29
SUPPLY AND SERV CLK	2040-2002		1
SUPPLY ASST MES	2005-5006	EAS-15	1
SUPPLY CLERK	2005-2002	EAS-07	2
SUPPLY CLERK	2040-07XX	PS-05	4
SUPPLY CLERK	2040-07XX	PS-04	17
SUPPLY CLERK (MES)	2040-2015	MESC-04	
SUPPLY CLK B	2005-02XX	OSD-04	1
SUPPLY SYSTEMS CATALOGER SR	2050-5004	EAS-19	3
SUPPLY&RPR PTS TECH	2010-5003	EAS-17	7
SUPPORT SERVICES CLERK	0341-3001	EAS-07	5
SUPPORT SERVICES SPECIALIST	0341-5054	EAS-24	1
SUPPORT SERVICES TECHNICIAN	0341-3002	EAS-11	2
SUPPORT SERVICES TECHNICIAN	0341-3003	EAS-17	1
SUPT ACCTBL PAPER DISPOS	0530-6007		5
SUPT ENG A	4704-6007	EAS-11	3
SUPT ENG B	4704-6008	EAS-14	20
SUPT MAIL MTEC	6951-6011	EAS-18	6
TUPT SPECIAL DELIVERY	2310-6025	EAS-20	1
SUPT TRANSPORTATION EQUIP CNTR A	6951-6012	EAS-16	
SUPT WHITE HOUSE MAIL SECT	2305-6038	EAS-20	1
SUPV ACCOUNTING SECT	0540-6045	EAS-21	1
SUPV ACCOUNTING SERVICES	0510-6043	EAS-19	14
SUPV ACCOUNTING SERVICES	0510-6044	EAS-21	68
SUPV ACCOUNTS PAYABLE SECTION	0540-6043		2
SUPV ACCT PAPER	0530-6009	EAS-15	90
SUPV ACCT PAPER DPSTRY	0530-6008		1
SUPV ACCTG (CUSTOMER SERVICE)	0501-6046	EAS-18	1
SUPV ADMIN SERVICES	0341-6032		1
SUPV AREA STAMP DISTRIBUTOR	2003-6026		6
SUPV BUSINESS MAIL ENTRY	2345-6055	EAS-16	220
SUPV CANCELLATION SERVICES (PFSC)	0530-6012	EAS-15	1
SUPV CPTR MAINT LABL PRNTG	0356-6003	EAS-19	2
SUPV CPTR MRK-UP UNIT	0301-6079	EAS-15	308
SUPV CPTR OPER LASL PRNTG	0332-6009	EAS-20	1
SUPV CUST SUPPT	0334-6034	EAS-21	7
SUPV CUSTODIAL SERVICES	3502-6006	EAS-12	3
SUPV CUSTOMER CLAIMS SERV SECT	0540-6021	EAS-18	I
SUPV CUSTOMER SERVICE SUPPORT	0341-6031	EAS-17	206
SUPV CUSTOMER SERVICES	2305-6121	EAS-16	14,520
SUPV CUSTOMER SERVICES (PFSC)	0530-6022	EAS-15	I
SUPV DATA COLL&MAIL CNTRL	0301-6036		5
SUPV DATA CONV	0356-6006		1
SUPV DATA PROCESSING UNIT	0334-6044	EAS-23	1
SUPV DISBURSING	0501-6032	EAS-18	1
SUPV DISBURSING SECTION	0501-6044	EAS-22	1
SUPV DISTRIBUTION OPERATIONS	2315-6076	EAS - 1 6	8,659
SUPV DLVY&COLL	2310-6032	EAS-15	5
SUPV ELEV OPER	5438-6005	EAS-IT	3
SUPV EXAMINATIONS PROCESSING	0301-6101	EAS-18	I
SUPV FOREGN ML PLNG	2305-6028	EAS-17	I
SUPV GENERAL ACCOUNTING SECT	0501-6033	EAS-20	1
SUPV HQ PAYABLES/ASSET CONTROL SEC	0501-6043	EAS-21	1
SUPV INTERNATIONAL ACCOUNTS CENTER	0510-6045		1
SUPV INTL ACCTS	0501-6028	EAS-15	I
SUPV INTL AIRMAIL RECORDS UNIT (B)	2340-6009		4
SUPV INTL AIRML REC UNIT A	2340-6025	EAS-13	1
SUPV VEHICLE SUPPLIES (8)	2003-6024	EAS-16	58
SUPV VEHICLE SUPPLIES ©	2003-6025	EAS-17	13
SUPV WAREHOUSING	696O-6007	EAS-15	9
SUPV WHT HSE DISP UNIT	2315-6040	EAS-13	1
SYS LIAISON SPEC	0334-4073	DCS-21	4

SYSTEM/BUDGET SPECIALIST (DNO)	2330-4037	EAS-17	
SYSTEM/PROCESS ENGINEER	0801-4060	EAS-23	2
SYSTEM/PROCESS ENGINEER	0801-4061	EAS-21	1
SYSTEM/PROCESS ENGINEER	0801-4062	EAS-25	3
SYSTEMS ACCT PDC	0510-4052	EAS-20	4
SYSTEMS ANALYST (MIN/MICRO)	0334-4075	EAS-24	14
SYSTEMS ARCHITECT	0334-6016	EAS-25	1
SYSTEMS DEVELOPMENT SPECIALIST	0334-4107		6
SYSTEMS INTEGRATION ANALYST	0334-5023		1
TAPE LIBRARIAN PDC	0335-2007	DCS-09	9
TECHNICAL DOCUMENTATION SPECIALIST	1083-5003	EAS-24	1
TECHNICAL SERVICES MANAGER	0334-4130	EAS-25	6
TECHNICAL TRAINING SPECIALIST	1712-5021	EAS-17	
TECHNICAL TRAINING SPECIALIST	1712-5022	EAS-18	
TECHNICAL TRAINING SPECIALIST	1712-5023	EAS-20	96
TECHNICAL TRAINING SPECIALIST	1712-5024	EAS-25	5
TECHNICAL WRITER	1083-5002	EAS-19	6
TECHNOLOGY ACQUISITION SPECIALIST	0801-4064	EAS-25	11
TECHNOLOGY ACQUISITION SPECIALIST	0801-4065	EAS-23	9
TECHNOLOGY ACQUISITION SPECIALIST	0601-4066	EAS-21	2
TELE HARDWR TECH	0856-3016	EAS-17	10
TELECOMM HARDWARE TECHNICIAN SR	0334-3062	EAS-19	2
TELECOMMUNICATIONS HARDWARE SPCLST	0334-4041	EAS-21	16
➤ TELECOMMUNICATIONS SPECAILIST(FLD)	0393-5001	EAS-17	82
TELEMARKETING ASSISTANTS	2005-2018	EAS-11	5
TELEPHONE OPERATOR	0382-01XX	PS-04	7
TELEPHONE OPERATOR	0382-2001	EAS-06	1
TELEPHONE OPERATOR	0382-2002	EAS-11	1
TELEPHONE OPERATOR	0382-2003	EAS-09	1
TELEPHONE SALES REPRESENTATIVE	1101-2001	EAS-11	2
TEXT&DATA SVC ASST	0332-2007	EAS-09	10
TIME AND ATTENDANCE CLK	0590-01XX	PS-05	427
TIME&ATTEND CLERK	0590-2006	EAS-08	1
TIRE REPAIRMAN	4504-01XX	PS-05	48
TOOL & PARTS CLK	6904-01XX	PS-06	2
TOOL & PARTS CLK	6904-OIXX	PS-05	838
TOOL AND DIE ENGINEER	3416-4001	EAS-18	1
TOOL AND PARTS CLERK (MES)	6904-1001	MESC-05	1
TOOL SPECIALIST (MES)	3416-3001	EAS-17	1
TOOL/DIE MAKER	3416-1002	EAS-14	3
TORT CLAIMS SPECIALIST (POC)	0540-5013	DCS-16	6
TORT CLAIMS SPECIALIST SR (PDC)	0540-5015	DCS-18	1
TOUR SUPT POSTAL OPERATIONS (A)	2305-6029	EAS-20	17
TRACTOR TRAILER OPER	5756-01XX	PS-06	4,633
TRAFFIC MANAGEMENT SPECIALIST	2330-4035	EAS-19	51
TRAINING TECHNICIAN	1702-5008	EAS-11	a
TRAINING TECHNICIAN	1702-5010		9
TRAINING TECHNICIAN, PEDC	1712-34XX	PS-06	580
TRANSFER CLK	2330-01XX		80
TRANSFER CLK AMF	2330-04XX		448
TRANSLATOR CORRESPONDENCE	1045-02XX	PS-07	7
TRANSPORTATION SPECIALIST	2330-5037	EAS-21	6
TRANSPORTATION SPECIALIST	2330-5038	EAS-23	11
TRANSPORTATION SPECIALIST	2330-5039	EAS-25	12
TREASURER	0505-7059	PCES-I	1
TYPIST	0322-2003	EAS-07	1
TYPIST	0322-2004	EAS-05	
TYPIST LABEL PRINTING	0322-04XX	MH-04	3
VEH OPER MAINT ASST	0341-06XX	PS-06	853
VEH OPNS ASST	2150-OBXX		9
VEH.TRAFFIC CONTROL TECHNICIAN-VCS	2330-75XX	PS-07	1
VEHICLE DISPATCHER	2151-01XX		15
VEHICLE DISPATCHER	2151-01XX	PS-06	4
VEHICLE MAINT PRGM ANALY(AREA OFC)	2150-5009	EAS-23	9
VEHICLE MAINTENANCE ANALYST	1601-08XX	PS-07	49
VEHICLE MAINTENANCE METHODS ANALYS	1601-4022	EAS-21	2

VEHICLE MAINTENANCE METHODS SPCLST	1601-4023	EAS-23	3
VEHICLE MAINTENANCE SPECIALIST	5823-5001	EAS-19	I
VEHICLE MAINTENANCE SPECIALIST(HQ)	1601-4021	EAS-25	
VEHICLE OPRNS ASST BULK MLS	2150-03XX	PS-06	267
VENDING MACHINES MECHANIC	4801-04XX		10
VIDEO PRODUCER	1071-5011	EAS-22	2
VIDEO PROGRAMMING SPECIALIST	1071-5013	EAS-24	1
VIDEOGRAPHER	1071-5012	EAS-21	1
VP AREA OPERATIONS	0340-7130	PCES-II	10
VP CONSUMER ADVOCATE	0301-7013		1
VP CONTROLLER	0505-7062		1
VP DIVERSITY DEVELOPMENT	0340-7102		1
VP ENGINEERING	0340-7104		1
VP FACILITIES	0340-7105		1
VP HUMAN RESOURCES	0340-7103		1
VP INFORMATION SYSTEMS	0340-7108		1
VP LABOR RELATIONS	0340-7109		1
VP LEGISLATIVE AFFAIRS	0340-7127		1
VP MARKETING SYSTEMS	0340-7126		1
VP OPERATIONS REDESIGN	0340-7136		1
VP OPERATIONS SUPPORT	0340-7111		1
VP PRODUCT MANAGEMENT	0340-7124		
VP PURCHASING	0340-7112		1
VP QUALITY	0340-7113	PCES-II	
VP RETAIL	0340-7138		
VP' SALES	0340-7134		1
VP TECHNOLOGY APPLICATIONS	0340-7125		1
VP WORKFORCE PLNG & SERVICE MGMT	0340-7135		1
WAREHOUSING SYSTEMS SPECIALIST	2030-5002	EAS-25	1
➤ WELDER	3704-02XX	PS-06	135
WINDOW CLEANER	3540-01XX	PS-04	5
WINDOW CLK	2320-01XX	PS-05	6,106
WINDOW SVC TECH	2320-29XX	PS-06	2,329
WLRS CONTROL CLERK	0301-94XX	PS-05	4
WORD PROCESSING OPERATOR	0322-2011	EAS-07	19
WORD PROCESSING OPERATOR	0322-2018	DCS-07	6
WORD PROCESSING OPERATOR SR	0322-2010	EAS-09	1
WORD PROCESSING OPERATOR SR	0322-2019	DCS-09	2
WORD PROCESSING TECHNICIAN	0301-4034	EAS-11	4
WORKFORCE PLANNING SPECIALIST	2305-5034	EAS-21	1
WORKFORCE PLANNING SPECIALIST	2305-5035	EAS-23	4
WORKFORCE PLANNING SPECIALIST	2305-5036	EAS-25	5
WORKING GP LDR DIST CLERKS	2315-25XX	PS-06	5
WRITER	1081-5023	EAS-21	1
WRITER/EDITOR	1082-5016	EAS-19	11
WRITER/EDITOR ASSISTANT	1081-5054		1

Chapter Eleven
Postal Inspectors

Postal Inspectors investigate criminal activities involving the security and integrity of the United States Postal System. Approximately 4,000 postal inspectors, evidence technicians, support staff and uniformed postal police ensure the safety of postal employees, the postal system, and the public. The inspection service investigates and enforces over 200 laws covering crimes that may adversely affect the mail, and provides considerable protection against identity theft and consumer fraud. Lee R. Health is the Chief Postal Inspector and the head of the Postal Inspection Service that reports directly to the Postmaster General.[1]

Inspectors carry firearms, make arrests, testify in court, serve subpoenas, and write comprehensive reports. It is a demanding position, often requiring frequent and extended travel and absences from home. Postal Inspectors may work under hazardous conditions, have irregular work hours, and be assigned anywhere in the country.

Beginning January 8, 2003, the U.S. Postal Inspection Service opened Postal Inspector recruitment for college graduates with no previous work experience. If you do not meet one of the special requirements in the *Application for U.S. Postal Inspector,* but have a conferred, four-year college degree with a minimum GPA of 3.0, or an advanced degree, you may apply to become a Postal Inspector. To apply, submit Form 168, *Application for U.S. Postal Inspector,* along with a copy of your college transcript.

Federal law enforcement agents in the GS-1811, Criminal Investigating Series, may apply through an expedited recruitment process by submitting a copy of a current SF 50, *Notification of Personnel Action,* with their application. If the applicant has Top Secret clearance, the process may be further expedited by including a letter from their agency's Security Control Officer certifying the clearance, the date it was originally issued and any updates, as well as copies of SF

---

[1]Fiscal Year 2003 United States Postal Service's Annual Performance Plan, September 2002.

86, *Questionnaire for National Security Positions,* for the original clearance and any updates.[2]

OVERVIEW

The United States Postal Service was founded by Benjamin Franklin and it is one of the oldest federal law enforcement agencies. The Postal Inspection Service has a long, proud and successful history of fighting criminals who attack our nation's postal system and misuse it to defraud, endanger or otherwise threaten the American public. As the primary law enforcement arm of the United States Postal Service, the U.S. Postal Inspection Service is a highly specialized, professional organization performing investigative and security functions essential to a stable and sound postal system.

Congress empowered the Postal Service "to investigate postal offenses and civil matters relating to the Postal Service." Through its security and enforcement functions, the Postal Inspection Service provides assurance to American businesses for the safe exchange of funds and securities through the U.S. Mail; to postal customers of the "sanctity of the seal" in transmitting correspondence and messages; and to postal employees of a safe work environment.

As fact-finding and investigative agents, Postal Inspectors are federal law enforcement officers who carry firearms, make arrests and serve federal search warrants and subpoenas. Inspectors work closely with U.S. Attorneys, other law enforcement agencies and local prosecutors to investigate postal cases and prepare them for court. There are approximately 2,000 Postal Inspectors stationed throughout the United States who enforce over 200 federal laws covering investigations of crimes that adversely affect or fraudulently use the U.S. Mail and postal system.

To assist in carrying out its responsibilities, the Postal Inspection Service maintains a Security Force staffed by 1,400 uniformed Postal Police Officers who are assigned to critical postal facilities throughout the country. The officers provide perimeter security, escort high-value mail shipments and perform other essential protective functions.

The Postal Inspection Service operates five forensic crime laboratories, strategically located in cities across the country. The labs are staffed with forensic scientists and technical specialists, who assist Inspectors in analyzing evidentiary material needed for identifying and tracing criminal suspects and in providing expert testimony for cases brought to trial.[3]

The Postal Inspection Service recruits for the following positions:

➤ Postal Inspectors
➤ Postal Police Officers
➤ Forensic Scientists

➤ Information Technology Specialists
➤ Security Electronic Technicians
➤ Administrative Support Specialists

---

[2] Postal Service web page, http://usps.com/postalinspectors/employmt.htm

[3] Excerpted from the Postal Inspection web page http://usps.com/postalinspectors/missmore.htm

Requirements for U.S. Postal Inspectors[4]

U.S. Postal Inspectors are federal law enforcement officers. Postal Inspectors have investigative jurisdiction in all criminal matters involving the integrity and security of the U.S. Postal Service.

Postal Inspectors investigate criminal, civil, and administrative violations of postal laws and are responsible for protecting the revenue and assets of the Postal Service. Inspectors are required to carry firearms, make arrests, testify in court, serve subpoenas, and write comprehensive reports. They must operate motor vehicles and may undergo moderate to arduous physical exertion under unusual environmental conditions. It is essential that Inspectors be in sound physical condition and be capable of performing vigorous physical activities on a sustained basis. The activities may require Inspectors to perform the following: climb ladders; work long and irregular hours; occupy cramped or crowded spaces for extended periods of time; exert physical force in the arrest, search, pursuit, and restraint of another person; and protect themselves and others from imminent danger.

The duties of the position require the ability to communicate with people from all walks of life, be proficient with firearms, have skills in self-defense, and have the ability to exercise good judgment. Inspectors may be relocated according to the needs of the Service.

The recruitment process is extremely thorough, and there is intense competition for relatively few positions. The recruitment and selection process must be completed prior to the applicant's 37th birthday.

This position is exempt from the Fair Labor Standards Act (FLSA) and does not qualify for overtime compensation. Postal Inspector salaries are based on the Inspection Service Law Enforcement (ISLE) pay system. The ISLE pay grades and steps correspond to the General Schedule (GS) pay scale for law enforcement officers.

Selection procedures include the following:

- ✓ Completion of this application.
- ✓ Written examination, including a business writing test and the 620 Entry Examination (cognitive abilities).
- ✓ Language proficiency test, if applicable.
- ✓ Completion of the *Comprehensive Application Packet.*
- ✓ Assessment Center evaluation of knowledge, skills, and abilities.
- ✓ Medical examination.
- ✓ Polygraph examination.
- ✓ Background suitability investigation.
- ✓ Management interview.
- ✓ Drug screening.

---

[4]Excerpted from Postal Inspector Application, Postal Service Publication 168

✓ Residential basic training program at Potomac, Maryland.

✓ Six-month probation period for nonpostal and nonfederal law enforcement applicants.

Recruiting Standards

Applicants must be U.S. citizens between 21 and 36 years of age and meet all the General Requirements to apply for the position of U.S. Postal Inspector. The Postal Inspection Service is currently seeking individuals that meet the General Requirements, as well as at least one of the Special Requirements, listed below. Applications that do not contain one of the Special Requirements will be kept on file for two years and then purged. If an applicant's skills change during the two-year period, the applicant should contact the Postal Inspection Service.

General Requirements

Applicants must meet the requirements below and undergo a full medical suitability exam to determine fitness to perform the duties of a Postal Inspector, including, but not limited to, the following

- A conferred, four-year degree from an accredited college or university.

- Binocular vision must test 20/40 (Snellen) without corrective lens.

  Uncorrected vision must test at least 20/100 in each eye. Each eye must be corrected to 20/20, with good color identification and discrimination, depth perception, and normal peripheral vision. Radial keratotomy or orthokeratology are not acceptable.

- Hearing loss, as measured by an audiometer, must not exceed 30 decibels

  (A.S.A. or equivalent I.S.O.) in either ear in the 500, 1,000, and 2,000 Hz ranges. The applicant must have the ability to perceive normal speech discrimination.

- In good physical condition (weight proportional to height) and possessing

  emotional and mental stability. Manual dexterity with comparatively free motion of fingers, wrists, elbows, shoulders, hips, and knee joints. Arms, hands, legs, and feet must be sufficiently intact and functioning in order to perform duties satisfactorily.

- No felony convictions (felony charges may also render applicant ineligible).

- No misdemeanor conviction of domestic violence (other misdemeanor charges or convictions may also render applicant ineligible).

- A current, valid state driver's license, held for at least two years.

• Ability to demonstrate these attributes, as measured by the Assessment Center:

✓ Write and speak English clearly.

✓ Schedule and complete activities in a logical, timely sequence.

✓ Comprehend and execute instructions written and spoken in English

✓ Think clearly and comprehend verbal and nonverbal information.

✓ Interact with others to obtain or exchange information or services

✓ Perceive or identify relevant details and associate them with other facts.

Special Requirements

Language Skills

Applicants seeking to enter the recruitment process under the language skills track must have advanced competency in a foreign language deemed as needed by the Postal Inspection Service to meet its investigative mission. The current list is as follows:

Arabic	Armenian	Cambodian	Cantonese
Czech	Dutch	Egyptian	Farsi (Persian)
French Creole	German	Greek (modern)	Haitian
Hebrew	Hindi	Hmong	Indonesian
Italian	Japanese	Korean	Lao
Mandarin	Norwegian	Polish	Portuguese
Punjabi	Russian	Serbo-Croatian	Slovak
Spanish	Swahili	Swedish	Tagalog
Thai	Turkish	Ukranian	Urdu
Vietnamese			

Applicants must pass a formal proficiency test administered by a contractor of the Postal Inspection Service. In addition to the language requirement, applicants in this track must have one year of full-time work experience with the same company or firm within two years of the date of their application.

Specialized Postal Experience

Applicants entering through the specialized postal experience track must be currently employed by the U.S. Postal Service and have at least one year of full-time work experience in one of the postal functional areas designated as critical to the needs of the Postal Inspection Service. Currently, critical needs exist in the following areas:

• Business Mail Entry

• Computer Analysis

• EEO Investigation

• Finance/Budget/Revenue Assurance

• Industrial Engineering

• Information/Computer/LAN Systems

• In-Plant Support

• Labor Relations/Workplace Intervention

• Media Relations

• Operations Support

• Safety/Health/Security/Injury Compensation

In addition, Postal Service supervisors in any functional area (including acting supervisors) with at least one year of supervisory experience will also be eligible under this entry track. A letter from the applicant's immediate supervisor must verify that the applicant has been a supervisor for at least one year. Also, Postal Inspection Service employees and/or contract employees with one year of full-time work experience with the Postal Inspection Service would qualify under this skill track.

Specialized Nonpostal Experience

Applicants seeking consideration under the specialized nonpostal skill track must have experience in one of the areas of expertise designated as critical to the needs of the Postal Inspection Service. The areas are as follows:

Law degree. Candidates must have a Juris Doctorate degree and one year of full-time work experience with the same company or firm within two years of the date of their application.

Certifications in auditing or investigations. Candidates with certifications in accounting, such as Certified Public Accountant (CPA), Certified Management

Accountant (CMA), Certified Internal Auditor (CIA), and Certified Information Systems Auditor (CISA), or investigative certifications in protection, security, or fraud examination, such as Certified Protection Professional (CPP) and Certified Fraud Examiner (CFE), are accepted under this skill track. Applicants in this track must have one year of full-time work experience with the same company or firm within two years of the date of their application. Applicants must also provide proof of certification.

Specialized computer education. Candidates with a four-year degree in one of the following fields: computer science, computer engineering, telecommunications, management information systems, electronic commerce, decision and information science, or computer information systems. Applicants in this track must have one year of full-time work experience with the same company or firm within two years of the date of their application.

Specialized computer expertise. Applicants with at least one year of specialized computer expertise, within the last two years, with the same company or firm and who are currently conducting computer or Internet investigations; computer forensics; or are currently employed in a position specializing in Internet, network, or information systems security for one year.

Certifications in computer systems. Candidates with one of the following certifications and one year of work experience with the same firm within two years of the date of their application: Microsoft Certified Systems Engineer (MCSE), Microsoft Certified Professional + Internet (MCP+I), Cisco Certified Network Professional (CCNP), Certified Novell Engineer (CNE), A+ Certified Computer Technician, Certified Information Systems Security Professional (CISSP), Linux certification, or Sun Systems Certified Administrator.

Law enforcement. Candidates with at least one year of full-time work experience, within the last two years, in the law enforcement field. This includes detectives, criminalists, and polygraph examiners; and patrol, probation, correction, and parole officers. This track excludes clerical or other technical support personnel. Applicants must provide examples of the type of work conducted.

Diversified Experience

To increase competitiveness and acquire a more diversified candidate pool, applicants may enter the recruitment process along a fourth track, which combines higher education and work experience, including:

- Bachelor's degree (B.A. Or B.S. in any field) plus two years of full-time work experience.

- Advanced degree (M.A., M.S., or Ph.D. in any field) plus one year of full-time work experience.

Applicants entering the recruitment process under the diversified experience entry track must have completed full-time work experience with the same company or firm, as stated above, within two years of the date of their application. This includes all U.S. Postal Service employees who have a four-year degree and meet the required minimum work experience.

Application for U.S. Postal Inspectors

You should not apply for this position if you answer "no" to any of questions 1-12. Go to http://www.usps.com/cpim/ftp/pub168/168forms.html to complete this form on line. This form is excerpted from this site.

Last Name		First Name		MI	Mr./Ms.
Home Address	Street Name			City	
State	ZIP Code	Date of Birth		Social Security Number	

blank	YES	NO
1. Have you possessed a valid state driver's license for 2 or more years?	▯	▯
2. Are you willing to investigate sensitive issues in the personal lives of others?	▯	▯
3. Are you willing to undergo a pre-employment investigation of your personal background?	▯	▯
4. Are you between the ages of 21 and 36?	▯	▯
5. Do you have a *conferred* 4-year baccalaureate degree from an accredited college or university? GPA: _____	▯	▯
6. Are you in good physical condition?	▯	▯
7. Are you willing to relocate within the continental United States, Puerto Rico, Alaska, or Hawaii?	▯	▯
8. Are you willing to carry a firearm?	▯	▯
9. Are you willing to work under hazardous conditions?	▯	▯
10. Are you willing to work an irregular schedule, such as nights or weekends, with possible extended absences from home?	▯	▯
11. Are you a U.S. citizen?	▯	▯
12. Are you willing to undergo a pre-employment polygraph exam?	▯	▯

Special Requirements (also see pages 2 through 4)

Second Languages
List any second languages you can speak and translate fluently:

(Must also complete Self-Appraisal of Second-Language Proficiency form)

Specialized Postal Experience	YES	NO
Business Mail Entry		
Computer Analysis		
EEO Investigation		
Financial/Revenue Assurance		
Industrial Engineering		
Information/Computer Systems		
In-Plant Support		
Labor Relations/Workplace		
Intervention		
Media Relations		
Operations Support		
Safety/Health/Security		

Specialized Nonpostal Experience	Yes	No
Law degree		
Certification in auditing or investigations		
Specialized computer education		
Specialized computer expertise		
Certification in computer science		
Law enforcement		

Diversified Experience	Yes	No
Bachelor's degree + 2 years' full-time work		
Advanced degree + 1 year of full-time work		

Privacy Act Statement. The collection of this information is authorized by 39 USC 401 1001. This information may be used to assist in determining your qualification for an appointment. As a routine use, this information may be disclosed to an appropriate government agency, domestic or foreign, for law enforcement purposes; where pertinent, in a legal proceeding to which the USPS is a party or has an interest; to a government agency upon its request when relevant to its decision concerning employment, security clearances, security or suitability investigations, contracts, licenses, grants or other benefits; to a government agency in order to obtain information relevant to a USPS decision concerning employment, security clearances, contracts, licenses, grants, permits or other benefits; to a congressional office at your request; to an expert, consultant, or other person under contract with the USPS to fulfill an agency function; to the Federal Records Center for storage; to the Office of Management and Budget for review of private relief legislation; to an independent certified public accountant during an official audit of USPS finances; to an investigator, administrative judge or complaints examiner appointed by the Equal Employment Opportunity Commission for investigation of a formal EEO complaint under 29 CFR 1614; to the Merit Systems Protection Board or Office of Special Counsel for proceedings or investigations involving personnel practices and other matters within their jurisdiction; and to a labor organization as required by the National Labor Relations Act. Completion of this form is voluntary; however, if this information is not provided, you may not receive full consideration for a position.

All qualified candidates will be considered for employment without regard to race, religion, color, national origin, sex, age, or mental or physical disability.

The law (39 USC 1002) prohibits political and certain other recommendations for appointments, promotions, assignments, transfers, or designations of persons in the Postal Service.

The answers I have provided are accurate to the best of my knowledge.

Applicant's Signature

Date

How did you learn of career opportunities with the U.S. Postal Inspection Service?

If your initial contact was with an Inspection Service employee, list the employee's name and work location:

U.S. Postal Inspection Service
Drug Policy

The U.S. Postal Inspection Service is firmly committed to a drug-free society and workplace. The unlawful use of drugs by Inspection Service employees is not tolerated, and those who apply for employment with the Inspection Service and currently use illegal drugs are considered unsuitable for employment. While we do not condone prior unlawful drug use by applicants, we realize some otherwise qualified applicants may have experimented with illegal drugs at some point in their past.

The following policy sets forth criteria for determining whether applicants' prior use of illegal drugs renders them unsuitable for employment. The policy balances the needs of the Inspection Service to maintain a drug-free workplace and the public integrity necessary to accomplish its law enforcement mission with the desirability of affording employment opportunities to the broadest segment of society, consistent with those needs.

Criteria

• Applicants who have illegally used drugs while in a law enforcement or prosecutorial position with a high level of responsibility or public trust are considered unsuitable for employment.

• Applicants who have deliberately misrepresented their drug history in their application are considered unsuitable for employment.

• Applicants who have sold an illegal drug are considered unsuitable for employment.

• Applicants who have illegally used any drug (other than marijuana) within the past 10 years are considered unsuitable for employment, absent compelling, mitigating circumstances. Applicants are also considered unsuitable if they used drugs other than marijuana on five or more occasions more than 10 years before applying for employment.

• Applicants who have used marijuana within the past five years are considered unsuitable for employment absent compelling, mitigating circumstances. Applicants are also considered unsuitable if they have used marijuana on 15 or more occasions more than five years before applying for employment.

I fully understand the need for the U.S. Postal Inspection Service Drug Policy and I am in compliance with the stated Drug Policy.

Applicant's Signature
Date

**Self-Appraisal of
Second-Language Proficiency**

Applicants must complete this form *ONLY* if claiming a second-language proficiency, as listed under the Special Requirements section.

Last Name	First Name	MI	Mr./Ms.
Date of Birth	Social Security Number	Home Telephone Number	

	YES	NO
1. Which second language do you speak? What is your country of birth?	blank	blank
2. How and where did you learn this language? (Circle all correct answers.) High School College Resident Native Self-Study	YES	NO
3. Can you use a minimum of 30 words in appropriate contexts (not just counting or reciting the days of the week)?	[ ]	[ ]
4. Can you tell someone how to get to the nearest hotel, restaurant, or post office?	[ ]	[ ]
5. Can you ask and tell the time of day, day of the week, and date?	[ ]	[ ]
6. Can you order a simple meal?	[ ]	[ ]
7. Can you negotiate for a hotel room or taxi ride at a just price?	[ ]	[ ]
8. Can you buy an item of clothing or a bus or train ticket?	[ ]	[ ]
9. Can you understand and respond correctly to questions about your nationality, marital status, occupation, date, and place of birth, etc.?	[ ]	[ ]
10. Can you make social introductions and use appropriate leave-taking expressions?	[ ]	[ ]
11. Can you use the language well enough to assist someone who doesn't know the language in coping with situations or problems referred to in items 4 through 10, above?	[ ]	[ ]
12. Can you describe your present or most recent job or activity in some detail?	[ ]	[ ]
13. Can you give detailed information about your family, house, or today's weather?	[ ]	[ ]
14. Can you give and take simple messages over the phone?	[ ]	[ ]
15. Can you hire an employee or arrange for special services (taking care of such details as salary, qualifications, hours, and specific duties)?	[ ]	[ ]

16. Can you give a brief autobiography and describe immediate plans and hopes?   [ ]   [ ]

17. Can you describe the geography of the United States or a familiar location?   [ ]   [ ]

18. Can you describe the purpose or function of the organization you represent?   [ ]   [ ]

19. Do you feel confident understanding native speakers on topics like those under items 12 through 18, and do they understand you (linguistically) at least 80 percent of the time?   [ ]   [ ]

20. Can you use the language well enough to assist someone else who doesn't know the language in coping with situations or problems in items 12 through 18?   [ ]   [ ]

21. Can you speak to educated native speakers on a professional subject and be sure you are communicating what you want to, without obviously amusing or irritating them linguistically?   [ ]   [ ]

22. Can you listen, take notes, and summarize accurately a speech or an informal discussion in your area of special interests, heard on the radio or over a public address system?   [ ]   [ ]

23. Can you cope with such trying linguistic situations as broken-down plumbing, an undeserved traffic ticket, or a serious social blunder made by you or a colleague?   [ ]   [ ]

24. Can you follow a connected discourse on a nontechnical subject, e.g., a panel discussion on the status of women?   [ ]   [ ]

25. Can you serve as an informal interpreter on subjects mentioned in items 21 through 24?   [ ]   [ ]

26. Are there grammatical features of the language that you try to avoid?   [ ]   [ ]

27. Do you sometimes find yourself in the middle of a sentence you cannot finish due to linguistic limitations (grammar or vocabulary)?   [ ]   [ ]

28. Do you find it difficult to follow and contribute to a conversation among native speakers who try to include you in their talk?   [ ]   [ ]

29. Are you afraid you will misunderstand information given to you over the telephone?   [ ]   [ ]

The answers I have given are accurate to the best of my knowledge. I understand I may also be required to complete a language proficiency test.

Applicant's Signature
Date

Completing Your Application

You will also need to complete a PS Form 2591. See Appendix C for blank forms or go to the USPS.com to download an electronic copy. You will be required to take entrance exams such as the writing test and the 620 Entry Examination and a language proficiency test, if applicable. Review

Chapter Seven to prepare for the interview. Postal Inspector jobs are highly competitive and the key to success is to strictly follow the guidance in the application package and to prepare a thorough PS Form 2591.

You can also contact one of the U.S. Postal Inspection Service Division offices for more information. A complete list is provided on the next page. Visit their web site frequently for updated information and new job announcements. You can also visit **http://federaljobs.net** to explore related federal government law enforcement occupations including positions with the new Department of Home Land Security.

U.S. Postal Inspection Service Divisions

Florida Division 3400 Lakeside Dr 6th Fl Miramar FL 33027-3242 (954) 436-7200 Fax: (954) 436-7282	**Newark Division** PO Box 509 Newark NJ 07101-0509 (973) 693-5400 Fax: (973) 645-0600	**Rocky Mountain Division** 1745 Stout St Ste 900 Denver CO 80202-3034 (303) 313-5320 Fax: (303) 313-5351
Gulf Coast Division PO Box 1276 Houston TX 77251-1276 (713) 238-4400 Fax: (713) 238-4460	**Northeast Division** 495 Summer St Ste 600 Boston MA 02210-2114 (617) 556-4400 Fax: (617) 556-0400	**Southeast Division** PO Box 16489 Atlanta GA 30321-0489 (404) 608-4500 Fax: (404) 608-4505
Michiana Division PO Box 330119 Detroit MI 48232-6119 (313) 226-8184 Fax: (313) 226-8220	**Northern California Division** PO Box 882528 San Francisco CA 94188-2528 (415) 778-5800 Fax: (415) 778-5822	**Southern California Division** PO Box 2000 Pasadena CA 91102-2000 (626) 405-1200 Fax: (626) 405-1207
Mid-Atlantic Division PO Box 3000 Charlotte NC 28228-3000 (704) 329-9120 Fax: (704) 357-0039	**Northern Illinois Division** 433 W Harrison St Rm 50190 Chicago IL 60669-2201 (312) 983-7900 Fax: (312) 983-6300	**Southwest Division** PO Box 162929 Ft. Worth TX 76161-2929 (817) 317-3400 Fax: (817) 317-3430
Midwest Division 1106 Walnut St St Louis MO 63199-2201 (314) 539-9300 Fax: (314) 539-9306	**Northwest Division** PO Box 400 Seattle WA 98111-4000 (206) 442-6300 Fax: (206) 442-6304	**Washington Metro Division** PO Box 96096 Washington DC 20066-6096 (202) 636-2300 or (301) 499-7585 Fax: (202) 636-2287
New York Metro Division PO Box 555 New York NY 10116-0555 (212) 330-3844 Fax: (212) 330-2720	**Philadelphia Metro Division** PO Box 7500 Philadelphia PA 19101-9000 (215) 895-8450 Fax: (215) 895-8470	**Western Allegheny Division** 1001 California Ave Rm 2101 Pittsburgh PA 15290-9000 (412) 359-7900 Fax: (412) 359-7682

Chapter Twelve
Civil Service Job Options

The majority of jobs in the postal service are mail carrier and clerk positions. However, like most large corporations the Postal Service requires a broad spectrum of occupations, everything from janitors to engineers, inspectors and administrative occupations of all types. Similar or related occupations exist in the federal civil service. There are over 900 occupational titles in the federal sector which provide abundant employment opportunities for those willing to seek them out.

Consider the numbers. Uncle Sam employs over **2,704,000** workers and hires an average of **305,452** new employees each year to replace workers who transfer to other federal or private jobs, retire, or stop working for other reasons.[1] Average annual salary of all full-time employees exceeded $55,932 as of January 2004. The U.S Government is the largest employer in the United States, hiring two percent of the nation's civilian work force. The Postal Service accounts for approximately 773,000 of Uncle Sam's total employment so many opportunities exist for those who know where to look.

Job hunters will find it easier today to locate job vacancies and to apply for federal jobs. Significant changes were implemented over the past 5 years to streamline the hiring process including simplified optional forms and resumes, and vacancies are posted online by most agencies. You should also be aware that civil service tests are now used for less than 20% of all occupations.

You need to know how to take advantage of the federal hiring system and recent changes to successfully land the job you want in government.

---

[1] The Fact Book, Federal Civilian Workforce Statistics, July 2003

Excellent job opportunities are available for those who know how to tap this lucrative job market. All government hiring is based on performance and qualifications regardless of your sex, race, color, creed, religion, disability, or national origin. Where else can you apply for a high paying entry-level job that offers employment at thousands of locations internationally, excellent career advancement opportunities, plus careers in hundreds of occupations?

This chapter will help you understand and explore civil service job options. Much of this chapter was excerpted from *The Book of U.S. Government Jobs*, 9th edition by Dennis V. Damp.

LOCATING JOB VACANCIES

Job vacancies are listed on the Office of Personnel Management's (OPM's) internet employment web site http://www.usajobs.opm.gov or visit hundreds of agency employment web sites through links on http://federaljobs.net. You can also call OPM's **USAJOBS** hotline 24 hours a day, seven days a week, for updated job information at 1-703-724-1850. Federal Career Opportunities publishes a consolidated list of thousands of federal job vacancies bi-weekly. You can also subscribe to Federal Jobs Central's on-line government job vacancy listings at http://www.fedjobs.com or you can search their on-line jobs database for specific occupations in your area.

Additional avenues are also available to locate open job announcements, including OPM and agency sponsored job hot lines, internet web sites, computer generated data bases, employment services, directories, and periodicals that publish job listings. These resources are listed under Common Job Sources In *The Book of U.S. Government Jobs,* 9th edition.

> Use the links listed on
> **http://federaljobs.net**
> to visit federal agency employment sites.

Individual agency personnel offices should also be contacted to obtain job announcements. Visit http://federaljobs.net for job listings and for direct links to over 200 federal agency recruiting sites.

NATURE OF FEDERAL EMPLOYMENT

The federal government affects the lives of Americans in countless ways.[1] It defends Americans from foreign aggressors, represents American interests abroad, provides important public services, creates and enforces laws, and administers social programs. Americans are aware of the federal government when

---

[1] Career Guide to Industries April 2000, U.S. Department of Labor

they pay their income taxes each year, but they are often unaware of government's influence when they watch a daily weather forecast, purchase fresh and uncontaminated groceries, travel on highways or by aircraft, or make a deposit in a bank. Workers employed by the federal government play a vital role in these and many other facets of American life.

The Constitution of the United States divides the federal government into the legislative, judicial, and executive branches. The executive is by far the largest of the branches, but each is equally vital in running the country. Appendix C provides detailed information for all of the branches of government.

The legislative branch is primarily responsible for forming and amending the legal structure of the nation. Its largest component is Congress, the primary U.S. legislative body, which is made up of the Senate and the House of Representatives. This body includes senators, representatives, and their staff members. The offices and employees of the legislative branch are concentrated in the Washington, D.C. area.

The judicial branch is responsible for interpreting the laws the legislative branch enacts. It employs the smallest number of people of the three branches, and, unlike the legislative branch, its offices and employees are dispersed throughout the country. The highest rulings are made by the Supreme Court, the nation's definitive judicial body. Its decisions generally follow an appeal of a decision made by the one of the regional Courts of Appeal, which hear cases appealed from U. S. District Courts. District Courts are located in each state and are the first to hear cases under federal jurisdiction.

Because of the scope of executive branch responsibility, it employs the vast, majority of federal workers. In 2001, it employed about 97 percent of all federal civilian employees (excluding postal workers). The legislative branch and the judicial branch each employed about one and a half percent.

The executive branch is composed of the Executive Office of the President, the 15 executive cabinet departments, and over 90 independent agencies, each of which has clearly defined duties. The Executive Office of the President is composed of several offices and councils that aid the President in policy decisions. These include the Office of Management and Budget, which oversees the administration of the federal budget; the National Security Council, which advises the President on matters of national defense; and the Council of Economic Advisers, which makes economic policy recommendations.

Each of the 15 executive cabinet departments oversees a vital element of American life. They are referred to as cabinet departments because the highest departmental official of each, the Secretary, is a member of the President's cabinet. The Department of Defense is by far the largest, employing roughly 1.5 million military personnel on active duty in addition to 670,568 civilian workers in 2001. It is responsible for providing the military forces that protect the country and contains the Departments of the Army, the Navy, the Air Force, and a number of smaller agencies.

The other executive departments are not nearly as large as Defense, primarily because their duties do not usually require as many workers. Each, listed by employment size, is described below.

Veterans Affairs (223,137 employees). Administers programs to aid U.S. veterans and their families, runs the veterans' hospital system, and operates our national cemeteries.

Treasury (159,274 employees). Regulates banks and other financial institutions, administers the public debt, prints currency, and performs law enforcement in a wide range including counterfeiting, tax, and customs.

Agriculture (100,084 employees). Promotes U.S. agriculture domestically and internationally and sets standards governing quality, quantity, and labeling of food sold in the U.S.

Homeland Security - Incorporates 22 agencies from other departments. Visit their web site at **http://www.dhs.gov** for more information. Staffing for this department will come from the agencies that are transferring functions to this newly formed department.

Justice (126,711 employees). Enforces federal law, prosecutes cases in federal courts, and runs Federal prisons.

Interior (72,982 employees). Manages federal lands including the national parks and forests, runs hydroelectric power systems, and promotes conservation of natural resources.

Transportation (64,131 employees). Sets national transportation policy, runs the Coast Guard, plans and funds the construction of highways and mass transit systems, and regulates railroad, aviation, and maritime operations.

Health and Human Services including SSA (63,323 employees). Sponsors medical research, approves use of new drugs and medical devices, runs the Public Health Service, and administers the Social Security and Medicaid programs.

Commerce (39,151 employees). Forecasts the weather, charts the oceans, regulates patents and trademarks, conducts the census and compiles statistics, and promotes U.S. economic growth by encouraging international trade.

State (28,054 employees). Runs the nation's embassies and consulates, issues passports, monitors U.S. interests abroad, and represents the U.S. before international organizations.

Energy (15,689 employees). Coordinates the national use and provision of energy, oversees the production and disposal of nuclear weapons, and plans for future energy needs.

Labor (16,016 employees). Enforces laws guaranteeing fair pay, workplace safety, equal job opportunity; administers unemployment insurance; regulates pension funds; and collects economic data.

Housing and Urban Development (10,154 employees). Funds public housing projects, enforces equal housing laws, and insures and finances mortgages.

Education (4,581 employees). Provides scholarships, student loans, and aid to schools.

Numerous independent agencies often perform tasks that fall between the jurisdictions of the executive departments, or that would be more efficiently executed by an autonomous agency. Although the majority of them are fairly small, employing fewer than 1,000 workers (many employ fewer than 100 workers), some are quite large.

National Aeronautics and Space Administration (18,850 employees). Oversees aviation research and exploration and research beyond the Earth's atmosphere.

Environmental Protection Agency (17,968 employees). Runs programs to control and reduce pollution of the nation's water, air, and lands.

General Services Administration (13,921 employees). Manages federal government property and records.

Some smaller, but well known independent agencies include the *Peace Corps*, the *Securities and Exchange Commission*, and the *Federal Communications Commission*.

WORKING CONDITIONS

Due to the broad scope of federal employment, almost every working condition found in the private sector can also be found in the federal government.[1] Most white-collar employees work in office buildings, hospitals, or laboratories, and most of the blue-collar workforce can be found in factories, warehouses, shipyards, military bases, construction sites, or national parks and forests. Work environments vary from the comfortable and relaxed to the hazardous and stressful, such as those experienced by law enforcement officers, astronauts, or air traffic controllers.

The vast majority of federal employees work full time, often on flexible "flexitime" schedules, which allow workers to tailor their own work week, within certain constraints. Some agencies also have "flexiplace" programs, which allow selected workers to perform some job duties at home or from regional centers.

The duties of some federal workers require they spend much of their time away from the offices in which they are based. Inspectors and compliance officers, for example, often visit businesses and work sites to ensure laws and regulations are obeyed. Few travel so far that they are unable to return home each night. Some federal workers, however, frequently travel long distances, spending days or weeks away from home. Auditors, for example, may spend weeks in distant locations.

EMPLOYMENT

In 2003, the federal government employed 2,703,000 workers, or about 2 percent of the nation's workforce. Because of the scope of government work, it employs workers in every major occupational group. Workers are not employed in

[1] Career Guide to Industries, U.S. Department of Labor, April, 2000

the same proportions in which they are employed throughout the rest of the economy, however (table 1-2). Because of the analytical and sometimes highly technical nature of many government duties, a much higher proportion of professionals and technicians are employed in the federal government compared with most industries. Conversely, the government sells very little, so it employs relatively few sales workers.

Table 1-2
Percent distribution of employment in the federal government and the private sector by major occupational group

Occupational Group	Federal Government	Private Sector
Total	*100*	*100*
Executive, administrative, and managerial	17.6	13.9
Professional speciality	30.8	13.7
Technicians and related support	8.3	3.8
Marketing and sales	0.7	10.4
Administrative support, including clerical	22.5	17.6
Service	6.8	15.5
Agriculture, forestry, fishing, and related	0.7	2.1
Precision production, craft, and repair	9.2	10.7
Operators, fabricators, and laborers	3.4	13.0

Although most federal departments and agencies are based in the Washington, D.C. area, only 16 percent of all federal employees worked in the vicinity of the nation's Capital. In addition to federal employees working throughout the United States, a small number are assigned overseas in embassies or defense installations.

OCCUPATIONS

The federal government employed workers in almost every occupation in 2001, including those found only in government, such as legislators or judges. About 71 percent of all federal workers were employed in professional specialty, administrative support, or executive, administrative, and managerial occupations.

Approximately 41 percent of all federal workers have a Bachelor's Degree or higher degree. For many jobs, any 4-year bachelor's degree will suffice, but some positions require a specific degree. A graduate or professional degree is necessary to enter some professional jobs.

Professional specialty and executive, administrative, and managerial occupations

Together, professional specialty and executive, administrative, and managerial occupations comprise about 47 percent of federal employment. Almost all professional specialty jobs require a 4-year college degree. Some, such as engineers, physicians and life and physical scientists require a bachelor's or higher degree in a specific field of study.

Engineers, such as chemical, civil, aeronautical, industrial, electrical, mechanical, and nuclear engineers, work in every department of the executive branch. In general, they apply physical laws toward design problems, such as building bridges or computer systems. Although most are employed in the Department of Defense, a significant number work in the National Aeronautic and Space Administration and the Department of Transportation.

Computer scientists, computer engineers, and systems analysts are employed throughout the government. They write computer programs, analyze problems related to data processing, and keep computer systems running smoothly.

Health professionals include registered nurses and physicians, with more than 3 out of 4 of these workers employed by the Department of Veterans Affairs (VA) at one of many VA hospitals. Other professionals included life scientists, such as biologists and foresters and conservation scientists, who research problems dealing with life processes, and physical scientists, such as geologists, meteorologists, and physicists, who examine the state of the earth and research physical phenomena. The Department of Agriculture employs the vast majority of life scientists, but physical scientists are distributed evenly throughout government.

Executive, administrative, and managerial workers are primarily responsible for overseeing operations. Legislators are included in this group, and are responsible for passing and amending the nation's laws. Because managers are generally promoted from professional occupations, most have at least a bachelor's degree. These workers include many types of managers who, at the highest levels, may head federal agencies or programs, such as general managers, top executives, and middle managers, who oversee one activity or aspect of a program.

Other executive, administrative, and managerial workers provide management support. Accountants and auditors prepare and analyze financial reports, review and record revenues and expenditures, and check operations for fraud and inefficiency. Inspectors and compliance officers enforce federal regulations governing everything from aircraft to food. Tax examiners determine and collect taxes. Management support workers include purchasing agents, who handle federal purchases of supplies, and management analysts, who study government operations and systems and suggest improvements.

Administrative support occupations

Almost one federal worker in four falls into this category, not counting the U.S. Postal Service. Administrative support workers usually only need a high school diploma, though any further training or experience, such as a junior college degree, or at least two years of relevant work experience, is an asset. Administrative support workers aid management staff with administrative duties. They include secretaries; bookkeepers; accounting, auditing, stock, traffic, shipping, and receiving clerks; receptionists; and switch-board operators.

Technicians and related support occupations

Technicians make up about eight percent of the federal workforce. They may aid professionals in research, analysis, or law enforcement. Often their tasks and skills are quite specialized, as with air traffic controllers. As a result, many technicians are required to have some vocational training or extensive work experience; many have two-year associate degrees.

Engineering technicians, who may work either directly with engineers or by themselves, are common. Other technician occupations include health technicians, such as dental hygienists and radiologists, who have specialized health service jobs, or legal assistants, who aid judges and attorneys.

Other occupations

Most federal jobs in other occupations require no more than a high school diploma, although some departments and agencies may prefer workers with some vocational training or previous experience. For instance, some precision production workers like mechanics or machinists, or service workers such as chefs or barbers need some specific training or experience. The federal government also offers apprenticeship programs, which train unskilled workers on the job for some skilled occupations.

Compared to the economy as a whole, service workers are relatively scarce in the federal government. Nearly half of all federal workers in these occupations are firefighters, police officers, and correctional officers. These workers protect the public from crime, oversee federal prisons, and stand ready to intervene in emergencies.

Over half of the federally employed precision production, craft, and repair occupations are mechanics, such as vehicle and mobile equipment mechanics, who fix and maintain all types of motor vehicles, aircraft, and heavy equipment, and electrical and electronic equipment operators. Other precision production workers are skilled in construction trades, such as painters, plumbers, and electricians.

The federal government employs relatively few workers in fabricator, operator, and laborer occupations; agriculture, forestry, fishing, and related occupations; and marketing and sales occupations.

OUTLOOK

Employment in the federal government was projected to decline by nine percent through the year 2008 due to efforts to balance the Federal budget, however, with the many new jobs now required to fight the war on terror this trend may reverse. Considerable opportunities remain in the federal sector. Uncle Sam hires an average of 305,342 new employees each year to replace workers who transfer to other federal or private jobs, retire, or stop working for other reasons. Competition will be keen for many federal positions, especially during times of economic uncertainty when workers seek the stability of federal government employment. The distribution of employment will change, however, toward a higher proportion of professional, technical, and managerial workers.

Factors that influence federal government staffing levels are unique. Unlike any other employer in the nation, the Congress and President determine the government's payroll budget prior to each fiscal year, which runs from October 1 through September 30 of the following year. Whether operating at a surplus or a deficit, the federal government generally adheres to its payroll budget. As a result, federal employment is not affected by cyclical fluctuations in the economy, as are employment levels in many construction, manufacturing, and other private sector industries; employment levels tend to be relatively stable in the short run.

Each presidential administration and Congress may have different public policy priorities, resulting in greater levels of federal employment in some programs and declines in others. Layoffs, called "reductions in force", have occurred in the past; however, they are uncommon and generally affect relatively few workers.

After major decreases following the dissolution of the Soviet Union, Department of Defense civilian employment, which makes up almost 40 percent of federal civilian employment, is expected to level off. Employment in many other agencies is expected to decrease. However, there will be numerous employment opportunities even in agencies in which employment is contracting due to the need to replace workers who leave the workforce, retire or obtain employment elsewhere. Furthermore, some occupations, especially professional, technical, and managerial occupations, will be in demand even as employment in other occupations is being reduced.

Employment of blue-collar workers will decrease the most because many of their functions will be contracted out to private companies. As in other industries, employment of some administrative support and clerical workers in the federal government will also be adversely affected by the growing use of private contractors for many functions. In addition, computerization will continue to eliminate many clerical positions.

GETTING STARTED

The Book Of U.S. Government Jobs by Dennis V. Damp is an excellent resource that will steer you to highly informative government and private sector Internet web sites, electronic bulletin boards, self-service job information centers, telephone job hotlines, and it explores all facets of the federal job search. This book is available at most libraries or you can order a copy by calling 1-800-782-7424. This book will complement your federal job search.

Readers will find up-to-date information on how the federal employment system works from an insider's perspective, how to locate job announcements through various methods, and complete a thorough application package. You'll learn about special hiring programs for the physically challenged, veterans, students, and scholars, thousands of job opportunities, Civil Service Exam requirements, overseas jobs, how to complete your employment application, and much more. Appendix A provides a comprehensive checklist that will take you through the entire federal employment process.

The three appendices include an easy to use federal job check list, complete lists of federal occupations, and comprehensive agency summaries and contact lists including employment office addresses and phone numbers.

This book will guide you step-by-step through the federal employment process, from filling out your first employment application to locating job announcements, networking resources and hiring agencies. Follow the guidelines set forth in this book to dramatically improve your chances of landing a federal job.

PAY & BENEFITS

Job security and excellent pay are among the top reasons most seek federal employment. There are eight predominant pay systems. Approximately half of the workforce is under the *General Schedule (GS)* pay scale, twenty percent are paid under the *Postal Service rates*, and about ten percent are paid under the *Prevailing Rate Schedule (WG) Wage Grade classification*. The remaining pay systems are for the *Executive Schedule, Foreign Service, Special Salary Rates, Nonappropriated Fund Instrumentalities pay scales*, and *Veterans Health Administration*.

General Schedule (GS) pay for locality area "Rest of U.S." pay varies from the GS-1 level at $14,757 per annum to $113,674 per annum at the top GS-15 grade (not including locality pay adjustments). The Senior Executive Service salary tops out at $158,000 per annum. The president adjusts federal salaries to levels that are competitive with the private sector. The average annual salary for full time non-postal employees increased to $55,932 in 2004.[1] Starting pay depends on the level of experience, education and complexity of the position applied for. A complete General Schedule (GS) pay schedule is available at http://federaljobs.net/.

---

[1] Profile of Federal Civilian Employees, January 2004, Central Personnel File.

Each GS grade has ten pay steps. Currently, a GS-9 starts at $36,478 for step one and reaches $47,422 per year at step ten (not including locality pay adjustments). At the GS-9 grade, each pay step adds $1216.00 to the annual salary. Pay steps are earned based on time in service and the employee's work performance. General Schedule employees are referred to as white collar workers under the federal classification system. Approximately 13.3 percent of total federal non-postal employment is classified under the Wage Grade (WG) blue collar pay schedules. See Appendix D for a complete list of occupations.

There are a number of special compensation systems that augment the general schedule. Physicians receive signing bonuses for a one year continued-service agreement and additional bonuses for two years. The Federal Aviation Administration pays employees in safety related careers under a "Core Compensation" multi payband system. Organizations such as the General Accounting Office (GAO), NASA, and the Commerce Department's National Institute of Standards and Technology are either exempt from or have exceptions to the GS pay system.

Pay reform has been implemented to offset competitive hiring pressures from private industry and local governments. Agencies can now offer allowances and bonuses when recruiting, match salary within certain limits, and they are authorized to pay interview travel expenses under certain conditions.

LOCATING A JOB

Fourteen cabinet departments and over 100 independent agencies comprise the federal government system. These departments and agencies have offices in all corners of the world. The size of each agency varies considerably. The larger the agency the more diverse the opportunities. These large agencies hire a broad spectrum of occupations, professional and blue collar.

If you desire to travel, the government offers abundant opportunities to relocate within the 50 states and throughout the world.

If you desire to travel, the government offers abundant opportunities to relocate within the 50 states and throughout the world. Chapter 7 provides information on thousands of overseas employment opportunities. Twelve federal agencies and departments offer employment abroad for over 60,000 U.S. citizens. The Department of Defense Dependent Schools system employees hundreds of teachers for military dependent schools overseas.

Washington, DC has the largest number of federal workers, 322,633, and Vermont the least with 2,853 workers. All of the 315 Metropolitan Statistical Areas (MSAs) in the U.S. and Puerto Rico have federal civilian employment as listed in the Central Personnel Data File. Small towns and rural areas outside of MSA's had approximately 18 percent of total non-postal federal workers.[1] The actual number of federal civilian employees is greater than the above figures. The Defense Intelligence Agency, Central Intelligence Agency, and the National Security Agency do not release this data.

EDUCATION REQUIREMENTS

In the federal government 59 percent of all workers do not have a college degree. The level of required education is dependent upon the job applied for. Each job announcement lists needed skills and abilities including education and work experience. However, the more education and work experience that you have the more competitive you will be when ranked against other applicants. A sample qualification statement is presented in Chapter 2 for Administration and Management Positions. The majority of positions within the government have a published qualifications standard similar to the provided example.

You can review and down-load a specific qualification standard on-line at http://federaljobs.net or visit your local Federal Depository Library. Many large college and private libraries are designated depository status and they can help you locate specific government publications including the Qualification Standards Handbook For General Schedule Positions.

SUMMARY

It took me two years to land my first competitive federal civil service job. I was not aware of the employment options available at that time and I simply sent written requests for job announcements every two weeks to the local OPM office. Today there are many options available through special emphasis hiring, case and direct hire authority, Outstanding Scholar Programs, student employment, and internships, to name a few. Also, use the many Internet sites that provide links to key job lists and informational resources such as http://federaljobs.net. Take advantage of as many of the programs and varied positions that you qualify for to expedite your career search. Don't give up or get overly frustrated with the paperwork that is required when applying for federal employment. There are software programs available today such as Quick and Easy Federal Jobs Kit and some jobs now accept on-line application for initial screening. Finally, I must add that it is unwise to get angry with the process; instead of getting mad, **GET INVOLVED.**

---

[1] Federal Civilian Employment By State & Metropolitan Areas (CPDF)

Appendix A
Job Hunter's Checklist

WHAT TO DO NOW

❑   Review Chapters One, Two and Three to fully understand the Postal Service job market, employee benefits, salary, and how they hire. Also review:

    ✔ Chapter Eight for Veteran's Hiring programs.

    ✔ Chapter Five for exam overviews. (All Tested Occupations)

    ✔ Chapter Six for the new **473 / 473-C Postal Exam Study Guide**

    ✔ The Occupation Directory in Chapter Ten.

    ✔ Chapter Eleven for Postal Inspector Jobs.

    ✔ Chapter Twelve for Related Federal Civil Service Occupations.

❑   Review the Postal Service occupations Listed in Chapter Three, Nine and Ten. Also review Chapter Eleven and Twelve for other job options. These chapters provide complete lists of postal jobs that you may qualify for — including job descriptions for over 40 job categories.

❑   Visit the following web site to locate examination announcements for mail carrier and clerk positions in your area:

    ✔ http://uspsapps.hr-services.org/ *(Job Vacancy Lists)*
    Note: *Apply on-line at this site to take tests that are scheduled for your area. If your area is not currently testing visit this site every week or so to check for updated testing dates.*

❑   See Chapter Four for a national list of Customer Service District Offices that you can contact for more information

❑   Contact the Postal Service's "National Job Listings" web site to locate corporate job listings that don't require entrance exams. Also, contact regional and local postal facilities including Customer Service District Sales Offices, General Mail Facilities, Sectional Center Facilities, Management Sectional Centers, or Bulk Mail Centers in your area. Don't forget to talk with the Postmaster at local the Post Office.

✔   http://usps.com/employment/ *(National corporate job listings)*

✔   http://postofficejobs.info/ *(Career Center)*.

✔   1/866-999-8777 *(Postal Service Job Hot Line)*
Note: *You must have a job announcement number to use the phone service.*

✔   http://usps.com/postalinspectors/employmt.htm
(Postal Inspector's website)

❑   Locate your school transcripts, military records, awards, and professional licenses. Collect past employment history; salary, addresses, phone numbers, dates employed, for the application. Use the forms printed in Appendix B to draft your application.

APPLYING FOR A JOB

❑   When you locate a job announcement it will list all required application forms and exams. You can apply online for exams or by phone. Blank application forms are in Appendix C.

❑   If no vacancies exist for your specialty, visit the listed web sites frequently to check on updated postings. The Postal Service also advertises in local newspapers and at State Employment Offices. You can also call or write your local District Office's Human Resource department to find out when tests may be scheduled for your area. Consider getting your foot in the door by taking the 473 Battery Test or any other written exam. Once hired you will have the opportunity to apply internally for vacancies in other occupations.

❏ Complete and sign **ALL** application forms received with the announcement including the PS Form 2591. *(Print or type them if possible)*. Follow all instructions.

Note: Corporate job vacancy announcements require applicants to complete write-ups for required knowledge and abilities. You **MUST** complete these statements on separate sheets addressing each requirement. If you neglect to do this your application may not be considered. *The Book of U.S. Government Jobs*, 9th edition by Dennis Damp provides guidance and recommendations on how to write Knowledge, Skills and Abilities statements. This book is available at many libraries or you can order a copy by calling 1-800-782-7424. It is also available through most bookstores and Amazon.com.

❏ Retain a copy of your application and all other forms required in the announcement. These copies can be used for other bids.

✔ You can copy your application and use it for other jobs. You must have an original signature on the application and the correct job title and announcement number. Therefore, type your application and don't enter this data until after you have copied the completed form. Then, on the copy you are sending to the Postal Service, sign it, add the job number and name.

❏ Send in the completed forms to the address specified on the announcement. Applications must be postmarked by no later than the closing date of the announcement for your application to be considered.

ADDITIONAL RESOURCES

NOTE: Internet access is required to contact the following services. You must have Internet access through a local provider or an online service such as America Online. Many libraries now offer on-line connectivity to their patrons.

❏ **http://federaljobs.net Federal Civil Service Jobs & Career Center** - One of the most popular federal employment sites on the internet today with over 100,000 visitors each month. Visit this site to explore federal job options including jobs with the USPS.

❑   **http://postofficejobs.info** **Post Office Jobs & Career Center** - A popular site for exploring Postal Service careers and for direct links to key Postal Service employment information.

❑   **http://opm.gov** **Office of Personnel Management (OPM)** This site posts thousands of job vacancies for the federal government,. Visit this site to search for related civil service job vacancies in your area. Some jobs can be applied for online. You can also register for email notification of job vacancies for specific job titles and occupational groups. Includes pay tables and benefits information.

❑   **http://www.usps.com** **Postal Service Home Page** - This highly informative service offers general information about the USPS and includes all recent press releases. Also visit their employment page listed above.

RESULTS

❑   Your application will be processed and results returned to you within several weeks. You will receive a *Notice* informing you of your eligibility and scheduled testing date and location. If rated eligible, your name will be placed on the list of eligible applicants for that position. Selected applicants must:

- ✔   Meet basic qualifications
- ✔   Score high on the exam (if required), and
- ✔   Successfully complete an interview

THE INTERVIEW

❑   Prepare for the interview. Review chapter Seven for guidance on how to present yourself and prepare for the interview. Most Postal Jobs books completely ignore the interview phase. If you don't impress the selecting officials, you may be passed over for the position.

Appendix B
Corporate Positions

Corporate positions include management and supervision, administrative, professional and technical occupations. Jobs that are open to the general public are listed on the Postal Service's web site http://usps.com/employment/. The jobs are advertised in the following categories, with a sampling of specific occupations:

- Engineering
  - Electrical
  - Electronic
- ERM/HR
  - Educational Psychologist
  - Training
  - Human Resources
- Facilities
  - Architect Engineer
- Finance
  - Accountant
  - Economist
  - Mathematical Statistician
- Information Technology
  - Business System Analyst
  - Information System Specialist
  - Systems Analyst
- Inspection Service
  - Security Architect/Engineer
- Marketing
  - Customer Service Support Analyst
- Network Operations
  - Transportation Specialist
- Engineering

When you apply for a corporate position with the Post Office, recruitment is similar to the federal civil service application process. The applicant is rating on his/her work experience, education, special knowledge, skills and abilities (KSAs). Job announcements are advertised on the USPS web site and the applicant must follow the job announcement application instructions precisely to be considered for the position. Any omissions can cause your application to be rejected. Many highly qualified applicants are excluded because of administrative errors or omissions.

This chapter guides you through the application process so that you can write an application or Postal Service resume that will get the attention of the selecting official. The PS Form 2591, "*Application for Employment*," is required when applying for most jobs. Resumes are also accepted however, you must be certain to include all of the information in your resume that is currently on the PS Form 2591 or they may not accept your application. Applicants must prepare their resumes and applications in accordance with specific guidelines. The Postal Service has developed the following enhanced application services:

✎   Diverse methods to collect information from job applicants – written, telephone, and automated techniques

✎   Applicant choices in how they submit written applications

✎   Updated PS 2501 application and an acceptable resume format

✎   Web site for job vacancies, http://usps.com/employment

✎   Customer Service District Sales Offices (See Chapter Four)

✎   Online applications for postal exams

All of the required information is currently included in the PS form 2591 application. You can use the sample application in Appendix B to draft your application ahead of time or download a copy of the form from the Postal Service's web site or from http://federaljobs.net/.

LOCATING JOB ANNOUNCEMENTS

Corporate jobs are advertised at http://usps.com/employment. Go directly to the *"corporate Jobs"* listing and following the links to the currently available job announcements. Jobs are listed in the categories noted on the previous page. The Postal Service posts announcements in federal, state, and municipal buildings open to the public, they advertise on the Internet, in local newspapers, and conduct and participate in job fairs, open houses, or other activities to reach the community.[1] I also suggest that if you visit the web site noted above and don't find jobs in occupations you are qualified for call the human resource department at your local customer Service District Office (see Chapter Four) and ask them when they anticipate hiring in your occupation.

You may also wish to consider related occupations to get your foot in the door. For example, if you are interested in an administrative position and the Postal Service is scheduled to give the 473 Battery Test for Carrier and Clerk positions,

---

[1] Handbook EL-312, September 2001, paragraph 223.12

apply to take the exam. If you are selected for the position you will have more opportunities within the system since most administrative jobs are first advertised to current employees. If none meet the qualification standards for the position or there are insufficient bidders, the position is then advertised to the local public. You may also find related lower paying jobs that will get your foot in the door as well. It all depends on what you can afford to do in this case. However, before deciding look at target occupations and salaries to determine if it will be worth your while to sacrifice initial salary for greater future salary and upward mobility potential.

APPLYING FOR JOBS

Many talented job seekers are frustrated by the paperwork and give up prematurely. If you take the time to thoroughly complete your application and seek out all available job vacancies, your chances for employment will increase substantially. All forms and KSA statements listed in the job announcement must be submitted with your package. If you need forms, most can now be downloaded off the Internet.

Don't limit your search to applying for only one job vacancy. Seek out all available job vacancies and continue to send in applications with every opportunity. The more often you apply the greater your chances. If you are having difficulty identifying jobs that fit your training, experience, and abilities, review the qualification standards in this book and view the Occupational directory in Chapter Ten.

COMPLETING YOUR APPLICATION

If you look at most Postal job announcements, the section titled "HOW TO APPLY" states, *"Applicants, must complete and submit a resume or Form 2591, Application for Employment, plus a separate statement of qualifications for each knowledge, skill, or ability (KSA) to the application address on or before the closing date."* Even though they permit the submission of a resume I suggest that you complete the PS Form 2591. This form includes critical data that the personnel staff uses to rate your application against other applicants. In the competitive federal civil service your resume must include 42 specific data elements to be considered. Therefore, your standard private sector resume will more than likely not include all required data. It doesn't hurt to submit both, but the Postal Service will focus on the PS Form 2591 since it includes the required information that is needed to apply for postal jobs.

Step One

Collect key data for your application. You will need the name, address, and contact phone numbers for previous and present employers. Locate or start compiling work histories, salary for each position, starting and stop dates. You will also need transcripts from schools and the dates attended including major undergraduate subjects. Include special qualifications such as licences, skills with machines, patents or inventions, publications, honors, awards and fellowships received. Use the PS 2591 as your guide. Make up a folder and compile needed data for when you sit down and start your application.

You should also include volunteer work, temporary details and other significant activities that were not work related. For example, if you managed a little league team you could capture management and organizational skill from that activity. Include this as a separate "Work History" entry under Section "C" on the application.

Step Two

Review the job announcement throughly before filling our your application. Highlight all keywords under the "Requirements" statements. Underline words that identify the key duties of the position. Do this with all job announcements and then incorporate relevant key words and duties in your "Work History" description of duties, responsibilities and accomplishments in your PS Form 2591 or resume work descriptions. If you have that skill or a related skill, include it in your application. The more you focus your application to key duties and responsibilities the higher your rating will be. This will also help you complete required KSA Statements.

Step Three

Complete the PS Form 2591 and type the form if possible. The electronic form is available in PDF format online. A PDF interactive form is currently being developed so that you will be able to type the data directly onto the form instead of using a standard typewriter. It should be available shortly online at our *Post Office Jobs Career Center* located at http://postofficejobs.info/.

Detailed work descriptions are included on the form. However, only four data blocks are devoted to present and past work history. You should go back a minimum of 10 years or to your 16th birthday, whichever is later. Don't limit your work history to your past four employers. Expand it to include any and all related work history, relevant volunteer and community service experience or temporary details that showcase required knowledge, skills and abilities including military experience if applicable. Use blank sheets of paper to expand your work descriptions and include your name, social security number, date and job experience at the top of each sheet.

When describing your experience use bullets to capture key KSAs. You have to show what you actually accomplished to achieve the stated skill or knowledge. Many who apply for federal jobs simply restate the skill, duty or accomplishment instead of describing how they attained them. If you don't provide specific examples you won't receive points for those items. Take your time and be thorough.

Step Four

In most cases you will be required to submit a detailed description of how you achieved each knowledge, skills and abilities statement listed on the job announcement. If your qualifications match the requirements, submit a separate sheet addressing each KSA along with your PS Form 2591 or resume to the address listed on the announcement.

Understanding and Completing KSAs

List each KSA title on a separate sheet of plain bond paper, and follow it with a description of what you did to meet this KSA. Include in each KSA any of these relevant elements:

- Education
- Training
- Experience
- Volunteer work
- Outside Activities
- Awards, Licenses, etc.

You must include a narrative that indicates the degree to which you possess the KSA and include as many of the bullets listed above that apply in that narrative. For each work example or accomplishment listed, describe the situation, problem, or objective of the assignment, what was done, and the results obtained. Following the narrative, the applicant must indicate the duration (date) of the activity, and the name and telephone number of a person who can verify the information provided, if available. Applicants may attach copies of any relevant documents that will help substantiate their statements, such as performance evaluations, awards, or work products. The applicant's narrative must indicate exactly how these documents relate to the KSA. DO NOT INCLUDE SUCH DOCUMENTS UNLESS THEY ARE DIRECTLY RELEVANT.

Formatting Your KSAs

You can format your KSAs in a narrative form starting with "I" or use bullets that start with a forceful verb such as organized, directed, managed, coordinated, analyzed, or conducted to provide action to your statements. If you don't refer directly to an experience block be sure to summarize the experience and provide the time and place where you performed that function. If you are applying for a supervisory position mention the number of people that you supervised, their status such as part time or full time and pay grade if applicable.

After writing your KSAs review them a number of times asking yourself "What did I do," "When did I do it," "Where did I perform these functions" and don't forget the proverbial question, "How often and how much did I do it." If you didn't answer these questions edit your work until it is included. Add examples either in the narrative or by attaching an example, which is permitted in most cases.

Another factor many applicants overlook is the depth of training completed. Include correspondence study, seminars, classes, lectures, computer based instruction, on-the-job training, every facet of training that you received including software programs that you taught yourself.

Include special licenses, registration exams, or certifications that you obtained in your specialty. If you are a medical assistant and passed the (RMA) Registered Medical Assistant Exam, annotate that on your application and in your KSAs. If you are in the trades and have various equipment operator's licenses list items such as "Fork Lift Operator" certification, list whatever is relevant to the job announcement.

The following KSAs are provided as examples to show formatting techniques. Sample Supplemental Qualification Statements are provided for two elements.[2] If special forms are not provided or if specific formats are not specified on the job announcement you can follow the sample outline to submit your narratives. Notice the use of bullets and short concise statements. You want the selecting official to focus on your key qualifications and good formatting techniques. The use of bullets, bold and underlined type will focus the reader's attention to your information. If you run everything together it is difficult for the selecting official to identify key elements that you accomplished to satisfy the rating factors. Include all required information and be sure to add your name, job announcement number and position title at the top of each page.

Sample KSAs

The following samples were excerpted from *"The Book of U.S. Government Jobs*, 9th edition. They present a format that you can use to draft your KSAs. Note that each KSA is on a separate page and that on each page you can address related knowledge, skills and abilities from multiple employers. You can use multiple pages for each KSA if needed. It is important to note that a rating of "no demonstration" on any of the KSAs will exclude an applicant from consideration for that position.[3]

Many applicants wonder why KSAs are needed when they already addressed their work experience in block C. KSAs are used by selecting officials to differentiate between the best qualified for the position. They present specific strengths and can point out weaknesses between candidates for the same position. It is important to take the time to draft clear and concise descriptions to improve your chances for the position. To keep the KSAs to one page you can change the formatting and font size. However, don't use a font size of less than 10 points because it is too difficult to read. I like to use a 11 or 12 point font size when writing applications. If you have significant accomplishments to add to a description include it even if the KSA is more than one page.

---

[2] KSA examples excerpted from *"The Book of U.S. Government Jobs"* 9th edition with permission.

[3] Handbook EL-312, paragraph 754.41, September 2001

Job Title: Administrative Officer
Announcement Number: XX-178A
Applicant's Name: John Smith
SSN: XXX-XX-XXXX

KSA #1 *Demonstrated ability to organize and coordinate work within schedule constraints and handle emergent requirements in a timely manner.*

I performed the following duties in my current position (Block C1):

- Managed the office suspense lists for all office supervisors. Transcribed meeting minutes and compiled action item lists, annotated due dates and listed responsible parties. Sent reminders to responsible parties, kept list current and upward reported accomplishments to the office manager weekly.
- Planned and coordinated two annual shareholder meetings for over 700 stock owners, key management and staff. Drafted the itinerary, set up the registration booth, arranged for morning breakout sessions, planned lunch and the shareholders meeting from 1:00 to 3:00 p.m. Also staffed the shareholders information booth after the meeting.

Award: Received an award for exemplary service for planning and organizing the 2001 meeting, copy attached.

- Required to frequently complete short notice work assignments including reports, transcribing meeting minutes, and payroll accounting tasks. I am the chief headquarters Payroll clerk and I provide backup to 12 field offices. If any of the field office clerks or supervisors are not available I complete their payroll reports prior to the cutoff time.

- Responsible for notifying management of pending funding shortfalls and providing justification for additional fund requests. I analyzed budget reports for trends, calculated spend rates and recommended reallocation of funds to satisfy pending or potential shortages.

Training:

1. Certificate: 24-hour Meeting Preparation and Planning seminar, March 2000
2. 40 - hour Time Management Course, RMC Services, April 2002

Job Title: Administrative Officer
Announcement Number: XX-178A
Applicant's Name: John Smith
SSN: XXX-XX-XXXX

KSA #2 *Demonstrated ability to monitor important and complex projects concurrently.*

Performed these duties in my present position from 1/1/99 to the present (Block C1):

- Budget analyst duties - Trend tracking, monitor and control of the Office's annual budget of $350,000. Performed budget data entry, compiled reports, tracked trends, anticipated fund shortages in various program areas and drafted requests for additional funds for management's signature. Audited program areas to insure fund expenditures were justified and properly classified.
- Payroll chief clerk - Insured timely submission of all payroll data before the cutoff date each pay period, entered amendments, and researched pay problems for 37 employees. I advised management of problems and notified them when to review and approve the attendance for each pay period.

Training: 80 - hour accounting software class, by Peachtree, January 1999.

Performed the following duties in my previous position as Administrative Officer, GS-0341-7, with the USDA from 10/4/96 to 12/31/98 (Block C2):

- Organizational Charts & Staffing - Processed revisions to and generated complex organizational charts based on input from the management team. Reviewed proposed changes to insure they conformed to authorized levels and that positions were properly classified. Concurrently, prepared, and tracked personnel actions for 124 employees and provided support in various program areas including payroll, benefits, staffing, and budget.
- Office of Workmen's Compensation Program (OWCP) Program - Conducted annual (OWCP) seminars for managers and supervisors. Seminars included guidance on procedures, claims processing and post accident interventions. Provided guidance to immediate supervisors of injured employees and maintained the OSHA 200 log for all accidents.

Award: Cash award, June 1998, for managing the OWCP program, copy attached.

Training: 60 - hours Position Management and Position Classification Course, 012-V-933, Graduate School, USDA Washington D.C., June 1997.

Job Title: Administrative Officer
Announcement Number: XX-178A
Applicant's Name: John Smith
SSN: XXX-XX-XXXX

KSA #3 *Knowledge of Microsoft Word, Excel, Powerpoint, and Lotus Notes/other email software.*
Performed these duties in present position from 1/1/99 to the present (Block C1):

- Proficient in Microsoft Office, Word, Excel, Powerpoint and Lotus and I use Lotus notes for office e-mail. Developed a 34 page Powerpoint presentation (copy attached) for our CEO to use at the 2004 annual stock holders meeting in Memphis. The presentation received rave reviews and I was asked to develop similar presentations for other meetings. Worked closely with accounting to compile the data and then integrated it into a succinct visual presentation. I use Microsoft Word for correspondence.

- Conducted Microsoft Word and Excel mini-training sessions for those less proficient in the office. Typically sessions ran 1-2 hours in length. Attended various software system seminars including Microsoft Office, Peachtree Accounting, and our new Lotus Notes e-mail program.

Volunteer Work: Performed these duties while working as a volunteer for United Way over past 6 years. Approximately 12 hours a week. (Block E):

- Developed our chapter's web site (http://www.xxxxxxxxxx.org) using Microsoft Frontpage 98. I consider myself very proficient in web site development and I learned Frontpage through self study and experimentation. This web site consists of 48 pages and two databases. We used a secure server for confidential requests. I'm the Webmaster. Contact the United Way Chairperson, Ms. Mary Jones for verification at XXX-123-4567.

Performed the following duties in my previous position as Administrative Officer, GS-0341-7, with the USDA from 10/4/96 to 12/31/98(Block B):

- Proficient in VISO. I used VISO to generate ORG Charts while at the USDA.

- Proficient in several Payroll & T&A software systems including IPPS, the USDA's Integrated Personnel and Payroll System.

Training Certificates: 24-hour VISO software course and a 16-hour IPPS software course both completed at our Regional Office, May 1998.

Job Title: Administrative Officer, GS-341-05/11
Announcement Number: XX-178A
Applicant's Name: John Smith
SSN: XXX-XX-XXXX

KSA #4 *Demonstrated ability to effectively communicate orally and in writing, to include writing and preparing memorandums, letters, and other official correspondence.*

Performed these duties in present position from 1/1/99 to the present (Block C1):

- **Written Guidance** - Developed Standard Operation Procedures (SOPs) for program areas including payroll administration, office suspense tracking, monitor and control, and general procedures. Adopted by the Regional Office for use throughout the organization, sample attached. I also wrote numerous internal memorandums within my program areas that provided direction for specific functions and clarified company policy issues.

  Prepare transmittal forms for project files, letters to share holders, fax cover letters, e-mail messages to team leads and customers, flip charts for meetings, Power Point presentations, proof and edit management draft correspondence, and prepare replies to organizational reports.

- **Oral Communications** - In current capacity I teach office software to small groups, brief management team of progress at meetings, give presentations at inter-office meetings and to small groups of share holders.

Volunteer Work

- I speak at various fund raisers for our local United Way and prepare written presentations to our work group and Chairperson. I organized and hosted a dozen fund raisers since 1994. Contact the United Way Chairperson, Ms. Mary Jones for verification at 890-123-4567.

Education: Completed 12 semester hours, 3 courses in communications, at Duquesne University in 1997; Report Writing, Oral Communications I and Effective Writing Techniques.

Training:

1) **Competent Toastmaster.** Joined Toastmasters International in 1995. Obtained Competent Toastmaster status in 1997. Chapter President, Dan McCormick, 321-6543-0987. Certificate attached.

2)   **Certificate;** <u>Constructive Communications With The Public</u>, USDA Course 01501, June 1996. <u>Interpersonal Communications</u>, Seminar 1996, sponsored by OPM.

KSA CHECKLIST

Use this list to insure that you have included key information.[4] It's important to consider these areas when drafting your KSA statements. When you first start to draft your KSAs don't worry about the specifics such as exact dates, contact information, etc. You can add that later. It is best to simply write down any and everything, even the least significant events. After you get it all down then add specifics and put them in logical sequence. Review and rewrite your KSAs at least three times and more if needed. Let your draft sit overnight and review it again the next day. You will be surprised at what you left out on the first draft.

❏ **Experience** - Include experience for all offices, departments or agencies that you worked for to show depth and range of experience. For example, include that you tracked inter-office correspondence at multiple locations, or that you tracked budgets for headquarters. Also show expertise in what you do well such as having A++ certification, maintain LANS/WANS for several locations, thoroughly familiar with Peachtree accounting software, proficient at office organization, etc.

❏ **Supervision -** If you don't have a supervisory background, did you work independently with minimal supervision and make decisions for your program areas? If so, state that in your KSA. Were you assigned to be an acting supervisor on several occasions? Do you draft memorandums and letters for your supervisor's signature? Do you manage/supervise programs or projects?

❏ **ComplexityFactors** - Did you write reports or work on large projects coordinating activities for various groups? Does your job impact the safety of others and what standards do you follow and utilize in your present and past jobs? Do you have certifications, licenses, specific training, or accreditation that would help you land this job?

❏ **Achievements and Impact** - How did you show initiative and creativity in your office while working under adverse conditions? Were you responsible for major programs, products, or activities? If so list them. What did you do to save time, money and resources or to improve the work environment?

❏ **Awards/Recognition -** Include all awards, monetary, letters of achievement, time-off awards, or write-ups in your office newsletter. Include scholastic nominations as well and any service awards or recognition received from volunteer work.

❏ **Contacts** - If you dealt with headquarters staff, the general public, EPA or OSHA inspectors, local authorities, or government officials, list them in your KSAs.

---

[4] Excerpted from *The Book of U.S. Government Jobs*, 9th edition

❏ **Fashionable Trends -** Mention current trends such as "Business Process Engineering (BPE), Model Work Environment (MWE) initiatives, Management by Objectives (MBO), Partnership, Quality Work Groups, etc. If you have exposure to these and other initiatives list them in your write-up.

OVERVIEW

Now that you have your application and KSAs completed you are ready to submit your package. Follow the instructions in the job announcement. Your application must reach the listed address on or before the specified closing date. If it is received after the closing date your application will not be considered.

If selected for the position, you will have to complete other forms such as a "Pre-Employment Screening - Authorization and Release Form," PS Form 2181-A. A copy of this form is included in Appendix C for your review.

KEYS TO SUCCESS

There are three basic ingredients to successfully finding federal employment for qualified applicants:

- Invest the time and energy needed to seek out all openings.

- Correctly fill out all required application forms.

- Don't give up when you receive your first rejection.

You can learn from rejections by contacting the selecting official. Ask what training and/or experience would enhance your application package for future positions. If they specify certain training or experience, then work to achieve the desired skills.

NETWORKING

Networking is a term used to define the establishment of a group of individuals that assist one another for mutual benefit. You can establish your own network by talking to personnel specialists, contacting Customer Service District Office Human Resource Departments, conducting informational interviews, and by bidding on all applicable job announcements. By following the guidelines outlined in the book and using your innate common sense your chances of success are increased substantially.

Visit http://federaljobs.net to explore viable civil service options in the competitive sector and to use the many resources offered on this site including direct links to hundreds of federal agency employment web sites. You will also find updates to this book posted on http://federaljobs.net as changes occur.

Appendix C
Application Forms

Depending on the job you apply for there are several forms required. This Appendix includes the *Application for Employment,* PS Form 2591, and the *Pre-Employment Screening - Authorization and Release,* PS Form 2181-A. You can also submit a Resume as long as the Resume includes all of the information that is included on the PS-2591 form. Review Chapter Eleven for the special form used for Postal Inspector positions. These forms can be downloaded from the Postal Service web site or from http://postofficejobs.info/.

The Postal Service will send a complete set of forms to applicants that call for information about a particular opening. Other forms may also be required depending on the type of job that you apply for.

A number of corporate jobs are filled without a written test, generally professional or highly skilled positions. It is important to thoroughly complete all application forms when applying for these positions including submission of required detailed knowledge and abilities statements. You will be examined and rated on a point system assessed through review of your knowledge, skills, and abilities that you submit on your resume and application forms. Your resume and application must be thorough and include all related experience, education and training that qualifies you for the position. Otherwise, you will lose points and others, who may be less qualified, will get the job.

Copy the forms that follow and use them to draft and refine your application prior to receipt of the official forms. This is an excellent time to compile your education, work, and military history. Draft concise work descriptions to place on your final application forms. You must provide your work history back at least 10 years. Go back further to include any work related experience that will help you qualify for this job, including military job experience. Take time to type these forms if possible and send a cover letter with the application package.

Application for Employment

The US Postal Service is an Equal Opportunity Employer

(Shaded Areas for Postal Service Use Only)

Rated Application			Veteran preference has been verified through proof that the separation was under honorable conditions, and other proof as required. *(See Section D below.)*	Check One:
Rated For	**Rating**	**Date Rcvd.**		☐ 10 pts. CPS
		Time Rcvd.	**Type of Proof Submitted & Date Issued**	☐ 10 pts. CP
Signature & Date			**Verifier's Signature, Title & Date**	☐ 10 pts. XP
				☐ 5 pts. TP

A. General Information

1. Name *(First, MI, Last)*

2. Social Security No. (SSN)

3. Home Telephone (   )

4. Mailing Address *(No., Street, City, State, ZIP Code)*

5. Date of Birth

6. Work Telephone (   )

7. Place of Birth *(City & State or City & Country)*

8. Kind of Job Applied for and Postal Facility Name & Location *(City & State)*

9. Will You Accept: Temporary/Casual (Noncareer) Work? ☐ Yes ☐ No

10. When Will You Be Available?

11. Are You Willing to Travel? *(Complete only if you are applying for an executive or professional position.)* ☐ Yes ☐ No

B. Educational History

1. Name and Location *(City & State)* **of Last High School Attended**

2. Are You a High School Graduate? Answer "Yes" if you expect to graduate within the next 9 months, or you have an official equivalency certificate of graduation.
☐ Yes - Month & Year:
☐ No - Highest Grade Completed:

3a. Name and Location of College or University *(City, State, and ZIP Code if known. If you expect to graduate within 9 months, give month and year you expect degree.)*	Dates Attended		No. of Credits Completed		Type Degree *(BA, etc.)*	Year of Degree
	From	To	Semester Hrs.	Quarter Hrs.		

3b. Chief Undergraduate College Subjects	Semester Hrs. Completed	Quarter Hrs. Completed	3c. Chief Graduate College Subjects	Semester Hrs. Completed	Quarter Hrs. Completed

4. Major Field of Study at Highest Level of College Work

5. Other Schools or Training *(For example, trade, vocational, armed forces, or business. Give for each: Name, City, State, and ZIP Code, if known, of school; dates attended; subjects studied; number of classroom hours of instruction per week; certificates; and any other pertinent information.)*

6. Honors, Awards, and Fellowships Received

7. Special Qualifications and Skills *(Licenses; skills with machines, patents or inventions; publications - do not submit copies unless requested; public speaking; memberships in professional or scientific societies; typing or shorthand speed, etc.)*

PS Form **2591**, March 1999 *(Page 1 of 4)*

Name (First, MI, Last)	Social Security No.	Date

C. Work History

(Start with your present position and go back for 10 years or to your 16th birthday, whichever is later. You may include volunteer work. Account for periods of unemployment in separate blocks in order. Include military service. Use blank sheets if you need more space. Include your name, SSN, and date on each sheet.)

May the US Postal Service ask your present employer about your character, qualifications, and employment record? A "No" will not affect your consideration for employment opportunities.   ☐ Yes   ☐ No

1.

Dates of Employment (Month & Year) From To **Present**	Grade If Postal, Federal Service or Military	Starting Salary/Earnings $ per
Exact Position Title Average Hours per Week	Number and Kind of Employees Supervised	Present Salary/Earnings $ per
Name of Employer and Complete Mailing Address	Kind of Business (Manufacturing, etc.)	Place of Employment (City & State)
	Name of Supervisor	Telephone No. (If known) ( )

Reason for Wanting to Leave

Description of Duties, Responsibilities, and Accomplishments

2.

Dates of Employment (Month & Year) From To	Grade If Postal, Federal Service or Military	Starting Salary/Earnings $ per
Exact Position Title Average Hours per Week	Number and Kind of Employees Supervised	Present Salary/Earnings $ per
Name of Employer and Complete Mailing Address	Kind of Business (Manufacturing, etc.)	Place of Employment (City & State)
	Name of Supervisor	Telephone No. (If known) ( )

Reason for Leaving

Description of Duties, Responsibilities, and Accomplishments

3.

Dates of Employment (Month & Year) From To	Grade If Postal, Federal Service or Military	Starting Salary/Earnings $ per
Exact Position Title Average Hours per Week	Number and Kind of Employees Supervised	Present Salary/Earnings $ per
Name of Employer and Complete Mailing Address	Kind of Business (Manufacturing, etc.)	Place of Employment (City & State)
	Name of Supervisor	Telephone No. (If known) ( )

Reason for Leaving

Description of Duties, Responsibilities, and Accomplishments

PS Form **2591**, March 1999 *(Page 2 of 4)*

Name *(First, MI, Last)*		Social Security No.	Date	
4.	Dates of Employment *(Month & Year)* From To	Grade If Postal, Federal Service or Military	Starting Salary/Earnings $ per	
	Exact Position Title Average Hours per Week	Number and Kind of Employees Supervised	Present Salary/Earnings $ per	
Name of Employer and Complete Mailing Address		Kind of Business *(Manufacturing, etc.)*	Place of Employment *(City & State)*	
		Name of Supervisor	Telephone No. *(If known)* ( )	

Reason for Leaving

Description of Duties, Responsibilities, and Accomplishments

D. Veteran Preference *(Answer all parts. If a part does not apply, answer "No".)*

	Yes	No
1. Have you ever served on active duty in the US military service? *(Exclude tours of active duty for training as a reservist or guardsman.)*		
2. Have you ever been discharged from the armed service under other than honorable conditions? You may omit any such discharge changed to honorable by a Discharge Review Board or similar authority. *(If "Yes," give details in Section F.)*		
3. Do you claim 5-point preference based on active duty in the armed forces? *(If "Yes," you will be required to furnish records to support your claim.)*		
4. Do you claim a 10-point preference? If "Yes," check type of preference claimed and attach Standard Form 15, *Claim for 10-Point Veteran Preference,* together with proof called for in that form.		

☐ Compensable Disability *(Less than 30%)*   ☐ Compensable Disability *(30% or more)*   ☐ Non-Compensable Disability *(includes Receipt of the Purple Heart)*   ☐ Wife/Husband

☐ Widow/Widower   ☐ Mother   ☐ Other:

5. List for All Military Service: *(Enter N/A if not applicable)*

Date (From - To)	Serial/Service Number	Branch of Service	Type of Discharge

THE LAW (39 U.S. CODE 1002) PROHIBITS POLITICAL AND CERTAIN OTHER RECOMMENDATIONS FOR APPOINTMENTS, PROMOTIONS, ASSIGNMENTS, TRANSFERS, OR DESIGNATIONS OF PERSONS IN THE POSTAL SERVICE. Statements relating solely to character and residence are permitted, but every other kind of statement or recommendation is prohibited unless it either is requested by the Postal Service and consists solely of an evaluation of the work performance, ability, aptitude, and general qualifications of an individual or is requested by a government representative investigating the individual's loyalty, suitability, and character. Anyone who requests or solicits a prohibited statement or recommendation is subject to disqualification from the Postal Service and anyone in the Postal Service who accepts such a statement may be suspended or removed from office.

Privacy Act Statement: The collection of this information is authorized by 39 USC 401 and 1001. This information will be used to determine your qualifications and suitability for USPS employment. As a routine use, the information may be disclosed to an appropriate government agency, domestic or foreign, for law enforcement purposes; where pertinent, in a legal proceeding to which the USPS is a party or has an interest; to a government agency in order to obtain information relevant to a USPS decision concerning employment, security clearances, contracts, licenses, grants, permits or other benefits; to a government agency upon its request when relevant to its decision concerning employment, security clearances, security or suitability investigations, contracts, licenses, grants or other benefits; to a congressional office at your request; to an expert, consultant, or other person under contract with the USPS to fulfill an agency function; to the Federal Records Center for storage; to the Office of Management and Budget for review of private relief legislation; to an independent certified public accountant during an official audit of USPS finances; to an investigator, administrative judge or complaints examiner appointed by the Equal Employment Opportunity Commission for investigation of a formal EEO complaint under 29 CFR 1613; to the Merit Systems Protection Board or Office of Special Counsel for proceedings or investigations involving personnel practices and other matters within their jurisdiction; and to a labor organization as required by the National Labor Relations Act. Completion of this form is voluntary; however, if this information is not provided, you may not receive full consideration for a position.

COMPUTER MATCHING: Limited information may be disclosed to a federal, state, or local government administering benefits or other programs pursuant to statute for the purpose of conducting computer matching programs under the Act. These programs include, but are not limited to, matches performed to verify an individual's initial or continuing eligibility for, indebtedness to, or compliance with requirements of a benefit program.

PS Form **2591**, March 1999 *(Page 3 of 4)*

Name (First, MI, Last)	Social Security No.	Date

E. Other Information

	Yes	No
1. Are you one of the following: a United States citizen, a permanent resident alien, a citizen of American Samoa or any other territory owing allegiance to the United States?		
2. RESERVED FOR OFFICIAL USE		
3. RESERVED FOR OFFICIAL USE		
If you answer "Yes" to question 4 and/or 5, give details in Section F below. Give the name, address (including ZIP Code) of employer, approximate date, and reasons in each case. ▶ 4. Have you ever been fired from any job for any reason?		
5. Have you ever quit a job after being notified that you would be fired?		
6. Do you receive or have you applied for retirement pay, pension, or other compensation based upon military, postal, or federal civilian service? (If you answer "Yes," give details in Section F.)		
7a. Have you ever been convicted of a crime or are you now under charges for any offense against the Law? You may omit: (1) any charges that were dismissed or resulted in acquittal; (2) any conviction that has been set aside, vacated, annulled, expunged, or sealed; (3) any offense that was finally adjudicated in a juvenile court or juvenile delinquency proceeding; and (4) any charges that resulted only in a conviction of a non-criminal offense. **All felony and misdemeanor convictions and all convictions in state and federal courts are criminal convictions and must be disclosed. Disclosure of such convictions is required even if you did not spend any time in jail and/or were not required to pay a fine.**		
7b. While in the military service were you ever convicted by special or general court martial? **If you answer "Yes" to question 7a and/or 7b, give details in Section F. Show for each offense: (1) Date of conviction; (2) Charge convicted of; (3) Court and location; (4) Action taken. Note: A conviction does not automatically mean that you cannot be appointed. What you were convicted of, and how long ago, are important. Give all of the facts so that a decision can be made.**		
8. Are you a former Postal Service or Federal Employee not now employed by the US Government? If you answer "Yes," give in Section F, name of employing agency(ies), position title(s), and date(s) employed.		
9. Does the US Postal Service employ any relative of yours by blood or marriage? Postal officials may not appoint any of their relatives or recommend them for appointment in the Postal Service. Any relative who is appointed in violation of this restriction can not be paid. Thus it is necessary to have information about your relatives who are working for the USPS. These include: mother, father, daughter, son, sister, brother, aunt, uncle, first cousin, niece, nephew, wife, husband, mother-in-law, father-in-law, daughter-in-law, son-in-law, sister-in-law, brother-in-law, stepfather, stepmother, stepdaughter, stepson, stepsister, stepbrother, half sister, and half brother. If you answer "Yes" to question 9, give in section F for such relatives: (1) Full name; (2) Present address and ZIP Code; (3) Relationship; (4) Position title; (5) Name and location of postal installation where employed.		
10. Are you now dependent on or a user of ANY addictive or hallucinogenic drug, including amphetamines, barbiturates, heroin, morphine, cocaine, mescaline, LSD, STP, hashish, marijuana, or methadone, other than for medical treatment under the supervision of a doctor?		

F. Use This Space for Detailed Answers (Use blank sheets if you need more space. Include your name, SSN, and date on each sheet.)

G. Certification

Enter number of additional sheets you have attached as part of this application:

I certify that all of the statements made in this application are true, complete, and correct to the best of my knowledge and belief and are in good faith.	Signature of Applicant	Date Signed

Disclosure by you of your Social Security Number (SSN) is mandatory to obtain the services, benefits, or processes that you are seeking. Solicitation of the SSN by the USPS is authorized under provisions of Executive Order 9397, dated November 22, 1943. The information gathered through the use of the number will be used only as necessary in authorized personnel administration processes.

A false or dishonest answer to any question in this application may be grounds for not employing you or for dismissing you after you begin work, and may be punishable by fine or imprisonment. (US Code, Title 18, Sec. 1001). All information you give will be considered in reviewing your application and is subject to investigation.

PS Form **2591**, March 1999 (Page 4 of 4)

UNITED STATES POSTAL SERVICE®   **Pre-Employment Screening — Authorization and Release**

Applicant: Carefully read the following information before you complete and sign this form.

Privacy Act Statement: The collection of this information is authorized by 39 USC 410(b) and 1001; it may be used to obtain information from organizations and individuals pertaining to your character and current or prior employment as may be relevant and necessary to determine your fitness and suitability for employment in the United States Postal Service. As a routine use, the information may be disclosed to an appropriate government agency, domestic or foreign, for law enforcement purposes; where pertinent, in a legal proceeding in which the USPS is a party or has an interest; to a government agency in order to obtain information relevant to a USPS decision concerning employment, security clearances, contracts, licenses, grants, permits or other benefits; to a government agency upon its request when relevant to its decision concerning employment, security clearances, security or suitability investigations, contracts, licenses, grants or other benefits; to a congressional office at your request; to an expert, consultant, or other person under contract with the USPS to fulfill an agency function; to the Federal Records Center for storage; to the Office of Management and Budget for review of private relief legislation; to an independent certified public accountant during an official audit of USPS finances; to an investigator, administrative judge or complaints examiner appointed by the Equal Employment Opportunity Commission for investigation of a formal EEO complaint under 29 CFR 1614; to the Merit Systems Protection Board or Office of Special Counsel for proceedings or investigations involving personnel practices and other matters within their jurisdiction; and to a labor organization as required by the National Labor Relations Act.

Completion of this form is voluntary; however, if consent to obtain this information is not given, it may have an adverse effect on your employment opportunities with the USPS.

Applicant's Name *(Last, First, Middle)*	Mailing Address
Date of Birth *(Month, Day, Year)* Home Phone Number ( )	

This constitutes my consent and authorization to the disclosure or furnishing of any relevant and necessary information or records to any duly authorized employment official of the USPS by any person, corporation, agency, or association concerning my character, employment, or military service as may be relevant and necessary for a determination of my suitability for employment with the USPS.

This authorization is executed with full knowledge and understanding that the USPS will take measures to protect the aforementioned information against unauthorized disclosure to any parties not having a legitimate need for it in the discharge of official business of the United States, or its agencies and instrumentalities.

I hereby RELEASE the aforementioned persons, corporators, agencies, associations and their employees, agents and representatives from any and all liability for damages resulting from a decision by the USPS not to employ me on account of compliance, or any attempts at compliance with this authorization, except for any damages resulting from knowingly providing false or misleading information or records about me.

A copy of this authorization shall be as effective and valid as the original. This authorization shall be valid for 12 months from the date it is signed.

Date Signed	Signature of Applicant

PS Form **2181-A,** March 1996

Index